Salome: The Image of a Woman Who Never Was

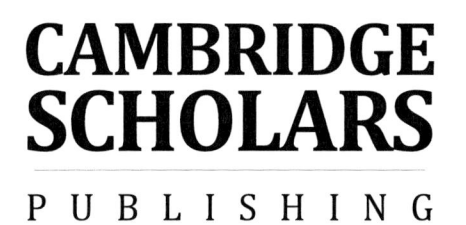

Salome: The Image of a Woman Who Never Was;
Salome: Nymph, Seducer, Destroyer

By

Rosina Neginsky

CAMBRIDGE
SCHOLARS
PUBLISHING

Salome: The Image of a Woman Who Never Was;
Salome: Nymph, Seducer, Destroyer,
By Rosina Neginsky

This book first published 2013

Cambridge Scholars Publishing

12 Back Chapman Street, Newcastle upon Tyne, NE6 2XX, UK

British Library Cataloguing in Publication Data
A catalogue record for this book is available from the British Library

Copyright © 2013 by Rosina Neginsky

All rights for this book reserved. No part of this book may be reproduced, stored in a retrieval system, or transmitted, in any form or by any means, electronic, mechanical, photocopying, recording or otherwise, without the prior permission of the copyright owner.

ISBN (10): 1-4438-4621-X, ISBN (13): 978-1-4438-4621-9

To those who crave love but are unable to love.

TABLE OF CONTENTS

List of Illustrations ix

Epigraph: Poem "Salome" by Rosina Neginsky xv

Preface xxi

Introduction 1

Part I: Creation of the Salome Myth

Chapter One 8
History and Myth in the Biblical Story

Chapter Two 23
The Evil Salome of Theology and Iconography: From the Church
Fathers to the Renaissance

Chapter Three 44
The Beautiful Salome in Renaissance Painting and Sculpture

Chapter Four 71
The Seducer-Destroyer Salome of Nineteenth-Century Art and Literature

**Part II: Salome and the Head of John the Baptist in Artists'
Self-Portraits**

Chapter Five 92
Painting: Titian, Bernard, Moreau

Chapter Six 125
Poetry: Stéphane Mallarmé

Part III: Salome in Story, Drama, Music

Chapter Seven 150
Salome's Dance in Flaubert's "Herodias": Pictorial or Ekphrastic?

Chapter Eight 167
Wilde's *Salome*

Chapter Nine 186
Wilde, Beardsley and Strauss

Conclusion 207

Appendix One 210

Appendix Two 215

Selected Bibliography 223

Index 236

LIST OF ILLUSTRATIONS

Cover

Vasilii Myazin, *Salome with the head of John the Baptist*, oil on canvas, 56 x 71 cm, circa 1980, private collection.

Part I

Chapter Two

Fig. I-2-1. *Herod's Banquet and John the Baptist's Decapitation*, a sixth-century miniature in the *Codex Sinopensis,* BNF, France.
Fig. I-2-2. *Dancing Salome* in the *Évangéliaire de Chartres*, the first part of the ninth century, BNF, France.
Fig. I-2-3. *Dancing Salome*, mosaic, fourteenth century, San Marco, Venice, Italy, Scala/Art Resource, NY.
Fig. I-2-4. Giovanni di Paolo, *The Head of John the Baptist brought to Herod*, tempera on panel, 68.5 x 40.2 cm, 1455/60, The Art Institute of Chicago.
Fig. I-2-5. Giovanni di Paolo, *John the Baptist's Beheading*, tempera on panel, 68.6 x 39.1 cm, 1455/60, The Art Institute of Chicago.
Fig. I-2-6. Cesare da Sesto, *Salome with the head of John the Baptist,* poplar, 136.5 x 79.6 cm, fifteenth century, Kunsthistorisches Museum, Gemaeldegalerie, Vienna, Austria.
Fig. I-2-7. Andrea Solario, *Salome with the Head of John the Baptist*, wood, 58.5 x 57.5 cm, sixteenth century, Kunsthistorisches Museum, Gemaeldegalerie, Vienna, Austria.
Fig. I-2-8. *Decapitation of John the Baptist*, mosaic, thirteenth century, Florence Baptistery, Scala/Art Resources, New York.
Fig. I-2-9. Bernardino Luini, *Salome Receiving the Head of John the Baptist*, oil on canvas, 62.5 x 55 cm, sixteenth century, Louvre, Departement des Peintures, Scala/Art Resource, New York.
Fig. I-2-10. Bernardino Luini, *Salome with the head of John the Baptist*, poplar, 55.5 x 42.5 cm, late sixteenth century, Kunsthistorisches Museum, Gemaeldegalerie, Vienna, Austria.

Fig. I-2-11. *Salome Presenting the Head of John the Baptist to Herodias*, mosaic, thirteenth century, Florence Baptistery, Scala/Art Resources, New York.

Fig. I-2-12. Andrea Pisano, *Salome Shows John's Head to Herodias*, 1330-36, gilded bronze, 49.7 x 43.2 cm, panel from the South Door of the Florence Baptistery.

Fig. I-2-13. Lorenzo Monaco, *Herod's Feast, Salome with the head of the Baptist*, left wing of a predella for an altar in Santa Maria degli Angeli, Florence, tempera on wood, 33.8 x 67.7 cm, 1387-1388, Louvre, Departement des Peintures.

Chapter Three

Fig. I-3-1. Donatello, *The Feast of Herod*, bronze relief, circa 1427, the Baptistery of the Siena Cathedral, Scala/Art Resource, New York.

Fig. I-3-2. Filippo Lippi, *The Banquet of Herod*, fresco, 1465, Capella Maggiore of Santo Stefano Cathedral, Prato, Italy, Scala/Art Resource, New York.

Fig. I-3-3. Rogier van der Weyden, *Saint John Altarpiece*, *The Beheading of John the Baptist,* rightmost panel, oil on oak panel, 77 x 48 cm, 1455-1460, Staatliche Museen, Berlin, Scala/Art Resource, New York.

Fig. I-3-4. Giotto, *The Feast of Herod* and *The Presentation of the Head of John the Baptist*, fresco, 280 x 450 cm, 1320, Santa Croce, Florence, Italy.

Fig. I-3-5. *Salome's Dance*, mosaic, thirteenth century, Florence Baptistery.

Fig. I-3-6. *John the Baptist's Martyrdom*, mosaic, thirteenth century, Florence Baptistery.

Fig. I-3-7. Andrea Pisano, the South Doors of the Florence Baptistery, gilded bronze, 1330-36.

Fig. I-3-8. Andrea Pisano, *The Dance of Salome,* gilded bronze, 49.7 x 43.2 cm, 1330-36, panel from the South Doors of the Florence Baptistery.

Fig. I-3-9. Andrea Pisano, *John's Head is Shown to King Herod*, gilded bronze, 1330-36, panel from the South Doors of the Florence Baptistery.

Fig. I-3-10. Guido Reni, *Salome with the Head of John the Baptist*, oil on canvas, 248.5 x 174 cm, 1639/42, The Art Institute of Chicago.

Chapter Four

Fig. I-4-1. L. Levy-Dhurmer, *Salome*, 1896, pastel. Photo is located at the Victorian Web: http://www.victorianweb.org/painting/france/ld1.html. The website used the image from Patrick Bade, *Femme Fatale: Images of Evil and Fascinating Women* (NY: Mayflower Books, 1979).

Fig. I-4-2. Gustave-Adolf Mossa, *Salome*. 1904. Photo: http://www.johncoulthart.com/feuilleton/2011/01/24/mossas-salomes/

Fig. I-4-3. Gustav-Adolf Mossa, *Salome*, 1906, Musée des Beaux Arts, Nice, France.

Fig. I-4-4. Gustave-Adolf Mossa, Salome, 1908. Photo: http://www.johncoulthart.com/feuilleton/2011/01/24/mossas-salomes/

Fig. I-4-5. Franz Von Stuck, *Salome Dancing,* oil, 45.7 x 24.7 cm, 1906, private collection, Scala/Art Resource, New York.

Fig. I-4-6. Pablo Picasso, *Dancing Salome*, drypoint on copper, 40 x 34.8 cm, 1905, BNF, Musée Picasso, Scala/Art Resource, New York.

Fig. I-4-7. Henri Regnault, *Salome*, oil on canvas, 160 x 102.9 cm, 1870, Metropolitan Museum of Art, New York, Scala/Art Resource, New York.

Fig. I-4-8. Jean-Sylvain Bieth, *Salome*, three pieces, 1985-88, private collection.

Fig. I-4-9. Sergei Chepik, *Salome*, oil on canvas, circa 1980, private collection.

Part II

Chapter Five

Fig. II-5-1. Michelangelo, *Last Judgment*, detail, fresco, 1340 x 1200 cm, 1537-1541, Sistine Chapel, Vatican City, Scala/Art Resource, New York.

Fig. II-5-2. Cristofano Allori, *Judith with the Head of Holofernes*, oil on canvas, 139 x 116 cm, 1613, Galleria Palatina (Palazzo Pitti), Florence, Scala/Art Resource, New York.

Fig. II-5-3. Titian, *Salome*, oil on canvas, 90 x 72 cm, 1515, Galleria Doria Pamphilj, Rome, Scala/Art Resource, New York.

Fig. II-5-4. Titian, *Lavinia as Salome*, oil on canvas, 87 x 80 cm, 1549, Museo del Prado, Madrid, Scala/Art Resource, New York.

Fig. II-5-5. Emile Bernard, *Salome with the Platter*, oil on canvas, 1897, reproduction taken from the book *Gustave Moreau et le Symbolisme* (Genève: Petit Palais, 1977).

Fig. II-5-6. Emile Bernard, *The Dancer or Salome*, oil on canvas, 1914, Galerie Larock-Granoff, Paris, France.

Fig. II-5-7. Gustave Moreau, *Salome Dancing Before Herod*, oil on canvas, 144 x 103.5 cm, 1876, The Hammer Museum, a public arts unit of the University of California, Los Angeles.

Fig. II-5-8. Gustave Moreau, *The Apparition*, watercolor on paper, 106 x 72 cm, 1876, Cabinet des dessins, Louvre, Scala/Art Resource, New York.

Fig. II-5-9. Gustave Moreau, *Dancing Salome (Tattooed Salome)*, oil painting, 92 x 60 cm, 1876, Musée Gustave Moreau, Scala/Art Resource, New York.

Fig. II-5-10. Gustave Moreau, *Salome in the Garden*, watercolor, 1878, private collection, Scala/Art Resource, New York.

Part III

Chapter Seven

Fig. III-7-1. Herrad de Landsberg, *The Whore of Babylon Inverted*, reproduction from Rosalie Green, ed., *The Hortus deliciarum of Herrad of Hohenbourg (Landsberg, 1176-96): A Reconstruction* (London: Warburg Institute/Brill, 1979), image 321.

Fig. III-7-2. Herrad de Landsberg, *The Whore of Babylon Falling*, reproduction from Rosalie Green, ed., *The Hortus deliciarum of Herrad of Hohenbourg (Landsberg, 1176-96): A Reconstruction* (London: Warburg Institute/Brill, 1979), image 351.

Fig. III-7-3. Herrad de Landsberg, *Lucifer Falling*, reproduction from Rosalie Green, ed., *The Hortus deliciarum of Herrad of Hohenbourg (Landsberg, 1176-96): A Reconstruction* (London: Warburg Institute/Brill, 1979), image 352.

Fig. III-7-4. Herrad de Landsberg, *Stairs that lead toward the skies*. Photo: http://museclio.over-blog.com/article-miniature-de-l-echelle-du-paradis-d-apres-l-hortus-deliciorum-de-herrade-de-landsberg-68600866.html

Fig. III-7-5. The goddess Isis in the acrobatic position known as the "bridge," reproduction from Myra Haase, *Reconciling Contradiction. The Myth of Salome*, Thesis for the Master of Theological Studies, Christian Theological Seminary, Indianapolis, Indiana, 1994.

Fig. III-7-6. Dancing Salome on the north tympanum of Rouen Cathedral, Scala/Art Resource, New York.

Chapter Nine

Fig. III-9-1. Aubrey Beardsley, *Salome with the head of John the Baptist*, 1893, Scala/Art Resource, New York.

Fig. III-9-1b. Aubrey Beardsley, *Climax,* reproduction from Bruce S. Harris, ed., *The Collected Drawings of Aubrey Beardsley* (New York: Bounty Books, A Division of Crown Publishers, Inc. 1967).

Fig. III-9-2. Aubrey Beardsley, Front Page, original version, reproduction from Bruce S. Harris, ed., *The Collected Drawings of Aubrey Beardsley* (New York: Bounty Books, A Division of Crown Publishers, Inc. 1967).

Fig. III-9-3. Aubrey Beardsley, *Enter Hérodiade,* Scala/Art Resource, New York.

Fig. III-9-4. Aubrey Beardsley, *The Woman in the Moon*, reproduction from Bruce S. Harris, ed., *The Collected Drawings of Aubrey Beardsley* (New York: Bounty Books, A Division of Crown Publishers, Inc. 1967).

Fig. III-9-5. Aubrey Beardsley, *The Toilette of Salome*, original version, Scala/Art Resource, New York.

Fig. III-9-5b. Aubrey Beardsley, *The Toilette of Salome,* Scala/Art Resource, New York.

Fig. III-9-6. Aubrey Beardsley, *John and Salome*, Scala/Art Resource, New York.

Fig. III-9-7. Aubrey Beardsley, *The Black Cape*, reproduction from Bruce S. Harris, ed., *The Collected Drawings of Aubrey Beardsley* (New York: Bounty Books, A Division of Crown Publishers, Inc. 1967).

Fig. III-9-8. Aubrey Beardsley, *The Peacock Skirt*, reproduction from Bruce S. Harris, ed., *The Collected Drawings of Aubrey Beardsley* (New York: Bounty Books, A Division of Crown Publishers, Inc. 1967).

Fig. III-9-9. Aubrey Beardsley, *The Dancer's Reward*, Scala/Art Resource, New York.

Fig. III-9-10. Aubrey Beardsley, *Tailpiece,* reproduction from Bruce S. Harris, ed., *The Collected Drawings of Aubrey Beardsley* (New York: Bounty Books, A Division of Crown Publishers, Inc. 1967).

Appendix One

Fig. App 1-1. Lovis Corinth, *Salome*, oil on canvas, 127 x 147 cm, 1900, Museum der Bildenden Künste Leipzig, Germany, Scala/Art Resource, New York.

Fig. App 1-2. Lovis Corinth, *Gertrud Eysoldt as Salome,* oil on canvas, 108 x 84.5 cm, 1903. Photo: http://publishing.cdlib.org/ucpressebooks/view?docId=ft1t1nb1gf&chunk.id=d0e4220&toc.id=&brand=ucpress

Appendix Two

Fig. App 2-1. Valentin Serov, *Ida Rubenstein as Salome*, oil and charcoal on canvas, 147x233 cm, 1910, Russian Museum, Saint Petersburg, Russia. Photo: www.abcgallery.com

Fig. App 2-2. Marianna Werefkina, 1911, *Salome with a Head of John the Baptist.* Photo: http://www.liveinternet.ru/journalshowcomments.php?journalid=3259969&jpostid=109962196

Epigraph

"Salome" by Rosina Neginsky[1]

The window's a stage.
Dolls are moving in the fog.
With wine-filled goblets in their hands,
Puppets dance the Minuet
To the music of Handel.

Sipping the wine of curiosity—
I look at them
The window stage opens
And a beautiful lady
Dressed in jewels
Flies out of it.

"My friend," she whispers to me,
"I am in love with you.
Would you dance the Minuet with me?
By the way,
My name's Salome."
I embraced Her.
She was naked and lovely.
Together we started
The rhythmical dance.

"I know,
You write about me,"
She said.
"Once in the castle of Herod
I was a twelve-year-old princess
And I did not know
How to dance at all.

For two thousand years
I've been Everything:
The beautiful whore
In Gustave Moreau's work—
I am dancing with you now
Her dance
In her costume.

I was the Princess Salome,
Who the other guy,
Whose name begins with M too—
I think Mallarmé—
Named Hérodiade.
He dressed me in jewels
And told me I was his self-portrait!
That one whose name begins with an M
Copied John the Baptist from Moreau.
Moreau severed the Baptist's head,
Painted himself as the Baptist,
Suspended his head in the air
And blamed it all on me!

There was also Flaubert.
In his story I'm truly young.
Imagine, he made me dance upside-down.
As a child he saw me in Rouen,
Shaped from stone:
My head down,
My legs above,
Flaubert reproduced this image.
But it wasn't me at all.
How could I, at 1,200 years old stand on my head?

The sculptors who put me on my head
Stole me from Herrad de Landsberg,
The learned nun.
She copied me from Isis,
The one who gave a second life to Osiris.
Isis was a good dancer.
She arched her body like a bridge
And danced on her hands
The dance of life.
But it wasn't me.

Today I'm two thousand years old.
I'm ancient.
For some reason however,
They still force me to dance,
The Dance of Seven Veils.

My friend, I ask you
Who haven't I been?
My friend, rescue me!"

Sounds of the Minuet.
The window's a stage.
Puppet-people drink wine.
The window closed.
The door opened.
I am waiting,
Sure She is about to come out.

A fat woman falls out of the castle.
But She?!
For sure this is her castle.

A woman yells,
Her husband hisses,
The car hums,
And I…

I am still dancing the Minuet with Her,
With a divine woman,
Two thousand years old.
I hear her whisper,
"My friend, rescue me!"

And it seems to me that she understood it all,
And blessed me to unravel
The eternal enigma of this mysterious life.

Notes

[1] Rosina Neginsky, "Salome," *Juggler. Poems* (New Orleans: University Press of the South, 2009), 106-115. I am including a Russian version of this poem, since originally it was written in Russian and then rewritten by the author in English.

Саломея

Сцена – окно.
Куклы движутся в тумане
Под музыку Генделя,
Менуэт вином запивая.

Я на них смотрю
И вино любопытства пью.

Окно-сцена проломилось,
И прекрасная дама,
В ожерельях вся
Вылетела из окна.
"Мой друг", --
Мне шепнула она.
"Я в вас влюблена
И вас Менуэт со мной
Танцевать приглашаю.
Саломея я" --
Невзначай бросила она.

Я обнял ее.
Она была нага, хороша,
И в танце ритмичном
Вдвоем закружились мы.

"Я знаю,
Вы пишете обо мне", -
Прошептала она.
"Когда-то в замке Ирода
Я принцессой была.
Мне было двенадцать лет,
И танцевать совсем не умела я.

За 2000 лет кем только я ни была?
Прекрасная проститутка
С картины Густава Моро,
В костюме которой
С вами сейчас танцую я.

Принцесса, которую другой,
Тоже на М.,
Кажется Малларме,
Иродиадой назвал,
В ожерелье одел
И своим портретом признал.

Иоанна Крестителя этот на М.
Списал с Моро:
Тот Крестителю голову отрубил
И себя Крестителем вообразил.

Голову он, висящей в воздухе, изобразил,
Ореолом ее окружил
И меня обвинил.

Был тоже Флобер.
У него я совсем юна.
Представьте себе,
На голове танцую я!

В Руане он видел меня.
Там из камня вылеплена я:
Голова вниз,
Ноги вверх!

Но то совем не я!
Разве в 1200 лет
На голове могла бы стоять я?!

Те, кто на голову поставили меня,
У Herrad de Landsberg,
Ученой монашки,
Украли меня.
А она срисовала меня с Изиз,
С той, что Озирису вторую жизнь дала.
Изиз большой танцовщицей была!
Мостиком и на голове
В танце жизни стояла она.

Сегодня мне 2000 лет.
Я очень стара.
Но танец семи вуалей все еще танцую я!

Мой друг,
Кем только я ни была!
Мой друг,
Спасите меня!"

Звуки Менуэта,
Сцена-окно,
Куклы – люди пьют вино.

Окно затворилось,
Дверь отворилась...
А я жду...
Вот-вот выйдет она.

Тут толстая баба
Вывалилась из дворца...
А Она?!
Ведь это замок Ее!

Баба шипит,
Муж ее кричит,
Машина гудит...

А я...
Я все еще Менуэт танцую
 С Ней,
С прекрасной женщиной,
Двух тысячи лет.

"Мой друг,
Спасите меня!" --
Все еще шепчет она.

И кажется мне,
Что она все поняла
И на разгадку вечной загадки
Благословила меня.

PREFACE

The origin of this book is in a conversation I had on a flight from Paris to Chicago. At the time I was reading Mireille Dottin-Orsini's book *Salome*. Seated next to me was a man who lived in Paris and was on his way to Chicago for vacation. At a certain point during the flight we began to talk. When he saw the book in my hand he said, "Ah, Salomé, la grande séductrice!" ("Ah, Salome, the great seducer!") I smiled and replied, "Really?" And then, hoping he would elaborate on the subject, provocatively added: "I did not know she was *la grande séductrice*." Alas, the conversation did not continue in this direction, but his statement left me puzzled. I asked myself: Was Salome, as a historical figure, really *la grande séductrice?* If this was not the case, why does she have this reputation?

These became troubling questions. Reputations often do not correspond to reality, but that does not stop them from influencing the destiny of an individual, a group of people, even a nation, society and the entire course of history. Such thoughts led me to write this book, *Salome: The Image of a Woman Who Never Was*. It is an investigation into Salome's reputation and the construction of such reputations. The result is a better understanding of woman's image in society and a study of how different outlets—theology, visual arts, literature and music—contribute to the creation and propagation of images and reputations. The focus is on Salome in particular, but my interest is also on myths in general. Thus, I use the story of Salome to inquire into the process of myth generation, one of the most fascinating and important of all cultural phenomena.

Work on this project has also reminded me of the personal component of myths and myth-building. As historians and scholars we often focus on the larger processes of history; it is important to remind ourselves that such processes take place at a human level. A key element behind the power of myths is their accessibility and adaptability to people's everyday lives.

One of the richest experiences on my own quest of discovering Salome's myth was my time in Florence, Italy, a city famously associated with John the Baptist and images of his life. During my stay I visited Prato, a small town less than half an hour from Florence by train, where the Renaissance painter Filippo Lippi lived and worked for a period. It was in Prato that Lippi painted one of the most fascinating fresco cycles depicting the story of John the Baptist and the associated dance of Salome. Woven into these beautiful images is the subtext of Lippi's own life, a story of love and loss, which left a profound impression on me. The scenes, which are at once historical and personal, speak to the power of myth on levels both large and small.

Work on any scholarly project is often lonely, as the nuts and bolts of research and writing is done alone with our books and thoughts in front of a computer screen. My experience writing this book was no different. Perhaps the interdisciplinary nature of this project and a necessity to work in art, literature, theology and even sociology kept me from settling too comfortably into one particular group. However, I was fortunate that throughout the process of writing this book I had people who supported me and were always interested in my progress.

My very sincere gratitude goes to my friend Larry Shiner, emeritus professor of Philosophy at the University of Illinois at Springfield, specialist in aesthetics, who was always present during my research and writing. He encouraged me throughout the entire process and was one of the most helpful and supportive readers of this book. My gratitude also goes to Peter Cooke and Brendan Cole, who shared with me their own work and made a number of valuable suggestions, and to David Boffa and Frank O'Leary.

INTRODUCTION

This is the study of a myth and its sources – the mythical image of Salome and its links to the broader cultural myths surrounding women. Although the root of the Hebrew name "Salome" is "peaceful," the image spawned by this famous woman to carry that name has been anything but peaceful. She and her story have long been linked to the beheading of John the Baptist, since Salome was the supposed catalyst for the prophet's execution. According to the Gospel accounts, it was the seductive beauty of Salome's dance at the banquet of her stepfather, Herod Antipas, that led to John's beheading.

Salome and her dance have been topics of literary and artistic works for centuries. The story's basic origins, however, provide little to suggest that this should be the case. In the Gospel she is nothing more than a tool in the drama of John the Baptist's martyrdom (Mark 6:14-29, and Matthew 14:1-12). In the Middle Ages her role was always secondary to John the Baptist's. She was part of *his* story. At the same time, however, she was also widely used as a cautionary example to shape and reinforce a cultural view of women and their place within society. Later, during the Renaissance, and especially in the nineteenth century, she became a fully independent cult figure. Her story was embellished and expanded, becoming a favorite subject of artists and writers. Though the meaning of her roles varied throughout the centuries according to the ideology of the period and the sensibilities of individual artists, she was always predominantly an incarnation of evil. From her humble beginnings, mentioned in a few lines of the Gospels, she had thus become a figure of mythic proportions, entirely independent from the historical Salome.

For the earliest disseminators of the Salome myth it was important to portray her as one of the main players in the execution of John the Baptist. Although he was executed for political reasons by Herod Antipas, in the Bible he became the victim of two women. One of them was the wife of Herod Antipas, Herodias, and the other was her daughter, a young unnamed dancing girl who later appears under the name of Salome.

The Bible and the Church fathers developed three main stereotypes of women: the saint, the sinner and the repenting sinner. The image of a saint, of an ideal woman, a woman-mother, was attached to the Virgin Mary. The image of an evil sinner who is going through the process of repentance was attributed to Mary Magdalene, whereas Salome belongs to the type of the inherently evil sinner who is without repentance, the descendent of the supposedly sinful Eve.

Her image, although always an embodiment of evil, went through a number of transformations. Church fathers and the artists who worked for the Church during the Middle Ages propagated the vision of Salome as evil through writings and the visual arts. When the shifting cultural and artistic norms of the Renaissance placed increasing emphasis on beauty and individuality, the stereotype of Salome as a purely evil destroyer began to falter. Salome's evil image was thus transformed into the image of a beautiful woman, a muse for artists. This development continued during the Baroque period, when Salome's cruelty and her already established ideology as an evil and mischievous woman were again emphasized alongside her status as a beautiful muse. As a result of these changes her image became representative of the more secular worldview of the time. Despite the various incarnations of Salome, one thing remained constant up to the nineteenth century: For centuries, she was not an entirely independent figure. Rather, she remained an appendix to John the Baptist and was always represented in association with him.

In the nineteenth century, however, the myth took a different shape. With the increasing independence of women and the appearance of feminist movements, women became a threat and potential competitors to men. Since society and social rules were largely made and governed by men, there was an effort to repress women and not let them break from social stereotypes to become equal, strong and independent. Ironically, it is through the process of a struggle against women and their potential power that Salome became a truly independent cult figure in her own right. She was used as a tool, a scarecrow of sorts, and as a symbol of the dangerous and destructive woman, manipulative through her beauty and through her ability to enslave and destroy men by awakening in them an uncontrollable sexual desire. The problem raised was that women, while physically and domestically indispensable, were considered by many to be socially destructive if given too much power. In the nineteenth century, Salome became a symbol of the dangerous and seductive woman who, once allowed to gain social power, would destroy man. Her image served as an inspiration for artists, poets and writers, who used her and her story to create new myths based partly on her existing reputation and partly on their own imaginations and philosophies.

In the nineteenth century, Salome became a symbol of woman-vampire, whore and murderess. Her supposedly Jewish origins were also stressed in order to emphasize the danger of a rising merchant class, many of whom were Jews. Her myth was thus made into a multifaceted expression of societal fears.

That image of Salome disappeared in the immediate aftermath the First World War, when feelings of hostility and struggle directed toward women were replaced by a real enemy and a true struggle for survival in Europe. The twentieth century created images of Salome in art and literature as well, but those images are only a tribute to the once-powerful myth. Freed of any real ideological foundation, these more recent appearances of Salome are little more than shadows of her former self.

The processes by which myths are created are among the most important of all cultural phenomena. In looking at Salome as a case study, this book examines those processes, considering how Salome and her story was transformed from history into myth. Particular attention is given to why and how Salome was presented as evil and how the purpose of her evil varied from one period to another.

The book is organized chronologically, looking at art and literature from Biblical times through the Middle Ages and Renaissance, and into the nineteenth century. The goal is not a survey, but a study of carefully selected works that serve as examples and evidence for my larger argument.

The first part, *Creation of the Salome Myth,* is divided into four chapters. The first chapter, History and Myth in the Biblical Story, examines the genesis of the story from historical, textual and literary viewpoints and considers the reasons for and results of that genesis. I begin with the Biblical story of Salome and its links to earlier folklore, specifically the story of the Roman consul Flaminius, who was expelled from the Roman Senate for having a prisoner killed to impress a young boy who was his lover. This story went through a variety of transformations, appearing in the accounts of different historians and serving as an inspiration for the Evangelists. I explain how they used the story of Salome and John the Baptist as a literary device to make their narrative emotionally and visually more effective, a tactic borrowed from contemporary Roman authors. For the Evangelists, the effect of their narrative was important not only as entertainment but also to construct a religious belief system based on the characters they were discussing. Their accounts of the life and death of John the Baptist—and of Salome and Herodias as archetypal, corrupting women and relatives of Eve—have become engraved in history and in people's psyche. The critical associations that develop at this early stage form the underpinnings of nearly all later expressions of this story.

The second chapter, The Evil Salome of Theology and Iconography:

From the Church Fathers to the Renaissance, analyzes the construction of Salome's image in Christian theology and how that image was applied to more general views on women. It demonstrates how her image contributed to the established myths of women as evil seducers and destroyers of men.

Chapter three, The Beautiful Salome of Renaissance Painting and Sculpture, is in some sense an extension of the previous chapter. It studies examples of the story of Salome created in different visual art forms from the fourteenth through seventeenth centuries. Close examination of these images reveals how they reflect the ideology and established artistic norms of a given period even while shaping new social ideologies and sensibilities. In this chapter I analyze new and unconventional images of Salome. One is by the Northern Renaissance artist Rogier van der Weyden. It was he who invented a new way of representing Salome by turning her head away from the bleeding head of John the Baptist. That iconography endowed Salome with a certain degree of shame and conscientiousness, changing the way in which her physical beauty could be considered.

The fourth chapter, The Seducer-Destroyer Salome of Nineteenth-Century Art, illustrates how the image of Salome was constructed in art and literature in order to neutralize the social, political and economic challenges created by the nascent feminist movements. It is during the nineteenth century, particularly in France, that Salome's ideological role and image as an independent figure were shaped.

The second part of the book, *Salome and the Head of John the Baptist in Artists' Self-Portraits*, examines how the image of Salome was used in the creation of personal myths. Chapter five, Painting: Titian, Bernard, Moreau, demonstrates the construction of the self-portrait in *decapité* and in disguise and examines the significance and hidden meaning of each self-portrait. I examine artworks that create a personal legend through the story of Salome and John the Baptist. In those representations, the artists I examine—Titian, Emile Bernard and Gustave Moreau—often convey a hidden biographical message as well as their philosophical stance on art. By portraying themselves in the guise of the beheaded John the Baptist these artists further complicate and personalize the imagery and story of Salome.

Chapter six, Poetry: Stéphane Mallarmé, studies the self-portrait in literature, concentrating specifically on Mallarmé's unfinished poem *Les Noces d'Hérodiade*. In this poem Mallarmé fully reinvents the mythical image of Hérodiade/Salome as a *femme fatale* in order to create an image of himself. Mallarmé's untraditional Salome-Hérodiade becomes a metaphor for the poet's mythical ego, his inner world and his philosophy of creativity.

Part three, *Salome in Story, Drama and Music*, explores literary examples and their manifestations in visual arts and music. Salome's Dance in Flaubert's "Herodias:" Pictorial or Ekphrastic? (chapter seven), is a detailed study of the dancing Salome and her relationship to the process of creativity in Flaubert's short story. I consider the history of the image and the complexity of Flaubert's creative process, which, partly subconsciously, partly consciously, reshaped an already established mythical image of Salome, making her a dangerous object of masculine desire.

Chapter eight, Wilde's Salome, is an in-depth literary analysis of Wilde's play *Salome*. Wilde's Salome appears almost androgynous and can be taken as a symbol of the writer's reflections on life and art. On a less sophisticated level, his Salome becomes a striptease dancer performing the dance of Seven Veils, which became famous after Wilde's invention. Wilde's characterization of Salome's dance and its seductive effect on Herod colorfully and explicitly illuminated what many of his predecessors had only suggested about her nature. This characterization contributed greatly to the propagation of Salome's myth in the twentieth century and to her reputation as a seducer and destroyer.

Chapter nine, Wilde, Beardsley, Strauss, discusses several interpretations of the play. The "androgynous" Salome of Oscar Wilde is highlighted in visual form in the work of the English artist Aubrey Beardsley, whose illustrations I examine in this chapter. In music, my study is centered around Richard Strauss's opera *Salome,* based on Wilde's play. In this opera the character of Salome is depicted through music, and music enhances her with features that make her an even more complex, multidimensional and ultimately tragic character. Overall in this chapter I demonstrate how Aubrey Beardsley and Richard Strauss selectively focused on some of the play's possible interpretations in order to create their own artistic masterpieces.

There are many more works of art and literature, both minor and major, which feature Salome as a character and which either contributed to the various myths of Salome or were instrumental in their propagation. Unfortunately, the constraints of time and space do not allow for an examination of all instances of the Salome myth.

For example, the main text of my book does not study any of the appearances of Salome in Eastern Europe or Russia. It is worth noting, however, that Salome made a significant entrance into Russian culture with the translation of Wilde's play, which inspired its performance in theaters and also a film with Alla Azimova in the role of Salome. Salome made a particularly distinctive appearance in Russian poetry, especially in that of the twentieth century.[1] In Russia, the image of Salome was not invented or reinvented, but rather propagated in the form that she had already taken earlier in the minds of other artists and poets.

This book strives to challenge of the social stigmas attached to Salome, and it also questions the notion of social stigma in general. Part of the goal is to explore why and how history attaches such stigma to certain individuals, nations and cultures—in short, how society at large elects its demons and chooses its scapegoats. Perhaps human social structures are such that they require an enemy in order to reinforce who we are and who we want to be. Perhaps Salome has been one of those enemies, a vital figure in the structure of societies struggling to establish their ideologies and shape their cultures.[2]

Notes

[1] See Appendix 2.
[2] See the theory of the scapegoat developed by the French philosopher René Girard.

Part I

Creation of the Salome Myth

CHAPTER ONE

HISTORY AND MYTH IN THE BIBLICAL STORY

The Bible

Three New Testament Gospels—Matthew, Mark and Luke—mention the death of John the Baptist, but only Matthew and Mark depict the participation and the roles of Salome and her mother, Herodias. Matthew's account is the shortest and contains the essentials of the story:

> At that time Herod, the tetrarch, heard about the fame of Jesus; and he said to his servants, "This is John, the Baptist, he has been raised from the dead; that is why these powers are at work in him." For Herod had seized John and bound him and put him in prison, for the sake of Herodias, his brother Philip's wife; because John said to him, "It is not lawful for you to have her." And though he wanted to put him to death, he feared the people, because they held him to be a prophet. But when Herod's birthday came, the daughter of Herodias danced before the company, and pleased Herod, so that he promised with an oath to give her whatever she might ask. Prompted by her mother, she said, "Give me the head of John the Baptist here on a platter." And the king was sorry; but because of his oaths and his guests he commanded it to be given; he sent and had John beheaded in the prison, and his head was brought on a platter and given to the girl, and she brought it to her mother. And his disciples came and took the body and buried it; and they went and told Jesus.[1]

Many critics, theologians and historians have tried to determine the real reason for and manner of John the Baptist's death. The only historical sources we have are the works by the historian Josephus Flavius, principally in his book *Antiquities of the Jews*, written around 93 or 94 AD. More extensive than any biblical account, *Antiquities* provides a comprehensive account of Jewish history of the period, including a description of Herod's family and the story of the death of John the Baptist. Nowhere in his account is there any mention of a dance performed by Salome or by any other woman, nor of any involvement of Herodias, nor of any women in the execution of John.[2]

It is from Josephus' *Antiquities of the Jews* that we learn the name of Herodias's daughter, Salome (the biblical accounts do not give the girl a name), and that she had an unremarkable but contented life. She was married twice. The first marriage was childless, but after the death of her first husband she was happily married to Aristobulus, the king of Armenia, with whom she had three sons. Her portrait, in old age, was etched on Armenian coins of the period, and it is the only image of the real Salome that has reached our century. Such a prosaic existence apparently did not stem the rise of the mythical Salome, since her life story never informed the accounts of the artists, poets and writers who, for centuries, have been inspired by the image of a much more controversial, though fictionalized, dancing princess.

Josephus was attached to the Roman court and appears to have been privy to most of the political history of this period. He is not shy of being critical of historical figures, and he upholds John's righteousness. What reason would he have had to omit the dramatic story of John's death, if it indeed happened as described in the Gospels?

Textual Problems in the Gospels

The study of the Gospel stories told by Matthew and Mark complicates the investigation of the role of Salome in the Baptist's death. Several scholars claim that the story of Salome was a later embellishment, before the Christian era, added to the account of John the Baptist's death. In any case, it bears no resemblance to the sparse and equivocal facts of John's death. It is suspicious, for example, that the unnamed young girl is simply mentioned as a daughter of Herodias. Jean Psichari suggests that the story gives

> the appearance of an anecdote circulating in the isolated small community, little informed of the events outside of it. . . . We are in the presence of those rumors, vaguely shaped, very general, that travel from mouth to mouth, without any historical precision—unless in the mind of the narrators the moral precision is such that it allows them to avoid any historical precision.[3]

Psichari's point is well taken. One issue concerning the text is the chronological problem. In *Antiquities*, Josephus tells us that Salome was married to Philip, her uncle on her father's side, who died in 34 AD. After his death she married her young cousin Aristobulus. We know that in 49 AD Aristobulus was too young to inherit the kingdom of Chalcis from his father, and he became king of Armenia Minor only in 54 AD. Salome was still a child in 30 AD, probably all of twelve years old, and thus a young, prepubescent girl.[4]

Unfortunately, none of this is clear in the Latin Vulgate version of the Bible, which makes a significant mistake in its translation of the original Greek. In the Greek text, Salome is described as a little girl who had not yet reached puberty. The Latin translation, by comparison, describes her as a young woman, a girl who had already reached puberty. In the main English translations, which are translations from the Latin Vulgate, her age is not indicated at all. The Gospel of Mark simply tells us that "when Herodias' daughter came in and danced, she pleased Herod and his guests; and the king said to the *girl* . . ." (italics mine). The Gospel of Matthew tells us: "But when Herod's birthday came, the daughter of Herodias danced before the company, and pleased Herod, so that he promised with an oath to give her whatever she might ask." Here the word "girl" is omitted entirely.

Based on the original text of the Gospels, we can assume that in 30 AD the daughter of Herodias was about twelve years old. Supposedly she reached puberty and married her uncle a year later. At the time of her first husband's death in 34 AD, she would have been sixteen years old. The question is how could she have married Aristobulus if he must have been a small child, or even a toddler, in 34 AD, and thus far too young to marry the widowed Salome in the immediate wake of her first husband's death?

The other option, that she would have waited until Aristobulus became of age in 54 AD, seems implausible, as she would then have been 36 years old, much older than him. That does not give her enough time to have three sons with him, even if it were acceptable for an older woman to marry a younger man. All of this means that if Herodias did have a daughter named Salome who married Aristobulus, she could not have been the one who danced for Herod at the banquet.

Nikos Kokkinos, in his article "Which Salome did Aristobulus Marry?", contends that Aristobulus married the daughter of Herod Antipas and his first wife, the daughter of the Nabataean king Aretas, who left Antipas' house when she found out that he had married Herodias.[5] According to Kokkinos, their daughter's name was Herodias II-Salome and she was a little child in 30 AD. Kokkinos believes she was known throughout history as Salome and he believes that this is the reason for the historical confusion.

Kokkinos suggests that Herodias was not married twice but three times, and Herod Antipas was her third husband, whereas Philip, Antipas' half brother, was her second husband, and that marriage was childless. Kokkinos suggests that Herodias' daughter Salome was by her first husband and was supposedly born in 1 AD, when Herodias was 16 years old. Thus in 30 AD the daughter of Herodias would have been too old, around 30 years old, to be that young girl who danced at the banquet. W. Lillie suggests that, if there was ever any dance, it was performed by the daughter of Herod Antipas and his first wife.[6] If that is the case, and if she is the one who married Aristobulus, she would have been a very young child at the banquet, perhaps simply entertaining and pleasing her father and subsequently receiving encouragement and compliments from him. However, if we follow the assumption that the girl was around twelve years old, then she could not have been the daughter of Herod and his first wife, nor could she have been the daughter of Herodias.[7] Thus, from a historical perspective, the question of the dancing daughter of Herodias depicted by Mark and Matthew as a cause of John the Baptist's death remains unresolved. There are too few historical sources that address this issue, and they seem to supply conflicting information.

There is also a problem with whether such a dance is likely to have been possible at the time. Jean Psichari, in his article "Salomé et la décollation de St Jean Baptiste" ("Salome and the Beheading of John the Baptist"), examines different scenes of dance throughout the Old Testament and argues for the impossibility of a Judaic princess, even one who was Hellenized, dancing before men at a banquet. He writes: "We are absolutely not familiar with any dance of this nature. . . . We do not see the feminine *solo* appear anywhere."[8]

Kathleen E. Corley, in "Were the Women around Jesus Really Prostitutes? Women in the Context of Greco-Roman Meals,"[9] demonstrates that Roman meal practices divided meals into two parts: the first part was the meal itself and the second part was reserved for drinking, entertainment, conversation, philosophical discourse or religious rituals. It was not proper for wives and children to remain for the second part of the meal, and they were required to leave after the completion of the meal proper. Corley explains that

> Unmarried women, that is, young maidens, were still excluded from public banquet settings, although they may have been allowed to be present at a private meal even if a stranger was present. One assumes that if present, daughters would be seated at their parents' feet, as all children were, until they came of age and were married.[10]

The only women who always participated in the banquets with men and remained present for the second part of the meal, the entertainment, were the prostitutes or courtesans. If a matron stayed for the second part of the evening she would be characterized as a prostitute.

As far as Jewish women are concerned, purely Jewish laws regarding women were extremely severe. As Tal Ilan explains: "The world has been fashioned along certain hierarchical lines, according to which men rule women. Josephus explains that in Judaism a woman is supposed always to obey her husband."[11] In order to justify women's exclusion from social life, various ancient Jewish books describe women as "deceitful and cunning but weak-hearted and fragile,"[12] or state that "women are more susceptible than men to promiscuity."[13] These sources also assert that "A woman can be seduced, a man cannot,"[14] and characterize women as "light-headed."[15] As a result there were many laws that regulated both the behavior of women and the behavior of men toward women. Since women were considered prone to evil, there were regulations regarding men's talking with women, or even looking at women; there were further rules for keeping women at home and rules for women on how not to attract the attention of men.[16]

Although Herod Antipas and his family were Hellenized, they were Jews and ruled a Jewish territory. That means they knew the Jewish tradition even though they distanced themselves from it and instead adopted Greco-Roman traditions, including its treatment of women. Nevertheless, as rulers of the Jewish territory they had to partly respect the Jewish laws, especially at public events. Herod's banquet could be considered a public event, since it seems to have been an official celebration of the ruler's birthday.

All of this makes the biblical account of Salome seem increasingly unlikely. As we saw, women in Greco-Roman culture were allowed to participate in meals during banquets, but only prostitutes could attend the second part of the banquet, the one that was not the proper meal and was designated for entertainment. Unmarried daughters, such as Salome, were allowed to be present at private meals and sit at their parents' feet during the meal proper, but they then had to leave the banquet. Historically and culturally it would not have been possible for the daughter of Herodias, the wife of the tetrarch of Galilee, to even be present for the second part of the banquet, and it is unthinkable and unimaginable that she would perform any kind of dance, either as a child or as a young girl.

The Gospels: Historical and Literary Interpretations

On the basis of the biblical text it is clear that Herod gave the order to kill John the Baptist. Such a move was arguably in Herod's interest, as John was inflaming Jewish public opinion against him and his status as a Roman representative and a Hellenized Jew governing a Jewish territory. Jews could easily have seen Herod as a traitor. By comparison, the motivation and involvement of Herodias and her daughter are equivocal in the historical record, even if we accept the Gospels as fact.

In general, the Gospel stories give a quite limited account of each person involved in John's execution. With so little biblical or historical description of the people involved in John's death, we might take a more literary approach to explore some possibilities of what can we infer from the text.

Herod Antipas is a politician, one who serves the Romans and whose reputation in the Roman world depends on what he does in the area under his control. He is ambivalent about John. On the one hand he recognizes John's ability and inclination to provoke rebellion amongst the already contentious Jews, and he wishes to avoid civil unrest in his protectorate. On the other hand, he is also aware of the popularity that John commands among Jews, and he may respect and fear John's fervor and charismatic leadership. Irrespective of Herod's relationship with his wife and his willingness to promote her views, John's death would thus be a politically convenient result, if only it could be managed with minimal personal responsibility and guilt. Orchestrating John's death through a dramatic event in a public forum at the insistence of someone else would be an effective way to do both.

In the Gospel stories, Herodias is represented as the instigator of John's death because, according to the evangelists, John chastised her for marrying Antipas while Antipas' half-brother, Philip—to whom supposedly she was originally married—was still alive. According to Jewish law, marrying the brother of a living husband was not allowed, though marrying the brother of a deceased husband was permitted and even encouraged. A woman was not allowed to leave and divorce her husband, whereas the husband could leave and divorce his wife.

According to Roman law, however, divorce was acceptable, and there was no prohibition against marrying the divorced husband's brother. Moreover, Roman law allowed a woman to leave her husband and to initiate a divorce. This was unthinkable in the Jewish tradition. But, given that Herod's family was culturally Hellenized, neither divorce nor remarriage presented any legal or moral problem, even if the marriage between Antipas and Herodias could be politically risky. Hoehner suggests that in

> John's denunciation of Antipas' and Herodias' marriage, as presented in the Gospels, there may have been more political overtone that one would suspect. It must be seen from two points of view. First, from the viewpoint of John's followers: John was urging people to repent and be baptized, because the Messiah's kingdom was at hand. . . . But he also made a scathing denunciation of their ruler for violating the commandments of

God. Such a denunciation is significant, for at the climax of Messianic expectation, the laws of God are heightened, and believers far less tolerant towards those who oppose the Law.

Antipas would have known full well that religious fanaticism is far more dangerous than political zeal. From the point of view of John's followers, therefore, Herod had defiled not only man's law but God's, and this was not to be tolerated.[17]

Additionally, Josephus explains that the marriage between Herodias and Antipas was a cause of war with the Nabataean royal family, to which Antipas' first wife, the daughter of king Aretas, belonged. The mere intention of marriage between Herodias and Antipas and the forthcoming divorce of Aretas' daughter were taken by the entire Nabataean royal family as an insult that they believed could not go unpunished. Within a few years of the marriage of Herodias and Antipas a war began between Aretas and Antipas. Antipas almost lost the war and would have been expelled from his territory had it not been for the Romans, who intervened and chased Aretas' troops out of Antipas' territory. As Hoehner points out: ". . . in view of the political situation John's denunciation 'was not only embarrassing, it was politically explosive.'"[18] He goes on to suggest that

> It is highly probable that Antipas was closely watching the Baptist's movements. When John denounced the marriage of Antipas and Herodias this could have been the 'straw that broke the camel's back.' At least, it furnished a good excuse for Antipas to say that it could have started a revolt. John's grip upon the people was sufficiently strong to be noticed by both Antipas and the religious leaders. It was better to nip it in the bud than to wait until it was too late. From Antipas' viewpoint this movement could have led to serious consequences.[19]

Thus our investigations into the political and psychological dimensions of John's death establish the likelihood that Herod gave the order to have John killed. There is some historical consensus that Herodias had ambitious goals for her new husband, Herod Antipas, and that the couple established a strong bond and developed political plans to protect it. Involving Herodias' young daughter in a scheme to diffuse blame for John's death is a possibility, albeit an unlikely one. The absence of the dance story from Josephus' account, the improbability of a female—and a princess, no less—performing for an assembled group, and, as we will see later, the survival of a similar story from centuries earlier and the use of it to embellish the Gospel narrative all cast serious doubts on the biblical accounts of Salome's involvement.

The Gospels as an Ancient Novel

Perhaps it should not be surprising that the Gospels contain so many inaccuracies. Some scholars suggest that the Gospels were an example of an ancient novel, written for a specific audience and with a specific purpose. Such writings would have been intended to illustrate the comfort of a divinity who, unlike the pagan gods, offered the possibility of a personal relationship. For the isolated Greco-Roman common man this relief from solitude might have been especially attractive. Biblical scholars such as Tolbert and Hagg believe that the Gospels' narrative is rooted in the ancient popular novel, which had to satisfy the psychological needs of the contemporary population in the changing Greco-Roman world. These ancient novels are defined as "literature composed in such a way as to be accessible to a wide spectrum of society, both literate and illiterate."[20] In order to reach such a wide spectrum of society, popular literature usually addressed the issues of the general population. By the first century AD, the population of the Roman empire could be characterized by its mobility, resulting in a level of insecurity and a consequent desire for stability. In this constantly changing, unstable new environment there was great importance placed on rhetorical skills, especially the ability to persuade, which was necessary for survival. The literature of the period would have aspired to address these issues.[21]

Ancient novels were often a combination of historiography and dramatic events. Structurally, they conformed to some established norms. Tolbert describes their principal characteristics as follows:

> (1) [the novels were] filled with anticipations, repetitions, and recapitulations of material, so that the audience is never in suspense about what is to happen. (2) Characters in the novels are fashioned as 'types' who illustrate concepts or ethical principles rather than the realistic figures such as are found in modern writings. (3) The novels end with extended recognition sequences in which the fundamental nature of all the characters is revealed and all the important persons and issues are identified.[22]

Although the Gospels are not ancient novels, they do bear structural similarities to such novels. As Tolbert explains:

> The Gospels' mixing together of historiographic form and dramatic force, its synthesizing of earlier genres such as biography, memorabilia of a sage, aretalogy, and apocalypse, its stylistic techniques of episodic plot, beginning with minimal introduction, central turning point, and final recognition scene, and most of all, its fairly crude, repetitious, and conventionalized narrative display striking *stylistic* similarities to the

popular Greek ancient novel.[23]

Tolbert argues that each of the Gospels is a "self-consciously crafted narrative, a fiction, resulting from literary imagination, not photographic recall."[24] As Haim Cohn notes,

> the Gospel traditions are "messages of faith and not historiography": any historical material in their hands the authors used "to add detail and graphic quality," . . . they freely exercised their fantasy "in presenting, and in meaning to present, not history but theology."[25]

Though the Gospels were at first narrated orally, they were constructed as ancient novels, designed to make people feel more secure through comfort in God.[26]

Since there is no historical evidence that the story of John's beheading, as it is told in the Gospels, really occurred, the details of Salome and her dance appear to be little more than a dramatic device. They highlight the passion of John the Baptist and heighten the story's effects. A natural tendency of the authors, who were not historians but "evangelists," was to use any available stories or traditions that might make vivid the point of their narrative. We know that a story similar to Salome's dance and its deadly outcome was available for this purpose, and the evangelists might have drawn from it.

Helen Zagona and John White explain that the general story which the evangelists used to create the story of the death of John the Baptist was well known in the early Christian era and was perceived with horror by the early Christians.[27] It is suggested that the original story took place in the year 184 BC, at the moment the consul Flamininus was expelled from the Roman Senate for having a prisoner killed to impress a young boy who was his lover. The first account of the story appears in Cicero's essay *De Senecute*, and later Plutarch (c. 46-120 AD) describes different forms that the story took in the hands of different historians. In his *Life of Flamininus*, Plutarch writes:

> Titus had a brother, Lucius Flamininus, very unlike him in all points of character, and, in particular, low and dissolute in his pleasures. . . . He kept as a companion a boy . . . One day at a drinking bout, when the youngster was wantoning with Lucius, "I love you, sir, so dearly," said he, "that preferring your satisfaction to my own, I came away without seeing the gladiators, though I have never seen a man killed in my life." Lucius, delighted with what the boy said, answered: "Let not that trouble you; I can satisfy that longing," and with that orders a condemned man to be fetched out of the prison, and the executioner to be sent for, and commands him to strike off the man's head, before they rose from table. Valerius Antius only

so far varies the story as to make it a woman for whom he did it. But Livy says that . . . a Gaulish deserter coming with his wife and children to the door, Lucius took him into the banqueting room, and killed him with his own hand, to gratify his paramour.[28]

The story was kept alive by historians and rhetoric teachers, who occasionally changed it by adding different elements. The Roman historian Valerius Maximus, in his narration of Flamininus' story, transforms the boy into a girl. In Seneca's version the paramour of Flamininus seduces him with a dance. She is rewarded with the head of a man who has offended her, bringing the details closer to those used by Matthew's and Mark's accounts of the Baptist's death. Some scholars thus argue that the Flamininus story was adapted by Matthew and Mark for their own purposes.

We might ask what prompted Mark, in inventing the story (and Matthew in repeating it), to represent Herod Antipas not as a true political figure—a leader, a tetrarch, a Roman representative in Galilee and the real executioner of John the Baptist—but as an ineffectual leader, a victim of his wife, Herodias, and the wife's unnamed daughter. The similarity with the Gospels' representation of the execution of Jesus Christ is striking. In the latter story, Pilate, the cruelest governor of Judea, is depicted as a poor and noble victim of "horrid" Jews. In this regard the Jews are similar to the women in the story of John the Baptist's execution: Neither the Jews nor the women had any real power and authority yet both were blamed for sins they never committed.[29]

It seems that in order to lighten the Roman persecutions the Gospel writers endeavored to unburden the Romans of their responsibility in the deaths of Christian heroes and show that Romans themselves were pro-Christian. In Cohan's opinion,

> This . . . is the motive which prompted the evangelists to depict the Passion story in a manner calculated to discharge the Roman governor of any responsibility for the crucifixion, placing it squarely upon the shoulders of the Jews.[30]

In the case of John the Baptist's beheading, which is a parallel to Jesus' Passion narrative, the evangelists consciously aspired to relieve the Roman representative—in this case, Herod Antipas—of any responsibility for the Baptist's death, just as they later exculpated Pilate. In the case of Christ, they assigned responsibility for the crucifixion to the Jews, and in the case of John the Baptist they place his death upon the shoulders of two women. It was convenient, since, as we saw earlier, women were depicted as devious and debauched, not to be looked at or talked to, acceptable only when sequestered. Only evil women, such as prostitutes, could influence men by being looked at and spoken to. Hence, once women were allowed to circulate freely they could do only evil. The way Herodias and her daughter are perceived and represented is an embodiment of this way of thinking. Furthermore, by making the main characters of the story—John the Baptist and Herod—the victims of two women, the evangelists accomplished two significant goals: They exculpated the Romans of the responsibility for the Baptist's death even while they implicitly criticized the Romans for giving their women more freedom than they deserved.

Thus, I believe that Psichari's argument that presenting the execution of John in so barbarous a way was a means by which the first Christians demonized Herod Antipas as a belated vengeance for the execution of the prophet is inaccurate.[31] As was shown earlier, the evangelists do not try to demonize Herod Antipas but rather do just the opposite. Similar to discharging Pilate of responsibility for the execution of Christ and blaming the Jews, the evangelists excused Herod Antipas of responsibility for the death of John the Baptist and placed the responsibility on the women's shoulders. Herod's wife, Herodias, and her unnamed daughter are thus assigned blame. Similar to the Jews in Christ's Passion story, these women are scapegoats for the Baptist's death.

We can see that the creation of the myth of John the Baptist's death and the involvement of Herodias and her daughter, which would go through further evolution in later times, already begins in the Gospels. The evangelists, using the techniques of the ancient novel, embellish the narration of their stories by adding the reshaped version of the dance and beheading that took place in the year 184 BC at the time of the consul Flamininus, whose story and cruelty were engraved in popular collective memory. The evangelists' embellishment endowed the story with impressive details that capture the imagination of the listener or the reader.

Notes

[1] (Matthew, 14:1-12). This citation and the following are all taken from the Revised Standard Version of the Bible, copyright 1952 (2nd edition, 1971) by the Division of Christian Education of the National Council of the Churches of Christ in the United States of America (available online at:
http://www.biblestudytools.com/rsv/matthew/passage.aspx?q=matthew+14:1-12):

King Herod heard of it; for Jesus' name had become known. Some said, "John the baptizer has been raised from the dead; that is why these powers are at work in him." But others said, "It is Elijah." And others said, "It is a prophet, like one of the prophets of old." But when Herod heard of it he said, "John, whom I beheaded, has been raised." For Herod had sent and seized John, and bound him in prison for the sake of Herodias, his brother Philip's wife; because he had married her. For

John said to Herod, "It is not lawful for you to have your brother's wife." And Herodias had a grudge against him, and wanted to kill him. But she could not, for Herod feared John, knowing that he was a righteous and holy man, and kept him safe. When he heard him, he was much perplexed; and yet he heard him gladly. But an opportunity came when Herod on his birthday gave a banquet for his courtiers and officers and the leading men of Galilee. For when Herodias' daughter came in and danced, she pleased Herod and his guests; and the king said to the girl, "Ask me for whatever you wish, and I will grant it." And he vowed to her, "Whatever you ask me, I will give you, even half of my kingdom." And she went out, and said to her mother, "What shall I ask?" And she said, "The head of John the baptizer." And she came and immediately with haste to the king, and asked, saying, "I want you to give me at once the head of John the Baptist on a platter." And the king was exceedingly sorry; but because of his oaths and his guests he did not want to break his word to her. And immediately the king sent a soldier of the guard and gave orders to bring his head. He went and beheaded him in the prison, and brought his head on a platter, and gave it to the girl; and the girl gave it her mother. When his disciples heard of it, they came and took his body, and laid it in a tomb. (Mark, 6: 14-29)

Now Herod the tetrarch heard of all that was done, and he was perplexed, because it was said by some that John had been raised from the dead, by some that Elijah had appeared, and by others that one of the old prophets had risen. Herod said, "John I beheaded; but who is this about whom I hear such things?" And he sought to see him. (Luke, 9: 7-9)

[2] Italic is mine. Here is the text of *Flavius Josephus*: "Now when [many] others came in crowds about him, for they were very greatly moved [or pleased] by hearing his words, Herod, who feared lest the great influence John had over the people might put it into his power and inclination to raise a rebellion, (for they seemed ready to do any thing he should advise,) thought it best, by putting him to death, to prevent any mischief he might cause, and not bring himself into difficulties, by sparing a man who might make him repent of it when it would be too late. Accordingly he was sent a prisoner, out of Herod's suspicious temper, to Macherus, the castle I before mentioned, and was there put to death. Now the Jews had an opinion that the destruction of this [Herod's in a later battle] army was sent as a punishment upon Herod, and a mark of God's displeasure to him." (Parenthetical additions and italics are mine.) *The Works of Flavius Josephus*, trans. William Whiston, (available online at:
http://www.ccel.org/j/josephus/works/ant-18.htm).

[3] Jean Psichari, "Salomé et la décollation de St. Jean-Baptiste," *Revue de l'Histoire des Religions* 72 (1915), 135. "Cela donne tout de suite au récit je ne sais quelle apparence d'anecdote circulant dans une communauté isolée, petite, peu informée des choses du dehors. . . . Nous sommes en présence d'un de ces oui-dires qu'on se passe de bouche en bouche, avec des contours un peu vagues, un peu flous, sans grande précision historique—à moins que, dans l'esprit des narrateurs, la précision morale ne soit telle . . . qu'ils ont pu et dû se passer de toute précision historique."

[4] Many scholars agree that the translation of the Bible is not based on the original

texts, written in Arameic and Greek, but on the Latin translation of the Bible, the Vulgate, which in turn contains a number of errors. See Harold W. Hoehner, *Herod Antipas* (Cambridge University Press, 1972), 154-156.

[5] Tal Ilan, *Jewish Woman in Greco-Roman Palestine* (Hendrickson Publishers, Inc., 1995), 51. Nikos Kokkinos, "Which Salome did Aristobulus Marry?" *Palestine Exploration Quarterly* 118 (1986): 33-50.

[6] W. Lillie, "Salome or Herodias?" *Expository Times* 65 (1953-4), 251.

[7] For more options and details see Ross S. Kraemer, "Implicating Herodias and Her Daughter in the Death of John the Baptizer: A (Christian) Theological Strategy?" *Journal of Biblical Literature* 125, N 2, Summer (2006): 321-349.

[8] Psichari, "Salomé et la décollation de St. Jean-Baptiste," 138-139. «On ne connaît absolument aucun exemple d'une danse de ce genre. . . . De solo féminin nous n'en voyons nulle part.» Mary Ann Tolbert points out that "What little is known about the way women's social roles were defined in the ancient world suggests that proper behavior for women was almost the direct opposite of proper behavior for men. Male honor depended, in public, on winning contests of wit, strength, or rhetoric among male peers and, in private, on asserting authority over women of their class and over men and women of lower status. For women, winning honor was virtually impossible, and any public display was strongly discouraged." See the Introduction to "Mark" in Carol A. Newsom and Sharon H. Ringe, eds., *Women's Bible Commentary* (Louisville, KY: Westminster John Knox Press, 1998), 351.

[9] Kathleen E. Corley, "Were the Women around Jesus Really Prostitutes? Women in the Context of Greco-Roman Meals," *Society of Biblical Literature, seminar papers* (1989), 487-521.

[10] Ibid., 494.

[11] Tal Ilan, *Jewish Women*, 122.

[12] Ibid., *Testament of Rueben*, 124.

[13] Ibid., 124.

[14] Ibid., in *Mekhilta de-Rabbi Shimeon bar Yohai*, 124.

[15] Ibid.

[16] Ibid. One of the most famous ancient Jewish sayings was "Talk not much with womankind." (126) Men were forbidden to look at women. Tal Ilan points out that "Ben Sira completely forbids looking at any woman other than one's wife. The danger of observing women, particularly beautiful women, is mentioned three times in the Testament of the Twelve Patriarchs. Reuben avows that had he not looked at Bilha he would not have sinned. Judah, too, lamenting that he fell into the net of the Canaanite woman because of her beauty, warns his sons against looking at women. Finally, Benjamin tells his sons that pure thoughts require not looking at any woman not one's own." (127). The solution for avoiding looking at women and talking to them was to lock them in. They were supposed to be secluded at their houses. (128) Although historical sources show that women did go out, the law discouraged it. For instance, in their interpretation of the biblical laws on rape, the rabbis' rule asserts: "And a man finds her in the city. If she had not gone out into the city he would not have happened upon her." (128) Rabbi

Meir states that a wicked man is the one "who sees his wife go outside with her head uncovered . . . and she spins in public." (128). The *Babylonian Talmud* asserts that the wicked woman is the one "who eats in public, drinks in public." (129) Hair was considered one of the most seductive parts of a woman's appearance, and for that reason the head of proper women had to be always covered.

[17] Harold W. Hoehner, *Herod Antipas*, 142.
[18] Ibid., 144.
[19] Ibid., 145.
[20] Mary Ann Tolbert, *Sowing the Gospel: Mark's World in Literary-Historical Perspective* (Minneapolis: Fortress Press, 1989), 70.
[21] Tolbert, *Sowing the Gospel*, 63-64, suggests: "What unites these works is a common myth, a common heritage, and a common conventionalized style, employed by the authors with varying degrees of sophistication. The myth is the Hellinistic myth of the isolated individual in a dangerous world. 'Unaccommodated man, man alone and thus without security, seeks security, in God or his fellow man, or woman. Lacking a social identity, he seeks to create for himself a personal one by becoming the object of the affections of his own kind or of the providence of the Almighty. He identifies himself by loving God or man or both.' (Reardon, "The Greek Novel," 294; see also Hagg, "The Novel in Antiquity," 89-90) The novels are full of religious concerns and themes. It is the gods who often step in to save or damn the hero and heroine. . . . all of these ancient novels betray a very serious, very religious underlying concern: salvation from isolation, chaos, and death."
[22] Ibid., 53.
[23] Ibid., 53.
[24] Ibid., 30.
[25] Haim Cohn, *The Trial and Death of Jesus* (New York: Ktav Publishing House, Inc., 1977), xv. Cohn is citing two other scholars in this quotation: E. Sjoeborg, *Der verborgene Menschensohn in den Evangelien* (Lund, 155), 214; and H. Lietzmann, *A History of the Early Church*, 4 vols. in 2 (New York: Meridian Books, 1961), 223.
[26] For instance, the Gospel text uses common folkloric expressions of the time. The expression "you can have even the half of my kingdom," which Herod Antipas offers to Salome as a recompense for her dance, by Antipas' time had become a common idiom that would not have been taken literally but would have indicated that the utterer was or would be very pleased. Although this expression is also used in the Old Testament in Esther's story, in which Ahasuerus promises Esther "half of his kingdom," Harold Hoehner, in his book *Herod Antipas*, claims that the expression "half of one's kingdom" was already a proverbial expression at the time of Ahasuerus, when the Esther's story took place. He writes: "Certainly to offer a half of one's possessions was a familiar expression. No one at the banquet would have taken it literally, for all of them (including Antipas) knew Antipas' position. They would have accepted it as a proverbial saying. . . . Neither Esther nor Herodias' daughter held the rulers to their promise, but only requested a favor which did not involve them in the surrender of any part of their domains. The

promise, therefore, was not to be taken literally; it merely indicated that the ruler in question was willing to do a reasonable favor for the person to whom he uttered this saying." Harold W. Hoehner, *Herod Antipas*, 151. Some commentators have dismissed the possibility that Antipas would have made such an offer, on the grounds that to Antipas it would have been meaningless. As Hoehner (151) notes, "Not only did he have no kingdom to give away, but as a vassal of Rome, his dominions were not even his."

[27] Helen Genéve Zagona, *The legend of Salome and the principle of art for art's sake* (Geneva: Droz, 1960), 14-15.

[28] Ibid., 15. She cites Plutarch, *Lives of the Noble Grecians and Romans*, trans. John Dryden (New York, 1932), 462. Also see John S. White, *The Salome Motive* (Eloquent Press Corporation, 1941).

[29] Cohn, *Trial and Death of Jesus*, 189-190, writes that probably "Pilate—and I would add Herod Antipas—would be very much surprised if they had been told that the poor little Jews who appeared before [them] . . . would cause [their] own names to be handed down in immortal stories. [They] did nothing to deserve [their] fame—just another routine . . . sentences of stubborn and foolish Jews; nor did [they] do anything to deserve to be slanderously misrepresented as so inept as to allow [themselves] to be made a tool in the hands of contemptible natives [and devious women] and do their bidding against their own better judgment. They had arrived at their own judgement, and pronounced it, and would see to it that it was punctually carried out. . . . For the sake of a good administrative order, they would make a routine report to the emperor of . . . the sentence that they had passed, probably as one item among many in a monthly return, and that would be the end of the matter."

[30] Ibid., xvi.

[31] See Psichari's article, especially pages 146-147 and 150. The Christian attempt to take revenge on Herod by presenting him as a monster is one of the points of the article. Psichari endeavors to stress that, among other things, the evangelists meant that it was Herod's daughter, rather than Herodias', who danced. He claims that they further imply that Herod had sexual love and attraction toward his own daughter. This is all questionable and not clear. Nonetheless, even if it were the case, the evangelists do not state that, but on the contrary cover that up by precisely stating that it was Herodias' daughter, and not Herod's, who danced. It is an additional proof that the evangelists wanted to present Herod in a positive light, while negatively depicting Herodias and her unnamed daughter.

CHAPTER TWO

THE EVIL SALOME OF THEOLOGY AND ICONOGRAPHY: FROM THE CHURCH FATHERS TO THE RENAISSANCE

> Figaro here, Figaro there.
> —*The Marriage of Figaro*

Salome in Theology

As we have seen, the origins of Salome's image are found in the Gospels, but a religious and theological interest in her came only in the fourth century, with the construction in Alexandria of a church in honor of John the Baptist. The veneration of John and the growing interest in his death brought about a corresponding interest in Salome, who became at that time the object of religious attacks. As Helena Grace Zagona points out: "In legends, the purer the hero, the blacker the villain, and the Salome story followed the rule."[1] The roots of Salome's representations in art and literature—which have persisted over the centuries—can be traced to Church theologians in Late Antiquity.

In the fourth century, the Church was still in the process of establishing its views on gender roles. These views were in part influenced by the larger Greco-Roman culture. But the Church Fathers also drew on images of biblical women to develop their ideas on women's roles in society. The model woman, especially for wives and mothers, was the Virgin Mary. She was a paragon of virtue and represented the feminine ideals of submissiveness and humility.[2] By calling on women to follow such an example, the Church Fathers sought to minimize women's role in social life and reduce their potential influence on politics and society. Salome and her mother Herodias, by comparison, did not fit the model of "good" women. Rather, they fit Eve's lineage, in which the woman is the embodiment of evil.

The Church Fathers and the Church used the dance and the images of Salome and Herodias as an educational tool. They attacked the dance and even invented details to emphasize its immorality. Their attack was aimed at the dance's alleged indecency, which they depicted in exceedingly graphic and provocative terms. The Church perceived these entertainments as a threat, associating them with pagan traditions and especially with the dancing Bacchants or Maenads, who followed the God of Wine, Dionysus. Members of his cult were reported to dress in the skins of fawns and panthers and celebrate Dionysian rites in the mountains, where they would stir themselves into a state of ecstatic frenzy. Later Church writers also saw in the dance the manifestations of the tradition of mimes and circuses, both of which the Church fought against and which existed in Byzantium until the fifteenth century.

Stories of Salome being punished for the indecency of her dance and for her role in John the Baptist's death proliferated in Early Christian writings. Nikos Kokkinos tells us that in the New Testament Apocrypha, in the so-called *Letter of Herod to Pilate* from one of the appendices to the *Acts of Pilate* (middle of the fourth century), Herod writes about his daughter Herodias, who was supposedly the young girl who danced. He writes that at one point she was playing upon the water (i.e. the ice) and fell in up to her neck. He grabbed at her head to save her but "it was cut off, and the water swept her body away."[3] The story was repeated in various versions down through the Middle Ages, although the name Salome is typically used.[4] In Jacobus de Voragine's *The Golden Legend*,[5] written around 1260, Salome's death is described in the following way:

> As she (Salome) was journeying once in the winter time, and a frozen river had to be crossed on foot, the ice broke beneath her, not without the providence of God. Straightway she sank down up to her neck. This made her dance and wriggle about with all the lower parts of her body, not on land, but in the water. Her wicked head was glazed with ice, and at length severed from her body by the sharp edges, not of iron, but of frozen water. Thus in the very ice she displayed the dance of death, and furnished a spectacle to all who beheld it, which brought to mind what she had done.[6]

Sometimes there are other versions of her death. The French, German and Italian mysteries make her dance with demons who came to take her to hell. Occasionally she becomes the Queen of Witches and is destroyed by her own evil.[7]

Thus, the role of Herodias and Salome in the Baptist's beheading served as a lesson for men, reminding them to keep their wives and daughters locked up at home, away from society, since only evil could come from giving women a public voice.

With the Crusades the popularity of John the Baptist grew and the reputation of Salome suffered. Many more invented details were added to the New Testament story. It is at that time that Salome was represented as enamored of John, desiring his head as vengeance for what she perceived as his rejection of her.[8]

Salome in Religious Iconography

Visual artists have long depicted the life of John the Baptist and his death, and they have been particularly drawn to the story of the dance of Salome, since its beauty contrasted so powerfully with its gruesome consequences. The art historian Daniel Arasse discusses three female types, which Christian iconography has strongly reinforced.[9] The first type is Eve, whom the Church perceived as evil: she is the source of original sin, a dangerous temptress, a manipulator, a destroyer and an eater of men. The second type is Mary, the mother of Christ, the ideal woman, the anti-Eve, through whom original sin was forgiven. That is why, according to Arasse, when the angel Gabriel announces to Mary her future as the mother of the Son of God, he greets her with "Ave," an anagram of Eva.[10] Finally, there is Mary Magdalene, a composite image who was invented to give immoral women an opportunity to redeem themselves. Since any woman is an incarnation of evil, any woman is like Mary Magdalene. But Mary Magdalene abandoned her sinful life, became a follower of Christ and went to the desert to atone for her sins, setting herself on the path to being an ideal woman. She is a passage from Eve to Mary, and though ordinary women could never attain the exalted status of Mary they could hope to reach the state of Magdalene.

In early Christian literature and art all three images of women were popular but the iconography of the image of Salome/Herodias, which falls into the category of the evil and destructive descendants of Eve, was especially in demand. The death of John the Baptist and the accompanying legend of Salome's role in it were particularly well-suited for moral teachings, especially via art. The story was given a variety of imaginative forms by artists over the centuries. From this array of interpretations, three major themes involving the evil nature of Salome and Herodias became predominant in the story's religious iconography. What follows is an outline of these three major themes.

A. *The first theme is the Banquet of Herod as a Background for the Dance of Salome.* This representation has many variations. Sometimes there are musicians playing at the banquet while Salome dances her fatal dance. Occasionally, Salome holds the platter with the Baptist's severed head on it above her own head while she performs her dance, thus conflating the two moments of the story (Figs. I-2-3, II-1-2). In medieval art, Salome is seen performing an acrobatic hand-stand dance (Fig. III-1-6). Sometimes the banquet scene is combined with the beheading scene.

The oldest known representation of Herod's Banquet and John the Baptist's decapitation is a sixth-century miniature from the Gospel of Saint Matthew in the *Codex Sinopensis* (fol. 10v).[11] In that work (Fig. I-2-1) Salome does not dance, although she participates in Herod's banquet. The first time we see a dancing Salome (Fig. I-2-2) is three centuries later, in the *Evangéliaire de Chartres* (fol. 146v),[12] painted in the first part of the ninth century.[13]

From the year 1000 on there is a proliferation of images representing Salome dancing. We can see Salome dancing on the windows, tympanums and column capitals of churches. In the twelfth century, she resembles the figures of Ancient Greek bacchants in procession. Her dance involves her entire body and she is accompanied by tambourines or bells.

In the thirteenth century, the dance becomes quite acrobatic. On the capitals that came from the chapter house of St-Georges de Boscherville, preserved in the Museum of Antiquities in Rouen, Salome is represented standing on her hands and dancing with her head down. The same dance can be found on the doors of the churches of San Zeno in Verona, Saint-Lazare d'Avallon in Burgundy, San Cugat Del Vallès in Catalonia; on the door of the cathedral of Rouen (Fig. III-7-6); and on the windows of the Saint-Jean chapel in the cathedral of Clermont-Ferrand.[14] The Rouen representation is the one that undoubtedly inspired Flaubert's novella "Herodias." Danièle Devynck, in the article "La Saulterelle déshonnête," describes the representation of Salome's acrobatic dance of the thirteenth century as "taken to the level of jugglers and the troubadours, known at the feudal courts of the Middle Ages,"[15] which were then very popular. The Church perceived these entertainers as a threat and fought against them during the Middle Ages. Representing the evil Salome dancing on her hands as an acrobat was a way to put a negative spin on any kind of entertainment associated with dance and the circus.

In the fourteenth century, Salome's dance is represented less acrobatically but becomes even more provocative and seductive. For example, the image of the dancing Salome as a dangerous seducer can be found in mosaics in the Baptistery of San Marco in Venice (Fig. I-2-3). Here she holds the platter with the head of John the Baptist above her own head while she dances.

Fig. I-2-1. *Herod's Banquet and John the Baptist's Decapitation* in the *Codex Sinopensis*

28   Chapter Two

Fig. I-2-2. *Dancing Salome* in the *Evangéliaire de Chartres*

Fig. I-2-3. *Dancing Salome*, San Marco.

The artists of the early, middle and later Renaissance and of the seventeenth and eighteenth centuries continued to be inspired by Salome's dance. In the early Renaissance, she is represented by such innovators as Giotto, Donatello and Andrea del Sarto. She dances in Filippo Lippi's *Feast of Herod* in Prato (Fig. I-3-2). Yet the young girl dancing for these artists seems to have nothing to do with the evil seducer of the previous centuries. Inspired by the revival of Classicism, Renaissance artists portrayed Salome as a beautiful dancing nymph, the symbol of feminine beauty.

B. *The second theme of John the Baptist's Passion in visual arts is the Beheading, or Decollation, of John the Baptist.* This representation also has many variations. The beheading is often associated with the executioner's presentation of the head to Salome. The oldest known representation of this scene is in the sixth-century *Codex Sinopensis* (fol. 10v), mentioned previously as the oldest source of Salome imagery. In that representation (Fig. I-2-1), Herod and Herodias are shown terrified by Salome's trophy. This also appears in some later examples, such as on the column capitals of Saint-Etienne de Toulouse, preserved in the Musée des Augustins, or in the painting *The Head of John the Baptist brought to Herod* (1454) by Giovanni di Paolo, now located at the Art Institute of Chicago (Fig. I-2-4).

Fig. I-2-4. Giovanni di Paolo, *The Head of John the Baptist brought to Herod*

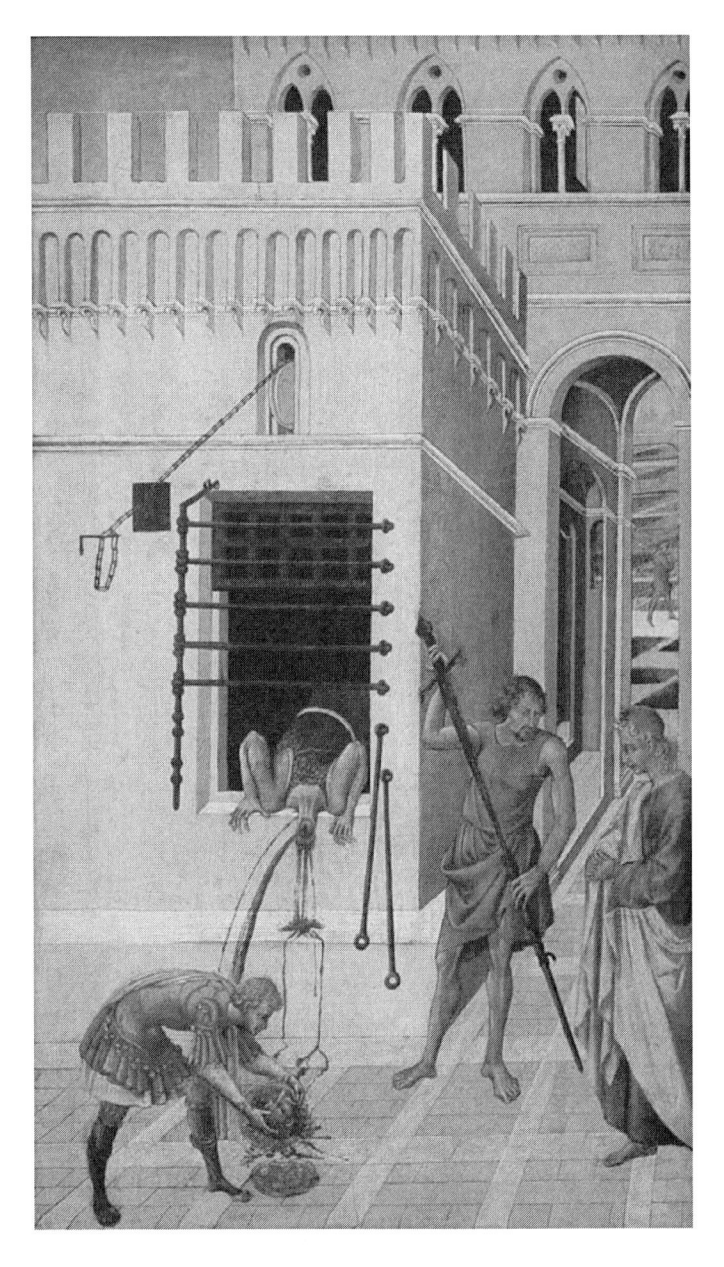

Fig. I-2-5. Giovanni di Paolo, *John the Baptist's Beheading*.

Fig. I-2-6. Cesare da Sesto, *Salome with the head of John the Baptist*, fifteenth century

The first known representation of the actual beheading is in the ninth-century *Evangeliaire de Chartres* (Fig. I-2-2). In this scene the beheading takes place without Salome present with the executioner during the execution. The same scene, without Salome present, was painted by Giovanni di Paolo (Fig. I-2-5).

In the version of a panel of English alabaster from the end of the fourteenth century, located in the museum of Mandet de Riom (Puy-de-Dome), the executioner gives John's head to Salome on the platter right after the execution. This scene inspired painters such as Rogier Van der Weyden, Hans Memling, Andrea del Sarto, Bernardino Luini (Fig. I-2-9) and others (Fig. I-2-6; Fig. I-2-7).

Fig. I-2-7. Andrea Solario, *Salome with the Head of John the Baptist*, sixteenth century

In execution scenes, John the Baptist is often depicted in a prison yard kneeling before an executioner with a sword (Fig. I-2-8). Often John's hands are tied behind his back and he is sometimes represented blindfolded. In some cases, Herod and Herodias are observing the beheading.

Fig. I-2-8. *Decapitation of Saint John the Baptist*, Florence Baptistery, thirteenth century

Images in which the executioner presents the platter with the saint's head to Salome slowly evolve over the centuries. In the fifteenth century, Rogier van der Weyden introduces the first important change, in which both Salome and the executioner turn away from the head on the platter (Fig. I-3-3). Barbara G. Lane, a van der Weyden scholar, believes that having Salome and the executioner turn away symbolizes their sinful character, since to contemplate John's head is a possible reference to the wafer on the paten.[16] Other scholars assert that Salome's act of turning away from the gruesome image is a symbol of her not being able or willing to confront the ugliness of death and the heinousness of her crime.[17]

Fig. I-2-9. Bernardino Luini, *Salome Receiving the Head of John the Baptist*, sixteenth century

Renaissance artists became more interested in Salome than in John, and they created half-length portraits of Salome using classical proportions of ideal feminine beauty. Her portraits slowly lost any religious dimension, although she was still represented holding the platter with the head on it. As Catherine Camboulives contends:

> The great innovation . . . is the conquest by Salome of her independence in true portraits of half-length portraits . . . the daughter of Herodias takes features of the young innocent beauty. . . . Salome . . . becomes a beauty which allows artists to prove their virtuosity.[18]

Similarly, Mireille Dottin-Orsini asserts:

> The subject allows an interesting pictorial contrast between youth and death, beauty and horror. Being depicted as a Madonna in glory, she holds the plate with the protective grace of Mary holding the Child Jesus. . . . Salome's beauty makes us forget John's sanctity.[19]

The sixteenth century thus brings a new feature to Salome, contrasting her innocent beauty with the cruelty of her action. This feature will evolve to its maximum effect in nineteenth-century art, in which Salome is transformed into a *femme fatale*.

The image of the executioner also undergoes changes. In the earliest works the executioner is painted as a full-length figure. With time his image becomes more and more repulsive. Rogier van der Weyden's executioner is an illustrative example, as he is portrayed with the facial features of contemporary images of Judas (Fig. I-3-3). The other interesting change to the executioner is his near-total disappearance from the picture space. Eventually, the only remaining attribute of the executioner is his hand holding the head of John while Salome holds the platter and turns away in disgust. Bernardino Luini's painting (Fig. I-2-9) in the Louvre is a striking example of such a representation. There we see only the executioner's hand as a reminder of his presence and his role in the saint's execution.

C. *The third theme of John the Baptist's Passion is Salome Presenting the Head of John the Baptist to Herodias*. In this scene, Salome is often depicted offering a dish with a head of John the Baptist on it to Herod and Herodias together at the banquet hall or to her mother alone in private. When the platter is presented to Herod and Herodias, they often, but not always, cover their eyes in horror (Fig. I-2-4).

Fig. I-2-10. Bernardino Luini, *Salome with the head of Saint John the Baptist*, late sixteenth century

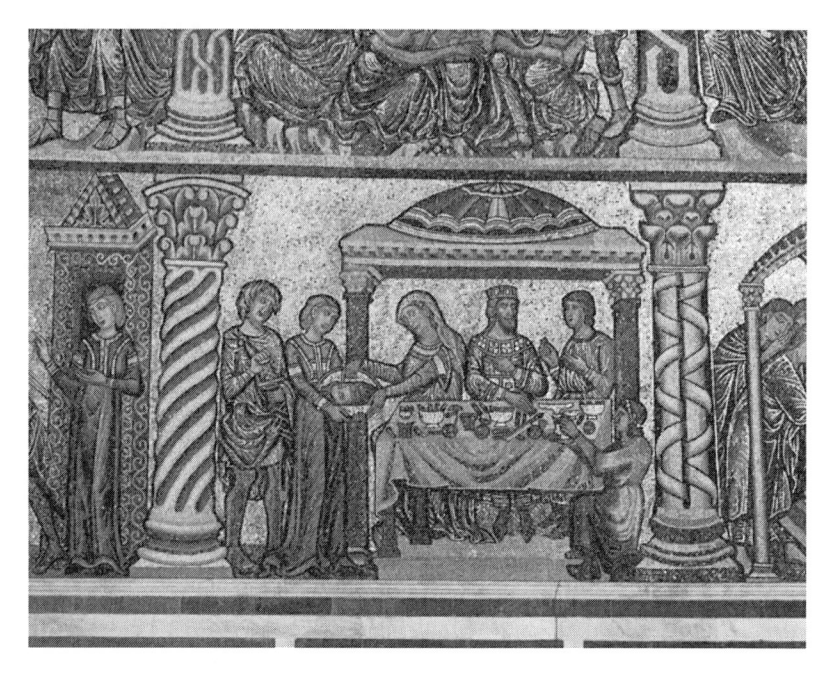

Fig. I-2-11. *Salome Presenting the Head of John the Baptist to Herodias*, Florence Baptistery

The earliest scenes of the Presentation in private to Herodias can be seen in scenes in the mosaics of the Florence Baptistery[20] (Fig. I-2-11) and on the Baptistery's South Doors (Fig. I-2-12). Such imagery is also visible in Giotto's painting of the same theme (1320) (Fig. I-3-4) and in the Presentation scenes that were modelled after Giotto, such as Lorenzo Monaco (Fig. I-2-13) or Filippo Lippi's in Prato (1464) (Fig. I-3-2). Salome is sometimes depicted kneeling before Herodias while she presents the head on the platter, as seen on the Baptistery's South Doors (Fig. I-2-12).

The Evil Salome of Theology and Iconography 39

Fig. I-2-12. Andrea Pisano, *Salome Shows John's Head to Herodias*, Baptistery South Door

Fig. I-2-13. Lorenzo Monaco, *Herod's Feast*

In some cases, Herodias pierces the head or the tongue of John the Baptist with a knife or hair-pin, which in earlier times was associated with the sacrifice of the lamb. This is the case in van der Weyden's work (Fig. I-3-3). A subset of this third theme is the head by itself on a platter, which seems to be a frequent subject starting at the end of the Middle Ages. At its origins, the interpretation of the head on a platter was associated with the wafer on the paten, as Lane and de Vos point out in their discussion of the symbolism in van der Weyden's St. John's Altarpiece.

As has been illustrated by the preceding discussion, the story of John the Baptist's Passion was a popular branch of religious iconography. As might be expected, the way Salome was depicted evolved throughout time. At first, her dance and her image served the Church and its teachings about women's role in society. Gradually, the story of Salome evolved to embody a new concept of feminine beauty, reflecting the revived classicism of the later Middle Ages and Renaissance. From her origins as an accessory of John's story, she slowly became almost an "independent" woman, represented solely for the sake of her alleged beauty. If, at the origin, her image served to stress the pain of John and to point out Salome's evil feminine role in the murder of the saint, with time the roles seem to have reversed, as if the representation of John's head were present solely to contrast the ugliness of death with the beauty of life, embodied in and by Salome.

Notes

[1] Helena Grace Zagona, *The Legend of Salome and the Principle of Art for Art's Sake* (Geneva: Droz; Paris: Minard, 1960), 20.

[2] For example, Tertullian, a Church Father, theologian and a writer, born in Carthage (c. 150/160—220), already in the second century begins to build the Church's views of women. For him, women represent an incarnation of the Devil; his main statement is "Beauty of Nature is the work of the Lord and Beauty of artifice is the work of a Devil." Thus, the Christian woman should be "natural." To be "natural" she should not use any makeup and protect her natural beauty by hiding herself from the world. He stresses the importance for the Christian woman to keep her body always hidden. Thus, the image of Salome and her dance, in which the body is the beautiful jewel, clearly does not correspond to Tertullian's image of a Christian woman. Similarly, the bishop of Carthage (d. 258) praises the importance of modesty for young girls and virgins. Such modesty clearly is incompatible with Salome's Dance. Finally Hilaire de Poitiers, the bishop of Poitiers (315—367), criticizes the importance of pleasure. Once again this contradicts the idea of the dance, which in its nature is a pleasurable activity, giving pleasure to both the dancer as well as those watching the dance. Jean

Chrysostome, in his Homely on the Gospel of Matthew, laments:

> When Herod celebrated his birthday, the daughter of Herodias danced in front of his guests and he liked her. . . . O, the diabolic celebration! O assembly of demons! O a cruel dance! O the reward that is even more cruel! . . . That girl is twice guilty: first for daring to dance; second for being liked by Herod and being liked in such a way that she obtains a homicide as a prize of her dance. (Mark Bochet, *Salome. Du voilé au dévoilé* [Paris: Les Editions du CERF, 2007], 23).

Chrysostome's conclusions in his Homely on Marriage are that women's role is to be docile and man should never allow women to have any authority. He is the master and women are at his service and should obey him blindly.

Saint Augustine, fourth-century theologian and philosopher, in his 15th Sermon cries:

> Poor young girl! Real demon possesses her; her soul and her body became the prays of extravagancies; there were not anymore the movements of her breasts which caused her move, but the diabolic manifestations. One should be either completely mad or drunk in order to dance!

In his 16th Sermon St. Augustine goes even further in inventing and imagining the details of Salome's dance, which in the Gospels is described in three words, *saltavit et placuit*:

> Under her light tunic the young girl appears naked, because in order to execute the dance she became inspired by diabolic thought. She wanted that the color of her clothes would emulate perfectly the color of her flesh. Either she shows her body or she parades her breasts. (Mark Bochet, *Salome. Du voilé au dévoilé* [Paris: Les Editions du CERF, 2007], 27).

The list can continue. French text is translated into English by Rosina Neginsky.
[3] Nikos Kokkinos, "Which Salome did Aristobulus Marry?" *Palestine Exploration Quarterly* 118 (1986): 45.
[4] The story was found in the *Life of John* by Eurippus and in the *Life of John* by Separion of Thmuis. Kokkinos explains that "As we learn from Schonfield, Separion's work was probably the source for Isho'dad of Merv, who repeats it in his commentaries, as does Cedrenus. In the Middle Ages the traditional death of 'the daughter of Antipas' has been popularly transformed as the death of 'the daughter of Herodias'. In Pseudo-Dorotheus the death of 'Salome' is described in the same way." Nicephorus Callistus, the fourteenth-century Greek Church historian who became especially popular between 1320 and 1330, and who was the author of the *Ecclesiastic History*, repeated the story and enriched it with graphic details.
[5] Ibid., 45.

[6] Ibid., 49.
[7] Nonetheless, as Kokkinos comments:

No matter how Christians have correspondingly punished the dancing girl, whom they wrongly identified with 'the daughter of Herodias', historically 'the daughter of Antipas' did not suffer any divine penalty. On the contrary, she prospered, at least in this life, by marrying Aristobulus, by producing for him three sons, and by being made queen of Lesser Armenia when the emperor Nero, late in A.D. 54, entrusted the area to her husband. (Ibid., 45.)

[8] This time also saw confusion between the names of the two women (Salome and her mother Herodias). Often the name of Herodias was used in reference to Salome, and Salome's in reference to Herodias. Such ambiguity is perhaps understandable when considering that Salome and Herodias were both women in the lineage of Eve and were therefore both personifications of evil.
[9] See Daniel Arasse, *On n'y voit rien. Descriptions* (Paris: Denoël, rééd. Folio-poche), 2002.
[10] Ibid. This is Arasse's take on Eva-Ave.
[11] Bibliothèque Nationale de France, Paris, MS Suppl. Gr. 1286.
[12] Bibliothèque Nationale de France, Paris, Lat. 9386.
[13] It is an example of art from what has been termed the Carolingian Renaissance. That trend in art began with Charlemagne, the Frankish King Charles who was crowned by Pope Leo III in the year 800 as Emperor of Rome. "The clearest picture of the Carolingian renaissance emerges not from the monumental arts but from a study of manuscript illumination and ivory carving, for it is only in these fields that abundant material survives," Marilyn Stokstad writes. (Marilyn Stokstad, *Medieval Art* [New York: Harper & Row, Publishers, 1988], 116) Traditionally the German and Celtic artists preferred geometrical abstractions with a great deal of energy. One of the new main features of Carolingian art and architecture expressed itself in underlying geometric design and the emulation of Roman Christian sources. In their new productions the artists had to reconcile symmetry, balance, imitation of ancient art, and three-dimensional representation with their natural inclinations of geometrical abstractions, two-dimensional linearism and personal imagination. These are the features that we find in the ninth-century *Evangeliaire de Chartres*. Another key feature of Carolingian manuscripts is the script employed, a relatively clear and legible script, which was developed under Charlemagne and was based on Roman letters.
[14] For more discussion of the Rouen image see Part III, Chapter Seven.
[15] Danièle Devynck, "La Saulterelle déshonnête" in *Salome dans les collections françaises* (Saint-Denis: Musée d'art et d'histoire, 1988), 18. Translation is mine (Rosina Neginsky).
[16] See Dirk De Voss, *Rogier Van Der Weyden: The Complete Works* (New York: Harry N. Abrams, 2000).
[17] See *Salome dans les collections françaises* (Saint-Denis: Musée d'art et

d'histoire, 1988).
[18] Ibid., 21.
[19] Ibid., 14.
[20] The Baptistery mosaics were conceived and executed in the thirteenth century. In 1271 there was an agreement between the city of Florence and the Arte di Calimala, which undertook financing the program; in 1281 there are records of other subsidies made to finance the work and finally a document of 1325 mentions fresh subsidies for the portion of mosaic being completed in the areas below the dome. The sixth and last register from the top, the most distant from the lantern, narrates fifteen stories of John the Baptist, the city's patron saint, to whom the Baptistery is dedicated.

Segment 12d, the south-east segment, represents Salome's Dance. This scene supposedly was created around the years 1290-1295. We do not know the name of the artist, but given the fact that the style of this particular segment is similar to two previous segments, *John sending two of his disciples to meet the Savior* and *John's disciples witness Christ's Miracles*, we assume that all were probably done by the same artist. The most distinguishing feature of these segments is the dynamic movement of figures, which creates an emotional tumult but also conveys the movement of Salome in the dance. Salome's dance takes place in the scene of Herod's feast.

CHAPTER THREE

THE BEAUTIFUL SALOME OF RENAISSANCE PAINTING AND SCULPTURE

The late Middle Ages and early Renaissance are surprising for the inventiveness and creativity of their artists, as well as for the development of new and increasingly naturalistic forms of artistic expression. Although images depicting the story of John the Baptist and Salome's associated dance provide only one of many examples of artistic exploration, it is still interesting to trace the ways various artists experimented with the subject and how they revealed themselves in their portrayal of John's Passion. Furthermore, the scene's appearance in a variety of formats allows for comparison across different media, such as painting, mosaic and sculpture.

Three especially striking examples come to us from the Renaissance. Two are from the Central Italian region of Tuscany: Donatello's *The Feast of Herod*, c. 1425 (Fig. I-3-1), in the Baptistery of Siena, and Filippo Lippi's fresco *The Banquet of Herod*, from his *Life of Saint John the Baptist* cycle of 1452-1465 (Fig. I-3-2) in the Cappella Maggiore of Prato's Santo Stefano Cathedral. The third example, Rogier van der Weyden's *Saint John Altarpiece*, dated to around 1455-1460 (Fig. I-3-3), is from Northern Europe. All three works contribute to the rich interpretations of Salome's myth and fit within the three representational categories of John's martyrdom.

Although original in style and interpretation, the paintings and the sculptural ensemble also show the influence of works that came before them. Two notable precedents come from Florence, where John the Baptist was the patron saint: Giotto's frescos depicting John the Baptist's life and martyrdom in the Peruzzi Chapel in Santa Croce (Fig. I-3-4) and Andrea Pisano's bronze doors for the city's Baptistery (Fig. I-3-7). Giotto and Pisano follow the traditional representations of John's martyrdom in the disposition of story's characters and in the representation of the sequence of the narrative, but their works are endowed with psychological subtleties and emotional life, characteristics absent in the works of their predecessors. Giotto borrows in part from the ceiling mosaic in Florence's

Baptistery (Figs. I-2-8, I-2-11, I-3-5, I-3-6), though his innovations in the representation of space and the psychological and theatrical components of the narrative are fully original. Undoubtedly, these innovations served as source material for the representation of Salome's story in works to come, such as those by Donatello, Filippo Lippi and van der Weyden. In the case of Andrea Pisano, an early follower of Giotto and the first artist known to cast the Baptist and Salome story in bronze, an emotional element is surprisingly real, and it undoubtedly influenced Donatello's relief and Lippi's fresco.

Giotto in The Peruzzi Chapel

As I mentioned above, John the Baptist is the patron saint of Florence, and there is an established tradition of depicting his life and passion in that city. Giotto, one of the most important early Renaissance artists, painted the story of John the Baptist in the Peruzzi Chapel in the Franciscan Church of Santa Croce in Florence (Fig. I-3-4).

Fig. I-3-4. Giotto, *The Feast of Herod* and *The Presentation of the Head of St. John the Baptist*

Giotto was responsible for four chapels and four polyptychs in the Church of Santa Croce. Of these, the most important are the Bardi chapel, where he painted the life of St. Francis, and the Peruzzi chapel, where he painted two scenes of the life of John the Baptist and two scenes of John the Evangelist. The left wall of the Peruzzi Chapel has scenes of the life of John the Baptist, while the right wall is devoted to the legend of John the Evangelist. Starting at the top, the frescos dedicated to the Baptist depict *The Annunciation to Zacharias*, *The Birth and Naming of St. John the Baptist* and events from his Passion, including *The Beheading*, *The Feast of Herod* and *The Presentation of the Head of St. John the Baptist* (Fig. I-3-4). In this lower fresco Giotto paints two different events in the same picture plane, a compositional device that was not typical for him.

One of the reasons Giotto uses that simultaneous representation could be related to his artistic experimentations with space and his move toward "the representation of a more spatially complicated composition."[1] Indeed, at the time when Giotto painted the frescos in the Peruzzi Chapel, he was very interested in the space-figure relationship, "which was already a perspective issue, tied tightly to the problem of the space-light relationship —in other words, chiaroscuro."[2] Thus, although his representation is in many ways traditional, Giotto places the narrative in an innovative and complex architectural design. On the lower left is the prison, shown as a tower, containing the decapitated body of John the Baptist; in the middle is a rectangular pavilion, in which *The Feast of Herod* takes place; and to the right of the pavilion is a little vaulted room, in which *The Presentation of the Baptist's Head* occurs. In *The Feast*, Salome, standing to the right of the table, seems to have interrupted her dance in order to stare at John's head. The head looks as though it has just been placed in front of Herod and his guests; perhaps only now do they all realize the outcome of Salome's actions. In *The Presentation*, Salome presents John's head to her mother Herodias. To show the connection between the two scenes—and to underscore Salome's role in the story—Giotto makes the hem of Salome's gown in *The Feast* touch the gown of Salome in *The Presentation*. In addition, to indicate that Salome and her mother are united in their actions and share the same guilt, Giotto paints both of them holding the platter in *The Presentation*, a motif borrowed from the Florence Baptistery mosaics (Fig. I-2-11).[3] However, Giotto represents Salome much smaller than her mother, perhaps to indicate the lesser responsibility of the former.

Although Giotto's iconography—the representation, the location of figures, the sequence of the narrative—is traditional and can be seen in the mosaics of the Florence Baptistery, the psychological intensity of the scene is his own invention. The characters' reactions to the events and

Giotto's attempt to convey something of what his characters feel bring the depiction of Salome to a higher emotional level. Through Giotto, Salome and her story are given greater development and drama, which in turn heighten the viewer's emotional involvement as well.

Fig. I-3-5. *Salome's Dance*, The Florence Baptistery mosaics

Fig. I-3-6. *John the Baptist's Martyrdom*, The Florence Baptistery mosaics, fragment

Andrea Pisano: The South Doors of the Florence Baptistery

The Florence Baptistery features two well-known depictions of the Baptist story from the Middle Ages and Early Renaissance: the mosaics on the interior and the bronze doors of Andrea Pisano. The mosaics, although artistically fascinating, do not offer new interpretations of the Salome story. In contrast, the Baptistery's oldest set of bronze doors, executed by Andrea Pisano and now located at the South entrance, do offer a new development, adding a level of psychological complexity to the story, especially to the interpretation of Salome's personality.

Although Andrea Pisano shares a name with Nicola and Giovanni Pisano—the father and son who were the leading sculptors of Italy in the thirteenth and early fourteenth centuries—he was not related to them and his artistic language was different from theirs. Giotto, rather than the Pisano carvers, shaped Andrea's style. The episodes on each of the doors' registers appear real and natural to us. As Annamaria Giusti suggests,

> Here the artist—who had been trained to master the 'ornate' manner of the goldsmith, based on decorative miniature—adapts wonderfully to the clarity required in a work to be taken in at a glance from a distance. . . . Pisano followed the iconographic models, which were already established in Florence at that time, such as the mosaics on the Baptistery dome and Giotto's frescoes in Sainte Croce's Peruzzi Chapel. But this was the first time that the life of Florence's patron Saint had been narrated with such a wealth of details. This perfectly balanced diptych fully covers his life and his sermons (left door), as well as his martyrdom and death (right door)."[4]

The panels associated with Salome and the execution of John the Baptist appear on the right-hand door (Fig. I-3-7). These include *The Dance of Salome* (Fig. I-3-8), *The Beheading of John, John's Head is Shown to King Herod* (Fig. I-3-9) and *Salome Shows John's Head to Herodias* (Fig. I-2-12). The influence of Giotto can be seen in the way Andrea Pisano has tempered his Gothic style with a degree of classicism, as well as in the representation of the narrative. Although the figures are slightly elongated per the conventions of Gothic art, they are all realistic, featuring well maintained proportions and emotionally expressive faces.

Fig. I-3-7. Andrea Pisano, *The South Door of the Florence Baptistery*

The Dance of Salome (Fig. I-3-8), following tradition, represents only men—three mature men with beards—sitting at the table of the feast. They turn their heads to their left to face the young woman who is presumably dancing very close to Herod. Strangely, it seems as if the dance takes place before the meal instead of after it. This is contrary to the Greek and Roman tradition, in which the second part of the Banquet was dedicated to the entertainment and during which only women of pleasure were allowed to be present. Perhaps it is an indication that Salome was a princess and not a woman of pleasure. It is also probable that Andrea Pisano did not think of it when he modelled *Herod's Banquet*. However, Andrea's depiction of the scene, like Giotto's, does not include Herodias. In this regard both images follow the accounts of Matthew and Mark, which state that Salome had to leave the room to ask her mother what she should request in return for her dance.

Fig. I-3-8. Andrea Pisano, *The Dance of Salome*

The men's faces are all expressive and Salome clearly holds their attention while dancing. But we can only assume that she is dancing because of the presence of the musician on the left and through our knowledge of the story and the positioning of her arms. Otherwise, her body appears static. She stands very close to Herod, and during her dance her eyes meet his, foreshadowing and stressing their intimate connection and mutual involvement in the forthcoming crime.

The panel *John's Head is Shown to King Herod* (Fig. I-3-9) is a continuation of *Salome's Dance*, with the same three men still sitting at the banquet table. In the panel of *Salome's Dance* the table is nearly empty but in the scene displaying the Baptist's head there are glasses of wine and some remnants of food on the table, showing that Herod and his guests have just feasted. Perhaps by serving the head on the platter possibly as a dish of a whole meal, Pisano makes an allusion to the Last Supper.[5] On the left is Salome, standing with her arms folded across her breast and a slightly insolent air, as though proud of her achievements. She looks at the platter with the head on it, which is presented to Herod by a young man kneeling on the right, probably the executioner. Herod, however, is not willing to receive the head, as if trying to deny his involvement and his guilt in John's execution. Instead he points to Salome, apparently stating that the head should be given to her since it was she who asked for it. The guest to Herod's right angrily looks at Salome and points to the head of the Baptist. Like an Old Testament prophet, he appears to threaten Salome with the forthcoming punishment. The other guest looks at Salome with the compassion and sympathy of an older and wiser person understanding the confusion of someone younger. The emotional range and the characters' reactions bring a degree of complexity to the interpretation of the story, something of a novelty for visual arts of the period.

In the panel *Salome Shows John's Head to Herodias* (Fig. I-2-12), Andrea Pisano follows the Gospel accounts by depicting Herodias outside of the banquet hall. The image shows a kneeling Salome offering her mother the platter with John's head. Both women hold the platter at the same time to symbolize their shared guilt, a motif also seen in Giotto's fresco and in the Baptistery mosaics. But contrary to Giotto, Andrea Pisano has shown both women very young, almost like two sisters, as if he wished to further stress their equal responsibility in crime and sin.

In all of the Salome panels, Andrea Pisano uses expressive faces and gestures to convey information about the story and its participants. The face of Herodias in the final panel, where she looks at the head of the Baptist, is calm. Perhaps it is a relief for her to be liberated from John, who had been so destructive to her life. Salome, however, seems to search for approbation from her mother, and she is perhaps confused and disappointed in seeing her mother so indifferent.

John's head appears almost to be alive, as though it were the head of someone sleeping rather than dead. His future lies in his resurrection, divine through his spiritual power and earthly through his Word, and thus he is only preparing himself for the anticipated triumph over death. Through the subtle manipulation of facial expressions, Andrea Pisano beautifully conveys complex psychological and spiritual states to the viewer, capturing the different states of the characters' minds and souls and stressing the mother and the daughter's unification in crime.

Fig. I-3-9. Andrea Pisano, *John's Head is Shown to King Herod*

These manipulations of characters' facial expressions and gestures are seen across the panels. The variations stress the figures' humanity and give the viewer access to their psychological states, especially in regard to their involvement in Salome's actions. Furthermore, Andrea Pisano convincingly depicts the changes in Salome's own mood among the panels. It starts with Salome's ambivalent interaction with Herod, continues to her state of apparent triumph in the panel representing *John's Head is Shown to King Herod* and ends with her disappointment and confusion in the final panel.

The psychological subtleties conveyed in the bronze, especially with small figures, are an extraordinary advancement in the visual arts in general and in the art of sculpture in particular. They endow the story of John's Martyrdom and Salome's dance with complexity and ambivalence, enriching the story and calling upon the viewer for various interpretations. In their power and expressive range, these images are almost theatrical, enticing the audience and making them to want to know what is coming next.

Donatello, *The Feast of Herod*, Siena Baptistery Font

The Florentine sculptor Donato di Niccolò di Betto Bardi, called Donatello (1386-1466), executed the bronze relief of *The Feast of Herod* (Fig. I-3-1) for the Siena Baptistery Font. The commission was entrusted to Donatello probably in May of 1423. Originally, the Sienese artist Jacopo della Quercia was commissioned to execute two bronze reliefs for the Baptistery but he did not complete the work. The records indicate that on 16 April 1417 Donatello accepted the offer. The modelling of the work was completed in the summer of 1425 and the finished relief was delivered on 13 April 1427.

Donatello captured the Salome story and imbued it with an amazing emotional power. He conveyed the passionate reactions of Herod, Herodias and the guests through vivid physical animation and powerful psychological expression. When the head is delivered to Herod and Herodias, Salome continues to dance, and her dance seems wild, contrary to her dance in the mosaics of the Baptistery in Florence, in Giotto's fresco in the Peruzzi Chapel and in Pisano's doors. Her face seems to express determination, as though saying that her audience has no choice but to endure the consequences of her actions. She is almost irritated at Herod's cowardice and the weakness of his character, expressed in his panic at the sight of the head.

In the foreground the eye of the viewer is directed toward Herod standing in horror in front of the head presented to him by the soldier. The curved back of the soldier suggests his own revulsion at the head, as though he were shying away from it, yet his hands thrust the platter forward. The effect seems to be of a soldier saying to Herod: "Here is what you wanted. Enjoy it now!" Herodias, sitting inclined toward Herod and pointing at the head, seems to try to calm Herod by telling him: "Is it not what we wanted? Now we have it. Do not be a coward!" She appears to be angry at his reaction—and with good reason. After all, it was he who ordered the beheading and now he is scared and unwilling to take responsibility for his own actions. Salome, meanwhile, continues to dance her wild dance. At the other side of the table we can see guests reacting with horror and disapproval to the events.

The vivacity, the expressiveness and the emotional power of the scene are stunning and draw the viewer fully in. It is an example of "art referred to as *storia*, a most lifelike portrayal of a scene from literature with the greatest possible variety of narrative motifs and objects."[6]

Donatello's representation of the scene's emotions is a reflection of the developing artistic theories of the period, embodied in the writings of men like Leon Battista Alberti. The sculptor has shown his figures to be reacting in ways that would be expected for an event of this caliber. Artistically and stylistically it was a stunning innovation that nobody before him had conveyed through bronze.

Fig. I-3-1. Donatello, *The Feast of Herod*

Donatello was responsible for a new way of depicting spatial depth in sculpture and relief, through the technique known as *relievo schiacciato*. Translated as "squashed relief," this refers to the appearance of recession into space through the progressively fainter delineation of forms. This contrasted with the more usual appearance of relief sculpture, in which the depicted space was reduced to the foreground figures. This is the technique that he uses in *The Feast of Herod*.

One of the first works to embody this new technique is Donatello's relief on the base of the tabernacle for his *St. George* statue on Orsanmichele, carved in 1417. *The Feast of Herod*, completed ten years after the *St. George* relief, is even more elaborate in its construction of space. The setting is the inside of a large palace constructed of ashlar masonry. Three arches separate the foreground from a series of rooms in the background.[7] The arrangement of space in the relief is very interesting and serves to assist in telling the story. As described by Joachim Poeschke, the relief is:

> the earliest example of a picture conceived as a unified perspective space, and it set a new standard for pictorial narrative. Instead of simply calling the work the *Feast of Herod* or the *Dance of Salome*, the payment record from October 8, 1427 (Bacci 1929), specifies that precise moment depicted: quando fu recata la testa di san giovanni a la mensa de'Re (just as the head of St. John was brought to the table of the king.)[8]

For Donatello, centralized perspective was very important for the organization of depicted space, but it was only one part of the ensemble. For this reason, he does not apply the rules of perspective with absolute rigidity. The narrative variety and the figures and events filled with life were as or more important than the other representational tools.

Donatello's *Feast of Herod* is the first representation in which emotions take over the events: People behave inappropriately in the scene. Herodias and Salome direct their accusations at Herod, as though to deny their own guilt while stressing that he was the one who ordered the execution. In light of such facts Herod's state of panic is almost laughable. In his artful pictorial narrative of *The Feast of Herod*, Donatello was able to achieve a stunning range of actions and characterizations.

Filippo Lippi, *Life of Saint John the Baptist: The Banquet of Herod*, in the Cappella Maggiore of Santo Stefano Cathedral, Prato

In 1452 Filippo Lippi was invited to decorate the Cappella Maggiore of Santo Stefano Cathedral, in Prato, with frescos of *The Lives of Saint Stephen and Saint John the Baptist*. Fra Angelico had earlier turned down the proposal of Geminiano Inghirmi, a humanist and the rector of the parish church. For the work on the frescos Lippi hired Fra Diamante as a principal collaborator and a few assistants such as Giannino della Magna, Domenico di Zanobi and the Master of the Nativity of Castello. It has been noted that, despite the diversity of the team, the cycle presents a homogenous appearance due to Lippi's close supervision and the finishing touches he added in tempera or "a secco."[9] Lippi finished the frescos in 1465, thirteen years after he started work.

The frescos entirely cover the walls of the Cappella Maggiore, a surface area of some 400 square meters. On the left are scenes from the life of Saint Stephen, patron of the city of Prato and of the cathedral; on the right are scenes from the life of Saint John the Baptist, the patron of Florence. The scenes describing the lives of the saints run parallel to each other and each consists of three registers. The lowest levels represent the martyrdom (or the Passion) of both saints. On the right there is the decapitation of John the Baptist, and on the left is the stoning of Saint Stephen.

The fresco which captures our attention for the purpose of this study is *The Banquet of Herod* (Fig. I-3-2), the third scene in the series of *The Life of Saint John the Baptist* and the last to be painted. By that time, Lippi's style had evolved to become graceful, elegant and full of vitality, even more so than in his earlier works. Donatello's banquet scene for the baptistery of Siena provided some of the inspiration for Lippi's rendition of the scene. Lippi situates the story in a large banquet hall, which at the back opens up to a landscape through a double arcade that also serves as a frame for the guests. With this arrangement, Lippi creates a new type of a spatial construction. The story in the fresco's narrative is unusually depicted from right to left, similar to writings in Aramaic or Hebrew, the original languages of the Old Testament, which unfold from right to left. The fresco is the epitome of his ability to create a narrative with multiple episodes spread across the pictorial field and placed deep within the depicted space. Lippi scholar Megan Holmes believes that the painter was particularly indebted to Ghiberti's *Gates of Paradise*, installed on the Florence Baptistery in 1452, for his ability to set the narrative episodes within the pictorial space and for the increasing clarity of his composition.[10]

Fig. I-3-2. Filippo Lippi, *The Banquet of Herod*

The principal character of this scene is Salome, who is represented in three different actions. On the left she is standing and looking away while receiving from the executioner the platter with the head of John the Baptist. In the middle she is shown as a beautiful and graceful young girl, dancing in front of the guests gathered around the banquet table. On the right, she appears younger still, kneeling and giving the plate with the head of John the Baptist to her mother, Herodias, who is dining at a table separated from the main banquet. In all three representations the beautiful white dress with green sleeves remains the same, whereas the hairstyle, facial expression and age of Salome change from one scene to another.

Isabella Lapi Ballerini interprets the changes in Salome's appearance in the context of Lippi's life. According to her, Filippo Lippi has depicted three ages of Lucrezia Buti, his model, lover and the mother of his two children, a daughter, Alexandra, and a son, Filippino Lippi, who later became a famous painter in his own right. Lucrezia was Lippi's model for a number of his paintings of the Madonna. Her facial features and figure also appear in his dancing Salome.

The pair met in 1456, when Lippi was a monk of forty-six and she was only seventeen. At the time, she was a novice of the Augustinian monastery of Saint Margaret in Prato. The image of Salome offering the head of John the Baptist to Herodias appears to show Lucrezia as a young girl, as she would have been when Fra Filippo came to Prato. In the scene of Salome dancing, Lucrezia is portrayed as a seductive young woman, although the dance is slow and her face is sad. For the image of Salome receiving the head of John from the executioner, Lippi has painted Lucrezia at a later stage of life: here she is a mother, a woman with a certain maturity and experience.

In Part II, *Self-Portrait in Disguise*, of this book, I mention the Renaissance tradition in which a woman and a man united by some kind of erotic feeling would be represented in the guises of Salome and the head of John the Baptist. Although in *Self-Portrait in Disguise* I discuss mainly the sixteenth-century tradition, it would be logical to assume that those representations have roots in the fifteenth century, in which case Filippo Lippi might be the origin of this tradition. Given the fact that Salome was modelled after Lucrezia Buti, whom Lippi met and fell in love with when she was only seventeen, it is quite possible that the paintings are a way to express his love for Lucrezia, especially if the head of John the Baptist on the platter that Salome is holding is the artist's self-portrait.

When Lippi represents Salome-Lucrezia as a dancing young woman, perhaps this image embodies the dance of life that she had to dance in order to survive. Her face is sad and her dance seems slow, almost static. Her dancing feet are red. Should we read this as the blood of John the Baptist or as the blood of Lucrezia Buti? If it is the latter then perhaps it represents the sacrifices Lucrezia herself must have made in order to live and love, no easy things for a young novice or nun in her time.

In the far left scene, when Salome receives the head of John from the executioner, she does not seem to be interested in it and in fact turns away from it. If the head represents Lippi and his head on the platter is a symbol of the pair's romantic involvement, then perhaps this scene indicates Lucrezia Buti's waning interest in Lippi. By the time Lippi finished the fresco in 1465, Lucrezia and he had already had two children and she had left him in order to return with her daughter Alexandra to live permanently in the monastery.

Lippi's Salome, his "flower of evil," might be perceived as a precursor of Sandro Botticelli's *Primavera* and other classical figures of Renaissance beauty. The beautiful incarnation of Salome with her wavy hair and clothes inflated by the wind embodies the aesthetic ideal described by Leon Battista Alberti in the second volume of his *De Pictura*:

> I desire, indeed, that [the depiction of] hair be treated according to all those seven movements, which I spoke of. Let [the hair], in fact, swirl attempting to make a knot; or better still, let it wave in the air while it imitates flames, and let it coil on some heads; let it rise sometimes in this or that direction. . . . one will present that loveliness: that the flanks of bodies which the wind hits appear almost nude under the covering of fabric, since the clothes stick to the body because of the wind. On the contrary, from the other sides, fabrics, stirred by the wind, will wave appropriately in the air.[11]

Salome and her dance are also the embodiment of Alberti's theory that the body's movements should express the sentiments of the soul. Stylistically, Lippi's fresco *The Banquet of Herod* stresses the importance of the dramatic unfolding of the narrative "through expressive, varied figure dispositions and the interrelationship between figures," and uses three-dimensional modeling or perspective, discreetly present, as "a design element or a conceptual framework."[12] Furthermore, the fresco creates the effect of being staged just in front of the viewer, like a play. The overall sensation is of the subjects' tangible and physical presence, such that the drama unfolds in the manner of a performance for the painting's audience. As viewers, we are invited to admire both the painting itself as well as the action—the dance especially—that takes place within it.

Rogier van der Weyden, *Saint John Altarpiece*

Between 1455 and 1460 the Flemish painter Rogier van der Weyden produced his *Saint John Altarpiece*. It is a fixed triptych with three equal panels. On the left is an image of the birth and naming of John the Baptist; in the center is Christ's baptism in the River Jordan; and on the right is the execution of the Baptist, in the background of which can be seen the courtyard and banquet hall of Herod's palace.[13]

As is customary in medieval and Northern Renaissance art, van der Weyden's images are constructed with consideration given to the laws of the spirit rather than according to strict visual laws. On the one hand, he knew how to represent the visible world in great detail and how to depict the minutiae of everyday life. On the other hand, at some level van der Weyden does not accept the idea that a painter should represent only what he sees. Like his teacher, Robert Campin, van der Weyden uses the representation of reality as a platform for the representation of the transcendental. As Panofsky points out, one of the most impressive features of his work is his ability to "subordinate the naturalism of detail to his supernatural intentions."[14]

Although the *Saint John Altarpiece* narrates the most important events of the Baptist's life—birth, baptizing and death—it also foreshadows Christ and his life story, placing "special emphasis on the role of Christ in the divine plan of salvation."[15] Around each panel, van der Weyden painted archivolts covered with sculptures, like the portals of a Gothic cathedral. These frames contain biblical scenes that contribute to the altarpiece's overall meaning and message of salvation. They are painted illusionistically, yet van der Weyden's frames are not designed to accentuate the scenes' status as paintings. Rather, the sensation is of events

Fig. I-3-3. Rogier van der Weyden, *Saint John Altarpiece. The Beheading of John the Baptist.* Rightmost panel

taking place in front of and beyond the Gothic frames, as though conflating the viewer's space with the painted space.

In each of the three panels, the spaces beyond the portal arches complement the narrative of the main scenes, similar to how the archivolts complement the primary image. Moreover, statues of the apostles are placed in the portal walls to make an allusion to the events of the New Testament. The perspective in the two side panels is oriented toward the central panel, the scene of Christ's baptism, which produces an overall unity of effect. This is accentuated by van der Weyden's use of the same type of light grey stone for the architecture and the sculptures decorating each panel.

The rightmost panel (Fig. I-3-3) is directly related to our study. This panel is divided into three parts and the action unfolds across three spatial zones. The first zone, closest to the viewer, is the decapitation, which takes place in front of the Gothic arch. In the scene's ambiguous spatial relationship to the viewer it is real and transcendental at the same time; death is thus a passage to resurrection and to eternal life. Van der Weyden represents the decapitation in the hallway of the palace, at the top of a set of stairs rather than in a prison, to stress its symbolic importance: The martyrdom of John presented at the front of the painting, in front of the "cathedral doors," is a symbol of the forthcoming Passion of Christ. Behind Salome and the executioner, serving almost as a stage, is the Gothic archway adorned with fictive sculptures. The scenes on the archway represent, clockwise, *The Priests and the Levites Asking John if he is a Messiah; John Pointing out Christ to Two of his Disciples; John Reproaching Herod for his Marriage to Herodias; the Incarceration of John; the Visit of Two Disciples to the Prison* and *The Dance of Salome.*

The innovation of van der Weyden is his representing both Salome and the executioner turning away from the head of the Baptist. Their sinful nature does not allow them to contemplate the head. If the head of the Baptist is also understood as a symbol of the wafer on the paten, then the figures' averted gazes also highlight their disconnect from Christ's salvation. Barbara Lane also points out that the executioner has been given features similar to those seen in contemporary depictions of Judas, in order to emphasize his vile nature and his betrayal.[16]

To the right of the execution scene, behind a stone wall, two of John's disciples watch the execution and mourn his death. Behind the disciples, the painter, experimenting with perspective, painted the courtyard of the palace and a distant archway that appears to offer access to the interior of the palace before opening up to the landscape. Van der Weyden often painted harmonious landscapes in the background of his paintings in order to create the impression of earthly reality being merely a vehicle for expression and not the real living world. These landscapes are represented not as individualized locales but as part of a very general and interchangeable world. This is what he does in the third panel of this altarpiece, and what we see through the arch is supposed to lead toward that landscape.

In the second zone, depicted a few steps up from the foreground scene, there is a hallway or passage with two individuals at leisure. The two men are shown much smaller than the figures on the first plane, smaller than would be expected based on the apparent recession of space. One of the men is looking through a window at the courtyard and the other is modestly lowering his eyes to avoid seeing the execution. This hallway features van der Weyden's experimentations with perspective. The floor looks tilted, the sizes of the characters are smaller than we would expect, and the space dramatically narrows as it recedes into the distance. But this zone is also a link between the execution scene and the feast that takes place in the background, which is where Salome has recently performed her dance and where she now brings the head of the Baptist. Thus the hallway, beyond linking two regions of the palace and two zones of the painting, also links several discrete moments in time. It could be that three rising levels and three steps uniting two of the levels -- with the number three being the symbol of trinity -- might symbolize the passage from the earthly realm of existence to the divine.

The third zone is beyond the hallway and three steps up. Herod and Herodias are having dinner in the company of guests, and they are "served" the head of John the Baptist on a platter. Herodias, upon seeing the head, stabs it with a knife.

Van der Weyden has painted a small dog lying down at the top of the stairs, a symbol of faithfulness, suggesting that the painter remains faithful to the symbolism of Christ's Prefiguration by using the story of John the Baptist to foreshadow the story and Passion of Christ. This panel, like the two other panels, is meant in part to foreshadow the story of Christ and in particular Christ's sacrifice, for which John the Baptist was a precursor. Perhaps the head of John the Baptist on the platter, served to Herodias during the feast, is also an evocation of the Last Supper. If this is the case, the bleeding head would then symbolically represent the body and blood of Christ, and the platter would have the same meaning as the paschal lamb lying on the table in the *Feast of Passover* panel from the *Altarpiece of the Holy Sacrament* by Dieric Bouts (Leuven, Cathedral Saint-Pierre).[17] This interpretation seems likely because contrary to typical representations of this scene the platter is depicted almost as a part of the meal.

Although each of the panels shows a separate scene, the panels, as a triptych, reinforce meanings through their relationships to each other. Stephan Kemperdick points out that the pictorial motifs of the two side panels express moral conflict:

> On the left, the chaste Virgin Mary holds the newborn baby in her arms; she and Zachary are looking at one another gravely, aware of the significance of the event. On the right, the unchaste Salome, in magnificent and seductive clothing, holds the Baptist's head. She and the executioner are turning away from each other and from their victim, as if painfully conscious of the crime that has been committed.[18]

Surprisingly, van der Weyden gave the figure of Salome a pose and face similar to that seen in his Madonna in the *Annunciation* scene of the *Saint Columbia Altarpiece* and the *Medici Madonna*. Kemperdick notes that

> Rogier was obviously able to make effective use of this elaborate and artificial pose [of Mary and Salome] in various circumstances, and only the worldly magnificence of Salome's dress and the context cause the viewer to assess it differently here."[19]

Furthermore, Salome and the Virgin of *The Annunciation* also share a detached facial expression, as though they are present without being present. According to Kemperdick, "The artist has not set out simply to make the figure of Salome merely despicable; indeed, in the context of this scene, her noble features give her a touch of complex ambivalence."[20]

Although Rogier van der Weyden follows in the tradition of Robert Campin and Jan van Eyck, his relationship to the representation of figures' individuality in painting was different from those two artists. In some ways van der Weyden was quite ambivalent by comparison. On the one hand, his portraits are very expressive. He is a great master of the representation of figures' emotional and psychological worlds and of the feelings associated with religious devotion. The characters he paints as portraits are often depicted with an object that is indicative of the subject's occupation or mood. On the other hand, there is often a similarity among the represented faces. All his portraits have a family air, which assists in determining van der Weyden's authorship. This familial resemblance is certainly the case with Salome's image.

Van der Weyden's representation of Salome opened a new tradition in her iconography, in which the beautiful Salome turns her head away from the ugly head on the platter. This motif subsequently became predominant during the Renaissance. The entire *Saint John Altarpiece* is an example of a very complex narrative and is an interesting experiment with using symbolism to narrate the transcendental while making it visually real. The work introduces a search for new and innovative ways of representing perspective, emotions and psychology. But the meaning embedded in van der Weyden's representation disappears in the Renaissance, and the image of Salome is transformed into a symbol of beauty and complexity. No longer just a spicy addendum to John the Baptist's Passion, she becomes a figure in her own right, embodied in the half-length portraits of her as a newly developed type of feminine beauty (Figs. I-2-6, Fig. I-2-7, I-2-9).

Guido Reni, *Salome with the Head of John the Baptist*

The Italian Baroque painter Guido Reni, who was born 4 November 1575 in Bologna and died in the same city in 1642, is responsible for one of the most interesting paintings of Salome, *Salome with the Head of John the Baptist* (Fig. I-3-10), probably painted around 1639.[21] Federico Zeri, who in 1960 was the first to identify and discover the authenticity of Reni's painting, described it in the following way:

> The luminous, almost ivory beauty of Salome, dressed in white blouse, yellow bodice and gown, and rose mantle, neatly described point, the precise focus, around which the figuration takes shape in a succession of zones of color increasingly tenuous and intangible ever closer to attaining the state of pure chromaticism, rapid annotations of an imagination for which the one and only means of expression is the brush with its load of color.[22]

What is quite striking in Reni's *Salome* are the paradoxical emotions that emanate from the feminine figures in response to the horror of the subject—the head of the Baptist on a platter. Luca Assarino, Reni's contemporary, was the first to write about the perception of the subject, stating in 1639 that

> I was completely overcome with horror at seeing with what cruelty, reaching out her arm, [Salome] seized by the hair that venerable head that had been the price of frivolous dance. That figure was so vividly depicted that, although inflamed by Christian zeal, my blood ran cold.[23]

Carlo Cesare Malvasia wrote about Luca Assarino's perception of the painting later:

> In the crimson color of Salome's mantle, draped by Reni with that special skill often noted in the early sources (Malvasia 1678/1841, 2:56), Assarino

saw "symbolized the fury of her utterly perfidious heart."[24]

It is worth noting that four of the five figures in the painting are women. The three women in the background space are probably servants, whereas the central figure is Salome, who is striking for the delicacy, refinement and almost sweet beauty of her facial features. Contrary to many earlier works, her face is not turned away from the platter; not only does she look at the head on the platter, she holds it by the hair. Her face does not exhibit any curiosity or fear—just complete indifference.

This detail might be attributed to Guido Reni's overall attitude toward women, well known in his lifetime. It is said that he was of an "asexual" nature, attracted neither to men nor to women. Yet he was not completely indifferent toward women. For Reni, women embodied evil, even more so than for his male contemporaries. In painting Salome, Reni incarnates the worst of her feminine evil: her perverse indifference to the murder of a person who will eventually be considered a saint, a murder that she has initiated. Reni shows Salome's beauty as untroubled. Her face remains peaceful, moved neither to satisfaction nor dissatisfaction. She has accomplished what she was asked of by her mother. Beyond the fulfillment of her filial duty this murder seems to mean nothing to Salome. The glances of the other women are also directed toward the Baptist's head, and they too remain beautiful, delicate, sweet and untroubled. Only the servant who draws the curtain aside exhibits any degree of curiosity.

The one face that manifests trouble is that of the page who delivers the platter to Salome. Although there are no records of Reni having amorous relationships with men, Richard Spear believes that his natural attraction was toward men. In Spear's view, only men were perceived by Reni as human beings with a range of feelings and a notion of good and evil, something absent in women (apart from the Virgin Mary). Thus, the boy, the only male character in the painting, is the only one to appear troubled by the death of the Baptist and the cruelty of Salome.

Salome with the Head of John the Baptist is a striking example of the tradition of representing Salome as an ideal beauty, a tradition whose origins are found in the Renaissance. The scene has been reinterpreted according to the conventions of Baroque art, with dramatic and selectively lit figures, deep shadows and an emphasis on human emotions. Yet here the overriding emotion is one of indifference, epitomized by Salome's inappropriately calm response to the situation.

***

Fig. I-3-10. Guido Reni, *Salome with the Head of John the Baptist*

The works I have examined summarize the major artistic innovations which occurred to Salome's imagery in the late Middle Ages and Renaissance and which had an impact on the art of subsequent periods. The story of Salome's dance and the events related to it as part of John the Baptist's martyrdom fascinated artists, inspiring them to apply their latest innovations to the biblical narrative.

Since Salome's story was quite provocative and could awaken a range of strong emotions in the characters as well as the viewers, this narrative was fertile ground for experimentation in representing characters' psychological and emotional states. Giotto and his followers, as well as Donatello, Filippo Lippi, Rogier van der Weyden and Guido Reni, all searched for ways to convey emotion in their art, and the story of John the Baptist's Martyrdom and the events leading to it offered especially rich source material.

Several of these artists searched for ways to convey the spiritual and transcendental essence of their works' religious iconography. The means of representing and symbolizing the transcendental went through numerous changes and developments during this period. Rogier van der Weyden was especially innovative in this regard, and he found his own personal way to convey religious symbolism. By accentuating certain characters and varying their locations in the painted space, by the skillful use and selection of color, by creating backgrounds and settings with special symbolic meanings and by varying the use of perspective, van der Weyden was able to imbue his works with a symbolic significance that was more than just the sum of its parts. Other artists also applied their advances to the narrative of Salome's dance and John's death, and these artistic experiments occurred in a range of media: panel painting, fresco, bronze, stone and mosaic.

It is also important to remember that Salome's image was shaped by the artistic and social ideology of the period in which she was depicted. Van der Weyden, for instance, was the first artist to portray Salome turning away from the gruesome image of the Baptist's head. He also shows her as a symbol of grace and beauty, as was customary in Renaissance portraits of women. During the same period artists began to use as models not only anonymous women but their lovers as well. Filippo Lippi seems to have excelled in this practice. Later, the nineteenth-century Pre-Raphaelite artists returned to that tradition, and Dante Gabrielle Rossetti, for instance, used as female models not only his lovers but also his family members, including his sister and his mother.

Notes

[1] Bruce Cole, *Giotto and Florentine Painting 1280-1375* (New York: Icon Editions, Harper & Row, 1976), 111.

[2] Francesca Flore d'Arcais, *Giotto* (New York: Abbeville Publishers, 1995), 252. She also asserts that "The Peruzzi Chapel represents the loftiest peak in Giotto's struggle with the issue of space."

[3] As Cole points out: "but never before had it appeared in such convincing space and thus seemed so real." Cole, *Giotto and Florentine Painting*, 111.
[4] Anna Maria Giusti, *The Baptistery of San Giovanni in Florence*, trans. Steven Grieco (Florence: Mandragora, 2000), 33-34.
[5] For more about it, please see the section on Rogier van der Weyden in this chapter.
[6] Joachim Poeschke, *Donatello and His World. Sculpture of the Italian Renaissance*, trans. Russell Stockman (New York: Harry N. Abrams, Inc., 1993), 23. The *varietas* is enhanced by the presence of the background scenes. The most distant chamber seems to represent the executioner on his way to taking the platter with John's head to the banquet room, whereas the chamber in the middle-ground depicts the musician who continues to play even after Salome has finished her dance and John has been executed. It feels like "life goes on." Hence it creates a very powerful contrast with the violent and emotional representation of the foreground. From this point on, the *varietas* embodied in this relief would be one of the objectives of Early Renaissance art, a characteristic that Alberti would require in his treatise on painting of 1435.
  Poeschke rightly points out that: "The palace architecture, with its massive pillared arcades and ashlar masonry, is obviously inspired by classical buildings. Although monumental in its effect, its surface articulation is highly varied, ornate, and full of detail. To achieve this, Donatello included all manner of structural details from classical architecture, even signs of deterioration in the masonry. The scene's perspective arrangement—especially apparent in the floor paving and the progressively smaller arches of the background arcades—follows the general rules of one-point perspective discovered by Brunelleschi and described in great detail by Alberti." (388)
[7] Poeschke, *Donatello and His World*, 22-23. Poeschke notes, "Here the setting is the interior of a large palace. A high, ashlar balustrade and three large arches separate the area of the main action from the sequence of connecting rooms to the back. This artful arrangement is novel both in its spaciousness and in its lack of a foreground frame."
[8] Ibid., 387-388.
[9] Megan Holmes, *Fra Filippo Lippi. The Carmelite Painter* (New Haven and London: Yale University Press, 1999), 41.
[10] That opening on the landscape is perhaps the result of Lippi's fascination with contemporary Netherlandish painting, which became well known in Florence in the 1450s and 1460s and which Lippi himself studied. He uses the window setting with the landscape visible through the window frame as a background for the set of portraits of subjects seated at the table at the time of the banquet.
[11] *Leon Battista Alberti: On Painting*, ed. and trans. Rocco Sinisgalli (New York: Cambridge University Press, 2011), 67. The relevant section from Alberti is mentioned in *Filippo et Filippino Lippi. La Renaissance à Prato* (Paris: Silvana Editoriale, Musée du Luxembourg, 2009), 50. At the table in the middle, raised by a step above the level of Herod's and Herodias' table, Lippi painted the donor, Francesco Datini, and his family.

[12] Holmes, *Fra Filippo Lippi*, 113-114.
[13] Described as "an unfoldable triptych consisting of three panels of equal size. . . . The panel on the left depicts the birth and naming of John the Baptist. . . . The central panel describes Christ's baptism by John the Baptist in the River Jordan. . . . The panel on the right shows the beheading of the Baptist in a vestibule in the palace of Herod, which opens onto a courtyard at the right, as well as the banquet hall in the background." In Stephan Kemperdick and Jochen Sander, eds., *The Master of Flémalle and Rogier van der Weyden* (Berlin: an exhibition organized by the Stadel Museum; Frankfurt am Main, and the Gemaldegalerie: Staatliche Museum), 352-353.

King Juan II of Castile presumably donated the *Saint John Altarpiece* to the Carthusian monastery of Miraflores near Burgos. He chose that monastery as his place of burial. It was moved to the Alcazar of Seville in 1810. The panels representing the Birth and the Baptism apparently made their way to London in 1816 and, via C.J. Nieuwnhuys, into the collection of King William II of the Netherlands in 1842; they were purchased for the Berlin museum in 1850 at the auction of the collection of William II in the Hague. The panel depicting the beheading was purchased at a Christie's auction on 19 May 1849 and acquired for the Berlin museums shortly thereafter.

There is a scaled-down version of the Berlin *Saint John Altarpiece* in the Stadel Museum in Frankfurt am Main. Not only it is different in size, but it is also lighter in coloring. Right after it was acquired by the Stadel Museum, it was determined that it was a work by "Rogier of Bruges," the name Rogier van der Weyden was mistakenly given. In 1843, Ernst Forster determined that it was a workshop copy since it was clearly inferior to the work then located in the collection of King William II of Netherlands. Dendrochronological analysis proved this supposition to be true. It indicates that the possible date for the execution of this work is not earlier than 1501. There is a supposition that it was done in Spain and was a commission of John II's daughter, Isabella the Catholic. There is also a supposition based on the comparative study that Juan de Flandres (ca. 1463-1519), the court painter of the queen, is the executioner of this work.

Rogier van der Weyden or Rogier de la Pasture—the name of van der Weyden before he settled in Brussels—was born in 1398 or 1399 in Tournai, the city located in the kingdom of Burgundy in the middle of the Netherlands' empire. He was the author of a complex and ambivalent art. He belonged to the second generation of Flemish painters. He was twenty years younger than Paul de Limbourg and Robert Campin, who was van der Weyden's teacher when he lived in his native town of Tournai before moving to Brussels.

[14] Erwin Panofsky, *Early Netherlandish Painting: Volume One* (New York: Harper & Row, 1971).
[15] Kemperdick and Sander, *The Master of Flémalle*, 352.
[16] See Dirk de Vos, *Rogier van der Weyden: The Complete Works* (New York: Harry N. Abrams, 2000).
[17] De Vos, *Rogier van der Weyden*, 3.
[18] Kemperdick and Sander, *The Master of Flémalle*, 116.

[19] Ibid., 116.
[20] Ibid., 116.
[21] Reni was a member of the Bolognese School. In 1601, he went to Rome to work as an assistant to Annibale Carracci on the Farnese ceiling commission (1597-1600; Palazzo Farnese). When he lived in Rome, he was very much influenced by the art of Caravaggio and began to experiment with his style. After he completed the work *Massacre of the Innocents* (1611; Bologna, Pinacoteca Nazionale), the last work painted in the style of Caravaggio, he moved to the style of classicism. His colors and the grace of his figures are akin to Michelangelo and Raphael, as exemplified by his *Aurora* (1613).

In 1613, Guido Reni returned to Bologna where he occupied the position of the city's leading master until his death in 1642. In 1620, Reni adopted a silvery palette and began to use silk instead of canvas. He decided to make this change because he came to the conclusion that silk is the material that would last beyond his life time. The portraits *Cardinal Roberto Ubaldini* (1625; Los Angeles, County Museum) and *Atalanta and Hippomenes* (1622-1625); Madrid, Prado) belong to Reni's silver phase.
[22] *Guido Reni 1575-1642* (Los Angeles: County Museum of Art, Nuova Alfa Editoriale, 1988), 87.
[23] Ibid., 308.
[24] Ibid., 308.

CHAPTER FOUR

THE SEDUCER-DESTROYER SALOME OF NINETEENTH-CENTURY ART AND LITERATURE

The eighteenth century—the century of the Enlightenment—produced very few representations of John the Baptist's life and Passion and Salome's dance. What few images were produced conformed to the traditions that had been established centuries earlier, in the Renaissance. The nineteenth century, by comparison, and especially the second half, seems almost obsessed with Salome and her images.[1] It was then that Salome was fully liberated and given an identity independent of the Baptist story. If previously she danced for the sake of John the Baptist— for the sake of narrating his Passion—in the nineteenth century she began to dance for her own sake, for the sake of the dance alone and in order to impress and to please the audience—us. She became an independent woman, an icon and a cult figure. Yet the irony is that the nineteenth century witnessed a surge in the repression of European women, especially French women, though it was France that produced more images of Salome in art and literature than any other country. The more women became dependent on men in the nineteenth century, the more Salome became independent of John and the more she danced for the sake of dance, pleasure, beauty and seduction.

The theme of Woman dominated the art and literature of the second half of the nineteenth century. As in Christian thought, there were two main views of women. One represented an idealized woman, either inaccessible and wholly pure or chaste and exceedingly religious.[2] We find idealized and dreamy images of women in the works of Maurice Denis, Aristide Maillol, Alphonse Mucha, in the later works of Puvis de Chavannes and even in the works of Gustave Moreau—*La Sulamite, Orphée* in the Musée d'Orsay—and Paul Gauguin.

Fig. I-4-1. L. Levy-Dhurmer, *Salome*

The other trend—represented by the majority of artists—tended to depict women as monsters, predators, seducers and destroyers of men, symbols of evil and perversity. The image of Woman became central in the works of Dante Gabriel Rossetti, who created a new type of Madonna—a woman who, with her penetrating glance and long red hair, was at once divine and earthly, saintly and demonic. The demonic woman is seen all across Europe: in the art of the German artist Franz von Stuck, the Austrian Gustave Klimt, the Belgian Fernand Khnopff, Norwegian painter Edvard Munch and French artist Gustave Moreau. Although Moreau also created inaccessible and virtuous women, such as his Galatée, the demonic beauty or the beauty of anguish incarnated in women is present in several of his works, including Eve, Dalila, Salomé and Messaline. All the above artists depicted women as seductive, evil destroyers, the lustful executioners of men.

Fig. I-4-2. Gustav-Adolf Mossa, *Salome*. 1904

The nineteenth century was fascinated with the notion of fragile yet strong, intelligent and dominating women who, in stories told about them, were always associated with blood and murder. Fantasies of feminine evil abound during this period and blossomed in *fin-de-siècle* culture, most notably in France, although they also existed to a lesser degree in other countries.[3] There was a proliferation of images of Delilah, traitorous lover of Samson; of Jezebel, a dangerous and destructive foreigner; of Judith, heroic murderess of Holofernes; of Cassandra, Cleopatra, Lilith and Lamia and, of course, Salome. This treatment differed profoundly from the treatment of women in the Renaissance, when strong or supposedly dangerous women were transformed into beautiful muses meant to serve as inspiration for artists.

Such nineteenth-century images of women undoubtedly demonstrate a fear of women, directly related to contemporary social changes and to the image of women then predominant in society. Increasing numbers of women had begun to enter the workforce and had taken on more active roles in society. As a result they came to be perceived by men as their competitors. Not only were men sexually dependent on women for reproduction—essential for the propagation of the human species—but now men also had to compete with women, though many men considered women to be their inferiors. Factors such as social recognition and a respected place within society were no longer restricted to men alone.[4] Art and literature were considered among the most effective means to fight this supposed feminine invasion.

Nineteenth-century artists and writers used the image of Salome to caution humanity against the dangers of women. In doing so they display a striking degree of aggression and hostility—occasionally mixed with admiration—toward what some male writers called the "woman's race," a notion invented in the period. The image of Salome, of a girl who murders through her charm, beauty and dance, became one of the most popular images of the *femme fatale*, the symbol of the beautiful destroyer: The nineteenth century produced some 2,789 works of art and literature in which Salome is the central figure. This image played a crucial role in creating the myth of women in the period. It also depicts the perception of women by men, an image shaped as much by men's efforts as by changing social conditions. The image of Salome encompassed a variety of characteristics, all of which reverberated with the nineteenth-century spirit. The century aspired to prove that "woman's race" was an inferior race.

The Seducer-Destroyer Salome of Nineteenth-Century Art and Literature 75

Fig. I-4-3. Gustav-Adolf Mossa, *Salome*. 1906

This view of women, however, is not original. Its origins can be found in the Bible as well as in the writings of the Church Fathers. But in the 19th century they were strongly reinforced by newly born Darwinian publications on evolution. In 1895, the French magazine *La Revue blanche* published an article under the title "Of the Inferiority of Woman," which asserted that there were obvious scientific reasons why women were inferior to men. Written by August Strindberg, the article is also a cry of the triumph of man over woman and a clear attempt to silence feminists. Strindberg writes: "It was reserved to our times to discover, among other things, that woman biologically is a limited version of a man; it is obvious that her physical development stopped between adolescence and full virility."[5]

The German philosopher Arthur Schopenhauer voiced similar thoughts: "The notion of the European Lady should not exist. . . . Women should only be used in the household. Young girls should be trained to aspire to that. They should not be shaped by arrogance but by work and submission."[6] To support and bolster these claims, the image of Salome was made to fit different characteristics that could supposedly prove the inferiority and evil of women. Nineteenth-century literature often perceived women as vampires, bloodsuckers and cold-blooded murderesses. Mireille Dottin-Orsini writes:

> The vampire male always remains a vampire, except for a few cases when he is feminized. As a vampire he is described as a supernatural being, a living dead who feeds himself with human blood and who can be destroyed only by the stake that would pierce his heart. This notion applied to a woman becomes very broad and very banal. It could mean any real woman if she is perceived to be dangerous for a man, for his health, his fortune, his intelligence, his honor, his soul. . . . The figure of a vampire might be associated with the notion of a *femme fatale*, and at the turn of the century the concept of vampirism could be envisioned as a purely feminine specialty.[7]

Dottin-Orsini gives many examples of women being perceived in these ways in literature and art. She points out that in relation to Salome's story, "The prophet's beheading reminds one of the bites of the vampire on the throat."[8]

A portrayal of Salome's supposed vampire tendencies appears in the 1894 play *The Love Council*, a satire on the Catholic Church written by Oskar Panizza, a German psychiatrist. In this play, Salome, the most immoral woman in hell—and a member of the Devil's harem—together with the Devil gives birth to syphilis as a punishment for humanity's immersion in sin. They do this at the request of God, Jesus and the Virgin Mary. The result of the Devil and Salome's union is personified in The

The Seducer-Destroyer Salome of Nineteenth-Century Art and Literature 77

Fig. I-4-4. Gustav-Adolf Mossa, *Salome*. 1908

"Spouse," the irresistibly beautiful woman who begins by contaminating the Pope with syphilis and eventually all of humanity. In the play, Salome admits to the Devil that she washes her fingers in the blood of John's head and she delights in having the platter overflow with blood—a characterization that readily calls to mind vampires' bloodlust. Salome's passionate kiss of John the Baptist in Oscar Wilde's play *Salome* also calls to mind the nature of a vampire. Holding John's head, she simultaneously triumphs and cries by saying: "I have kissed thy mouth, Iokanaan, I have kissed thy mouth. There was a bitter taste on my lips. Was it the taste of blood?... Nay; ... it was a taste of love."[9]

An 1896 pastel, *Salome*, by Levy-Dhurmer (Fig. I-4-1), in which Salome passionately kisses the Prophet's head, resonates with the kiss of Wilde's Salome and is similarly vampire-like. The French Symbolist painter Gustave-Adolf Mossa created a number of paintings of Salome, each with its own particularity. Salome's vampire tendencies are most pronounced in Mossa's 1904[10] *Salome*, in which she—a woman-child surrounded by blooming roses, each containing the bleeding head of John the Baptist—licks the blood from the sword used to behead the prophet (Fig. I-4-2). His 1906 *Salome*, in which she is dressed in red, the color of blood, with her fingers in the shape of scissors and blood stains all over the painting, also conjures images of vampires (Fig. I-4-3). She is once again depicted as the bloodsucker. Mossa's 1908 *Salome* (Fig. I-4-4), which resembles the pose used in Aubrey Beardsley's lithograph *Salome's Toilette*, depicts her as a natural murderess. In this painting, Mossa portrays Salome as his contemporary, an upper-class woman who enjoys reading and the comfortable life and who looks perfectly innocent. The only aberration is that one of the items of her household décor is the severed head of John the Baptist lying on a bloodied sword at her feet. The head, the blood and the other attributes are as innocent for her as the book and beautiful objects that surround her, all of which appear to be nothing more than part of the interior decoration. She is indifferent to her bloody right hand, for murder is a natural part of her nature. Franz Von Stuck's two paintings of a voluptuous *Salome* dancing with joy over the head of the Baptist could also fit this description (Fig. I-4-5). In both cases, we see the murderess joyfully celebrating the murder she has just conspired in.

Nineteenth-century artists and writers also portrayed Salome as a courtesan or a prostitute, which, according to that century's theorists, was in line with the innate tendencies of women. Female figures were depicted as hungry for the gold that could be obtained through the male seed. Bram Dijkstra discusses the notion of:

[the] virgin vampire, adolescent lusting after seed, unconscious whore who drained the veins of man's intellect. She was out to atrophy his head. . . . Symbolic castration, woman's lust for man's severed head, the seat of the brain, that 'great clot of seminal fluid' Ezra Pound would still be talking about in the 1920s, was obviously the supreme act of the male's physical submission to woman's predatory desire.[11]

Fig. I-4-5. Franz Von Stuck, *Salome Dancing*

Salome was prostituting herself through her dance, which was seen as a tool of seduction and a means to reach her "gold" or goal: the death and—importantly—the head of the Baptist, the seat of the brain. In the eyes of late nineteenth- and early twentieth-century artists, Salome undoubtedly knew how to use her predatory instincts and her naked body to masterful effect. Pablo Picasso's 1905 drawing of Salome has her throwing her legs in the air (Fig. I-4-6), as described by the Church Fathers, dancing naked while the executioner sits behind her with the head of John the Baptist on a platter, looking at her with lust and admiration, ready to do anything she desires.[12] The drawing of Henri-Léopold Levy, *A Sketch for Salome,* also depicts her dancing naked. Jules Desbois's bronze *Salome* is an image of a naked Salome, whose sensuality, as in Flaubert's *Herodias,* is overwhelming for the viewer. Franz Von Stuck's *Salome* (Fig. I-4-5) is dancing half naked, and her dance is sensual, seductive and irresistible. Fritz Erler's mural, *Dance,* which represents a half-naked woman holding the head in her lap, is undoubtedly Salome, dancing her provocative, seductive and ultimately fatal dance. Hugo von Habermann's 1896 *Salome* (or *Herodias*) goes even further: She is a naked beast dancing with untamed lust and passion while holding the head of John. There is a sense that she would lure into death any other man caught looking at her irresistible dance, her naked body and her lustful nature.[13]

Salome had another characteristic that was appealing to many in the nineteenth century: She was portrayed as a Jewess. Although historically Salome and her family from a religious point of view were pagans, Herod Antipas was a tetrarch of Galilee and thus a governor in the land of Hebrews living under the Roman Empire. Hence nineteenth-century artists, mirroring the ideology of their era, including new ideas on evolution, often depicted Salome not only with the attributes of a woman and a *femme fatale* but also with what were considered to be the attributes of a Jewess.[14] Bram Dijkstra, for instance, believes that in Albert von Keller's painting *Love* the woman casually holding the sword with which she has just decapitated her lover—whose head, as a forgotten and neglected object, is lying on the floor—is both "Salome and Judith rolled into one" and, according to him, is painted with Semitic features.[15] Dijkstra also stresses that

> While the theme of Salome as a bestial virgin Jewess, whose dance revived the dead embers of carnal life in even the most chaste of men, was passed around among the writers of the period's most determinedly purple prose, the painters became involved in their own scientific-archeological explorations of the link between gender and race in the reels of degeneration.[16]

Fig. I-4-6. Pablo Picasso, *Dancing Salome*

He goes on to tell us that

> Friedrich Fuchs, in *Venus* (1905), a monumental two-volume study of the representation of women in art, commended the French painters of the later nineteenth century for having been among the first to emphasize Salome's Semitic origins. He pointed to these painters' concern for bringing out Salome's 'racial nuances' and marveled gratefully at their 'ethnographic thoroughness,' which he linked to the Orientalist vogue among French painters.[17]

Dijkstra also quotes an anonymous writer of *Famous Pictures Reproduced*, in which the writer, commenting on Jules Lefebvre's *Salome*, states that she represents

> an essentially Semitic type of the antique period, with the sensuous and soulless beauty of the tigress rather than the woman, bearing the charger which is to receive the head of John the Baptist, and the sword which is to decapitate him, as indifferently as if it were a dish of fruit.[18]

But perhaps what made Salome most Jewish is that all the buyers of the most beautiful paintings of Salome were believed to be Jews. In France, a number of nineteenth-century articles not only pointed this out but also found it offensive since, according to them, Jews were deprived of taste. They saw these purchases as insolent attempts at pretending to understand art and acquire its most beautiful productions. For example, a French writer, Jean Lorrain, who also wrote about Salome and presented her with all the features attributed to women in general and to Salome in particular, stresses that all of Moreau's Salomes went to collections of Hayems and Ephrussis, collectors of Jewish origins.

A famous *Affaire Salomé* occurred in France in 1912, when the *Mona Lisa* was stolen from the Louvre (it was recovered a year later). As Mireille Dottin-Orsini describes it, "this curious business opposed the anti-Semite Léon Daudet to a converted Jew Arthur Meyer, as well as Mona Lisa to Salome, the Jew."[19] The *Mona Lisa* was stolen from the Louvre at the time when Henri Regnault's *Salome* (Fig. I-4-7) was for sale at auction, ready to be acquired by an American merchant for 480,000 francs. Arthur Meyer, the editor of the newspaper *Le Gaulois*, hoped that the Louvre or another French museum would buy it, especially because Regnault was a famous French painter killed during the war with Prussia in 1871. Léon Daudet, a member of the extreme-right movement *Action française*, fought furiously against this idea, boldly implying that Jews supposedly stole the *Mona Lisa* from the Louvre in order to replace her with *Salome*, a Jewess. He claimed that for the Louvre—or any other French museum—to buy Regnault's painting of *Salome* would be an insult to the French nation. In the end, Daudet won and an American merchant bought Regnault's *Salome*, which eventually ended up in New York's Metropolitan Museum of Art.

Fig. I-4-7. Henri Regnault, *Salome/Herodias*

Fig. I-4-8. Jean-Sylvain Bieth, *Salome*

The production of Salome images decreased markedly after the First World War. The War occupied people's minds to such an extent that there was neither the time nor the energy left to fight women, "woman's race," and everything associated with it. Now men had to fight for their own survival and for the survival of their nations and cultures. The energy that had been lavished on defining gender differences and "woman" as the enemy was now directed at a different enemy. Thus, only limited numbers of artworks inspired by Salome were produced after the First World War, and Salome's appearance after World War II is even less frequent. The issue of economic competition was difficult for critics to frame because of the critical role that women played in the Second World War.

Progressive movements in the second half of the twentieth century established ethical positions that brought increased parity between the genders socially, professionally, legally and parentally, though these changes did not occur simultaneously in all countries. Thus changes in social attitudes changed the status and the portrayal of women as well as the ways in which men and women perceived gender. Social and aesthetic theories based on questionable nineteenth-century pseudoscience now seem silly, and the art which illustrated such theories has become a curiosity. Performance art, like Strauss' opera *Salome*, offers the director and singers an opportunity to interpret a nineteenth-century work in a variety of ways that are not hamstrung with that century's social attitudes and *mores*. While the *femme fatale* has remained an archetype in modern art and literature and examples may exhibit human depravity in characterization, such characters are more likely to be interpreted as instances of psychological and ethical breaches rather than as proof of gender characteristics.

In the visual arts, Salome became little more than a name and an ancient story. Jean-Sylvain Bieth's 1988 abstract sculpture *Salome* (Fig. I-4-8) carries little of the dramatic narrative of its nineteenth- and early twentieth-century cousins. In this sculpture, Salome's sensuality, seductiveness and *femme fatale* attributes are reduced to three quadrangles in blue, red and white.

Two modern images, by the Russian artists Sergei Chepik and Vasyli Myazin, however, deserve special attention. *Salome* by Sergei Chepik (Fig. I-4-9) shows a female figure that is provocatively naked, irresistibly beautiful and shamelessly evil. As a contemporary figurative painter largely influenced by the artistic tradition of the second half of the nineteenth-century, Chepik remains faithful to that tradition without bringing in his own perceptions of women in general and Salome in particular. Vasyli Myazin's *Salome* (Cover), by comparison, follows more in the tradition of the Renaissance and Oscar Wilde's portrayal. Myazin seems to have sympathy for Salome. He represents her holding the head of John the Baptist on the platter but paints her as innocently beautiful and profoundly sad, as though contemplating the loss of her beloved, whose

Fig. I-4-9. Sergei Chepik, *Salome*

face she can finally contemplate but who is now gone. It belongs to her and to her alone. Although Myazin is influenced by different variations of the myth of Salome, he endows her representation with his own personal touch and his own sympathetic view of Salome as a beautiful, almost mournful woman who, on the one hand, has just lost her beloved, but, on the other, finally has him forever and fully for herself.

* * *

Nonetheless, one might confidently state that if we think of Salome's "master(s)" she has only one, and that master is Ideology with a capital "I," manifested mainly in social tendencies and aspirations, which determined the usage of the name of Salome. Although ideology has changed throughout periods, it was always Ideology that Salome's image was at the service of. At first Salome's function was to contrast her evil role with the sainthood of the Baptist: the darker her image, the purer the saint. The Church used her in order to deprive women of any social, religious or political power or influence, depicting her as an incarnation of Evil and a sister of Eve, the first sinner. Renaissance artists occasionally veiled Salome's evil role and she appeared instead as a muse and a symbol of beauty. In the nineteenth century, the century of a growing fear of women and their rise in social and political power, Salome was once again a tool to darken the image of women and to fight a new "sub race," the rising "race" of women, which was threatening to compete with men in order to further their social influence and power. In the period after the First World War, once ideology lost its importance, representations of Salome fell considerably. Today, for instance, Richard Strauss' opera *Salome* is popular not for the sake of any one ideology but for being an impressive, musically innovative work of art. The Salome of the late twentieth century has thus become little more than a reminiscence of her infamous self, a curiosity or spectacle from centuries past, now divorced from whatever ideology she once represented.

Notes

[1] The secularization of Christian art occurred with the move from Baroque art to the Rococo and Neoclassical styles of the seventeenth and eighteenth centuries and with the increasingly secularized views of the world that came with the Enlightenment. Themes such as portraiture, genre scenes, still life, and historical and mythological stories replaced religious themes. Diana Apostolos-Cappadona explains that "In the nineteenth century with the evolution of the romantic movement, there was a revival of interest in religious themes in art, literature, and music, although not always for spiritual purposes. . . By the end of the nineteenth century, the image of Salome erupted into one of the most popular themes of

symbolist painting. With the development of the *femme fatale*, the classical figures of Helen of Troy, Cleopatra, and Medusa were rediscovered in conjunction with the apocryphal heroine, Judith, and the scriptural dancer, Salome." Diane Apostolos-Cappadona, "Spiritual Women Who Danced," in *Dance as religious studies*, ed. Doug Adams (New York, NY: Crossroad Pub. Co., 2001), 103.

[2] For more information see the article by Brendan Cole, "Nature and the Ideal in Khnopff's *Avec Verhaeren: Un Ange* and *Art, or the Caresses*," *The Art Bulletin* 91 (September 2009), 325-342.

[3] A promulgation of one view of woman might be directly linked to the Napoleonic Code—or *Code Napoléon*—established under Napoleon I in 1804. On the one hand, the code forbade privileges based on birth, allowed freedom of religion, and specified that government jobs should go to the most qualified. On the other hand, it deprived women of all human rights and gave them the status of the mentally impaired. It was the first modern legal code to be adopted within all European countries "liberated" or occupied by Napoleon, and it strongly influenced the laws of many of the countries formed during and after the Napoleonic Wars.

[4] France, the country that produced more misogynistic images in art and literature than any other country in the second part of the nineteenth century, was the first to give birth to the Feminist movement, which instilled even greater fear and repulsion in men. The birth of Feminism in France, however, was directly related to women's dependency on men. Zinaida Vengerova, a Russian literary critic and journalist who lived in France at the turn of the twentieth century, explains in her article "Feminism and Woman's Freedom" that in France "The French woman has been created by the demands of French men and as such is, by her nature, an absolutely passive creature. She does not have any life of her own and exists exclusively in relation to man, her master and her slave, which two roles are essentially the same because the power of the French woman, however great it is in social life, in art and in the ideals of French men, is in reality spiritual slavery." (Zinaida Vengerova, "Feminism and Woman's Freedom," in *Russian Women Writers*, ed. Christine D. Tomei, trans. Rosina Neginsky, Volume 2 [Garland Publishing, Inc., 1999], 895). Vengerova believes that French literature preaches that "Man should live for abstract interests; a woman, for a man." Hence, "when news came to France about the ability of women in other countries to work, participate in social life, occupy professions that had up to that point been considered the exceptional privilege of men and simultaneously become equal members of society independent of traditional societal and family roles, . . . the concept of external freedom as promised by emancipation caused working [French] women to struggle to obtain it from their Motherland, and thus the question about feminine freedom in France transformed itself into an aspiration to improve the conditions of the working woman," (Tomei, 896-897), since in France the life of working women was miserable. Working French women were despised by upper class women who, because of the French constitution which treated them as minors and deprived them of all human and property rights, believed that it was their birth right to live off men; if a woman failed to do so, she was a failure. French working women were also despised by men, because men perceived working women as the

most miserable creatures, failures who could not find husbands and live off them—fully and completely a social expectation. Instead they had to work and to earn their living. These working women were subjected to many psychological and physical abuses and were objects of general contempt. As Vengerova explains: "Feminism in France is directed mainly toward the improvement of a woman's economic life and toward giving her an opportunity to survive as an independent worker when fate fails to realize her life-ideals of security and social status through marriage." (Tomei, 897)

In France the protests against the laws that deprived French women of any rights first reverberated in 1848. However, no one paid attention to those protests, largely because of the power of a then-existing opinion expressed by the well-respected French writer Pierre-Joseph Prudhon, who perceived woman as "the courtesan or the housewife." However, in 1860 the question of the condition of women in France was again brought to public attention, this time by Marie Deraim, the first literary French feminist and an active defender of women's rights. In her own right, she was a writer and a journalist, a literary critic and a playwright. In 1878, Marie Deraim was the representative of the congress of women's rights. Because of her efforts, women were accepted as members of Freemasons and she was instrumental in establishing a mixed Freemason obedience. In 1890 there were a number of women like Louise Michel, Pauline Mink and Jeanne Chmaal, for whom women's freedom was part of their political campaign and convictions.

Thus, the birth of a Feminist movement in a country like France, known as "the most central and the most cultured," in which a woman existed only for a man, could only terrify its male population, which consciously or subconsciously began to defend its "birth right," to apply its power and strength to limit the invasion of society by that dangerous and at the same time necessary "race," "woman's race," as they called it. The first male reaction was that the ideal solution would be to exterminate that race (gynocide), but if that were not possible, women should be locked up and eliminated from the social scene.

[5] Quoted in Mireille Dottin-Orsini, *Cette femme qu'ils disent fatale* (Paris: Bernard Grasset, 1993), 301. All citations from Dottin-Orsini are translated by Rosina Neginsky.
[6] Ibid., 341.
[7] Ibid., 277.
[8] Ibid., 277.
[9] Oscar Wilde, *Salome* (Boston, MA: Branden Publishing Company), 34.
[10] The date of this *Salome* is controversial. Sometimes it is indicated as 1901 and sometimes as 1904.
[11] Bram Dijkstra, *Idols of Perversity. Fantasies of Feminine Evil in fin-de-siècle culture* (New York, Oxford: Oxford University Press, 1986), 375. The point that Dijkstra is making also explains the proliferation of a fascination with beheadings in the nineteenth century. The essence of the decapitated head, however, is related to the idea expressed by Cazotte in his poem in prose *L'Olivier* (1762), in which the decapitated heads are depicted as true bearers of the life which remains in heads once the body is separated from the head. It is one of the reasons for the fascination with

90   Chapter Four

and representation of Orpheus—who was torn apart by the Maenads and whose head survived and was found by a young girl who was touched by the song it still sung—as well as the representation of the head of John the Baptist. In both cases, the head could be perceived as a symbol of everlasting life.
[12] This *Salome* is the part of the collection from *The Santimbanques,* printed and published in 1913 by Louis Fort and Ambroise Vollard. The majority of the images in *The Santimbanques* are not related to the biblical theme, but two images, *Salome* and *The Barbarous Dance* (*In Front of Salomé and Hérode*) are based on the story of Salome's dance and John the Baptist's beheading, although the dance itself is inspired by the figures of real performers at the *Cirque Médrano.* In *Salome* the striking figure is the executioner/servant who holds and cradles the head of John the Baptist. One would say that here Picasso is largely mocking. He represents the lustful executioner/servant with a male face in lust with Salome, but his body has female attributes, two large breasts. The lustful executioner/servant holds the head as a baby, cradling it and ready to feed it with his/her big breasts. Although androgyny was "fashionable" at the time when Picasso created this image, Picasso inverses the androgyny propagated at that time – female face and effeminate body with male sexual organs – and creates a male face with a masculine body but with two large breasts, female attributes. *The Barbarous Dance* deserves a special attention. It is a brilliant caricature of the representations of *Herod's Banquet,* in which Salome does not dance, but she, as a lover of Herod, sits naked next to him and together with him watches the crazy dance, which perhaps mirrors the dance that she has just finished dancing. Her head is turned toward the beautiful androgyne, an effeminate male, John the Baptist, the man of her heart, with whom she exchanges tender and loving glances. At the same time, the platter with the fruit on it served by the longhaired servant foreshadows the future of Salome's and John's "love affair." Some scholars believe that *Salome* and *The Barbarous Dance* in some ways represent the caricature of Apollinaire's poem "Salome," which was published in 1905, the same year as Picasso created his two images based on Salome's story.
[13] Ibid., 386.
[14] In the emerging capitalism of the nineteenth century, Jews were finding their place as business owners, merchants and bank owners—for centuries the only professions opened to Jews. Their success was seen as threatening by their gentile compatriots. The nineteenth century set as one of its goals to prove that Jews were a race of degenerates. To establish degenerate Jewish nature, among a number of characteristics attributed to Jews was that theirs was an effeminate race lacking maturity, much like "woman's race." Who could be more degenerate than a Jewish woman? In art, women, especially those who hold swords and behead men, were depicted more and more with what were considered to be "Jewish features."
[15] Dijkstra, *Idols of Perversity,* 400.
[16] Ibid., 386-387.
[17] Ibid., 386.
[18] Ibid., 387.
[19] Mireille Dottin-Orsini, *Cette femme qu'ils disent fatale,* 328.

PART II

SALOME AND THE HEAD OF JOHN THE BAPTIST IN ARTISTS' SELF-PORTRAITS

# CHAPTER FIVE

PAINTING: TITIAN, BERNARD, MOREAU

> The mirror is the attribute of Lust, and also of Truth, or Pride and Vanity, but also of Prudence: it is an attribute of sight. Contradictory, irreconcilable virtues. The mirror, of itself indifferent, loses its neutrality through the look focused upon it: the look creates it.
> . . .
> The mirror is knowledge. The mirror is the assassin. Mirrors open up an abyss.
>
> —Pascal Bonafoux, *Portraits of the Artists*[1]

In western civilization, artists have created self-portraits in brush, stone and the written word throughout the centuries, going back at least as far as classical antiquity.[2] The birth of self-portraiture that reflects the likeness of the artist begins in the Renaissance. Although Renaissance artists and humanists knew of the self-portraits of classical Antiquity, the source of their inspiration and search for self-representation did not come from the revival of Antiquity but from a new perception of humanity and of individual human complexity. That new perception was reflected in the increasing importance of portraiture and the development of the self-portrait as an independent genre. An early example of a self-portrait—and the earliest known instance of an artist inserting himself into a religious narrative—was executed in 1359 by Andrea Orcagna, who included himself in the *Dormition and Assumption of the Virgin* scene on his marble tabernacle for Florence's Orsanmichele. Taddeo di Bartolo did likewise in his own *Assumption of the Virgin*, painted in 1401.[3]

During the Renaissance one of the major roles of the self-portrait was to express the social status of artists. A self-portrait was partly an attempt to prove that painting and sculpture were not merely the products of manual labor, but that both were born out of the same source of creative genius as poetry, namely from the spirit. "Painting is a mental occupation," wrote Leonardo da Vinci. "We paint with our brain, not with our hands," asserted Michelangelo.[4]

The Renaissance gave us many of the types of self-portraits that artists from later periods used while creating their own self-portraits. These common motifs can be divided into a number of categories. *Assistenza* is when the artist represents himself as one of the figures in his multi-figure composition without necessarily indicating that he is the artist; he often shows himself as a member of his patron's court. *Verkapptes Selbstbildnis*, or "self-portrait in disguise," is in some ways very similar to *Assistenza* but is more complex. In this category of self-portraits, "the artist masquerades as one of the personages in his painting on a religious or poetic subject." In the category *Selbstbildnis zu Studienzwecken*, "self-portrait as an object for study," the artist uses himself as a model for study. In *Selbständiges Selbstbildnis*, the "independent" or autonomous self-portrait, "the artist challenges the spectator with an imposing image of himself as an artist."[5]

For the purpose of this study, I am only interested in the second category, *a self-portrait in disguise*, where the artist masquerades as one of the characters in a painting of a religious or poetic subject and thus paints himself as a historical, mythological or poetic figure. Instances of this practice abound in the history of art. A good example is Dürer's 1500 portrait of himself as a Christ-like figure. In 1833 Samuel Palmer followed Dürer's example and painted a *Self-Portrait as Christ*, and in 1889 Paul Gauguin created *Self-Portrait as Christ in the Garden of Olives*. In 1499 Henrik Bornemann the Younger depicted himself as *St. Luke painting the Virgin*; in 1596-1598 Caravaggio represented his own features in his *The Head of the Medusa*; in 1635 Rembrandt painted himself as *The Prodigal Son*; and in 1638 Artemisia Gentileschi created her self-portrait as *La Pittura*. It is also known that Titian imparted his own features to several mythological and biblical figures, including St. Jerome in his *Pietà*, for example.

Within the category of self-portraits in disguise is a sub-category of particular interest to this study, in which the artist portrays himself in the guise of a martyr or victim. The category bears two sides: one is the artist representing himself as a martyr and as a victim of love; the other is the artist as a saint and a martyr and therefore a victim of circumstance. The category is the extension and the inverse of the category in which the artist creates his portrait in the guise of a hero and/or a conqueror.[6] The classic example is Michelangelo's self-portrait in his *Last Judgment* in the Sistine Chapel (1534-1541), in which the artist depicted himself on the flayed skin held by St. Bartholomew (Fig. II-5-1).

Many self-portraits of this type show the artist *en decapité*—decapitated. We know of a painting by Cristofano Allori (Fig. II-5-2) in which he portrayed himself as Holofernes and his mistress as Judith (early seventeenth century). We also know of works by Cranach and Caravaggio in which the artists allegedly painted the head of Holofernes with their self-portraits (1530 and 1598-99, respectively).

Fig. II-5-1. Michelangelo, *Last Judgment*, detail

Fig. II-5-2. Cristofano Allori, *Judith*

In the following chapters, I will discuss examples of self-portraits in disguise—and more specifically *en decapité*—by looking at five works that pertain to the story of John the Baptist's beheading and Salome's dance. Four of these self-portraits are visual and will be discussed in this chapter; the fifth is a textual self-portrait and will be discussed in chapter six. The four visual works are: Titian's *Salome,* painted ca. 1515 and now located in the Galleria Doria in Rome; Emile Bernard's *Salome (The Head of John the Baptist representing the portrait of Emile Bernard),* painted in 1897, and his *Dancing Salome,* painted in 1914; and the watercolor *The Apparition,* by Gustave Moreau, presented at the 1876 Salon in Paris and now located in the Louvre. The fifth self-portrait, the literary one, is Stéphane Mallarmé's unfinished poem *Les Noces d'Hérodiade.* All of these works bear hidden meanings, which in some cases reflect external biographical and historical events of the artist's life. But overall these works are a reflection of the inner life of the artist, of his philosophy of art and of his creativity.

Titian

In Titian's painting *Salome* (Fig. II-5-3), Salome holds a platter with the head of John the Baptist. As in many late Renaissance paintings of the subject, Salome turns her head away from her trophy. Erwin Panofsky describes this painting in the following terms:

> Salome carrying the charger with the head of the Baptist is shown in front of a piece of masonry which, as indicated by a lock, represents the Saint's prison and is somewhat mysteriously connected with a frontal wall pierced by an arch. Meditative, sad and a little benumbed, she seems to recoil from the face of St. John which yet attracts her side-long glances with irresistible force; a handmaiden—normally found in renderings of Judith rather than Salome but here included, possibly for the first time, in order to produce a poignant psychological contrast—looks at the heroine with the eyes of a faithful dog who feels and shares his master's distress without comprehending its cause.[7]

In the background, Titian represented a cupid, thus reviving the medieval version of Salome's legend, according to which she orders John's beheading out of amorous frustration. Titian has portrayed the head of the Baptist with his own features, making it into a self-portrait. According to Panofsky, Titian's *Salome* is

> the earliest example of those self-portraits *en decapité* in which a love-stricken painter lent his own features to either Holofernes (as is the case with Cristofano Allori's famous *Judith* [Fig. II-5-2] in the Pitti Palace, where the heroine is impersonated by Allori's mistress, "La Mazafirra") or to Goliath (as is the case with Caravaggio's *David* in the Galleria Borghese).[8]

Fig. II-5-3. Titian, *Salome*

The legend of Salome's passion for John the Baptist and his subsequent rejection of her first appeared in the twelve-century writings of Nivardus, a canon and *scholasticus* of St. Pharaildis in Ghent. A patron saint of that city, St. Pharaildis (the Latinized name of the Flemish St. Verelde) was directly connected to Salome (who was often erroneously called Herodias through Late Antiquity and the Middle Ages). In medieval German mysteries Salome was equated with Frau Hulda, Fru Helle or Fru Helde, the old, Germanic storm goddess. The association came about due to the claim in some German legends that "she was blown into the sky by a blast of air miraculously rushing forth from the mouth of the Baptist's head,"[9] as retribution for her role in the Baptist's execution. She was therefore given a place in the *Wild Hunt (Wilde Jagd* or *Wildes Heer)*, riding the clouds by night. In that capacity she had been worshipped from the tenth to the twelfth century. The phonetic similarity of "Frau Helde" and the Flemish "Verylde/Verelde" resulted in a conflation of the figures of Salome and St. Verelde (Pharaildis).[10]

Nivardus transformed the story of the Baptist's death into a love story, in which Salome (whom he calls Herodias) "was madly in love with the Baptist and vowed not to marry any other man."[11] In response, a bitter and indignant Herod orders the execution of John. Salome, in her amorous despair, requests his head. She embraces the head, covers it with her tears and tries unsuccessfully to kiss it. The head rebuffs her advances and blows her into the air, where she is pursued by the spirit of the Baptist. Her only comfort during this period of suffering is the veneration she is accorded by millions of admirers, who eventually revere her as a saint, possibly because she—like the real Pharaildis—remained a virgin. Nivardus stresses the conflation of the two figures, stating:

> Now known as Pharaïldis—once Herodias—
> Unrivaled as a dancer now and evermore.[12]

Titian's self-portrait in his *Salome* suggests another version of the idea of a beautiful young woman in love with the man whose head she holds on a platter. In his book *The Youth of Titian (La jeunesse de Titian)*, Louis Hourticq asserts that Titian's *Salome* is one of many examples of sixteenth-century portraits depicting two people united by a love affair or some kind of erotic feeling. The woman would often be depicted as Salome and the man as the head of John the Baptist on a platter held by the woman. Hourticq implies that the presence of a cupid suggests Titian's self-portrait as John the Baptist is a love painting, in which Titian states his love for the lady depicted as Salome. The implication is that he is ready to offer her his life. Hourticq writes:

> The face of the beheaded always has the kind of tender and fatal romantic beauty, that would make the heart of the tigress melt. Those Saint Johns with beautiful beards are portraits like the Salomes who hold them. In Berlin, in the painting attributed to Romanino, a *grand seigneur* is present at the execution of Saint John, and the head given to Salome is so similar to

the one of the grand seigneur that there is no doubt that this handsome aristocrat is ready to offer his life for the beautiful eyes of a lady.[13]

Although this meaning in Titian's painting may be obvious in light of the established tradition, there may be another, deeper level of significance disguised under the literal representation. To see this possibility, we might go back to the early sixteenth century and read the draft preface that was intended to open Dürer's book on the *Theory of Human Proportions*. From its preface, Pascal Bonafoux draws the following conclusion:

> To be a painter is to be in the image of God; it is a life that imitates that of Jesus, and, further, it is the 'Schola Crucis' of St. Augustine: *'Tota vita Christiani hominis, si secundum Evangelium vivat, crux est'* (The whole life of a Christian, if he lives according to the Gospels, is a cross). . . . to paint oneself as Christ is to paint oneself as a painter.[14]

For Dürer, the painter is both prophet and victim: He brings a new message to humanity but he is also chastised for bringing this message. In his *Salome*, Titian paints himself as John the Baptist, the saint, who is like Christ in that he was killed for the message he brought. By inserting a cupid, the symbol of love, between Salome and the latter, Titian implies that Salome in this painting represents humanity, loved by the saint and Christ alike, and for whom John, like Christ, brings a message of love. Titian, a great artist who brings his own message to humanity through his art, seems to be saying that he too may suffer; he paints himself in the image of John the Baptist, the precursor and the harbinger of Christ. Like John, he suffers by sacrificing himself and giving himself to humanity through the mission of his art and by bringing a divine message through his creative process.

Another possible interpretation of Titian's *Salome* is that he is representing his self-sacrifice for art, and the pain that he endures in the process of creation. Titian painted his *Salome* in his youth, in 1515, when he was not yet established as an artist. Although his career had promise, it was also uncertain. Perhaps his Salome is a symbol of art itself, the art that he passionately loved and that gave meaning to his life. Or perhaps she represents a fear of the failure that might ultimately make his beloved art become his executioner.

Titian painted a second *Salome* (Fig. II-5-4) in the 1550s, when he was at the height of his artistic career. Now located in Madrid at the Prado, it is also called *Lavinia as Salome* after Lavinia, Titian's daughter.[15] In this work, Titian used his daughter as a model for Salome. She dances and holds the platter with the head of the Baptist above her own head.[16] She turns to the viewer, away from the head. Her face, her gaze and her lips are impressively sensual. She does not wear any necklaces, which makes her shoulders and her neck that much more open and erotic. If we were to think of Titian's daughter Lavinia as a symbol of a finished work of art, her depiction as Salome, the executioner, could imply that the work of art is always a mortal danger to those who are willing to live for it, love it and give it everything they possess. Titian's two *Salomes*, in isolation and considered together, are rich in such possible meanings.

Fig. II-5-4. Titian, *Lavinia as Salome*

Emile Bernard

In the case of Emile Bernard's *Salome* (Fig. II-5-5) of 1897 we do not need to speculate on whether the head of John the Baptist is a self-portrait, as Bernard added parentheses to the title indicating the work's status as such. In composition and spirit, the painting bears similarities to Titian's *Salome* in the Galleria Doria Pamphilj in Rome, except for the presence of the servant and the cupid. Both are absent in Bernard's work. Bernard was familiar with Titian's works in general and with his *Salome* in particular. In 1893 he spent time travelling in Italy and studying Italian Renaissance art.

In Bernard's half-length portrait, Salome's glance toward the spectator and away from the Baptist's head on the platter, her way of holding the platter on the left side and the position of the Baptist's head on the platter are all very much Titian's. However, Titian's Salome looks almost like a child or a teenager, striking in her innocent glance, whereas Bernard's Salome is older, and although she is still young and beautiful her face is notable for a certain maturity and lack of innocence.[17]

Despite the painting's superficial and stylistic resemblance to sixteenth-century love portraiture, the absence of a cupid in Bernard's work indicates that the focus of Bernard's Salome is not on a "love affair." In his painting, Bernard portrays his features in the Baptist's head lying on the platter. Salome's face is reminiscent of Bernard's Egyptian wife, Hanénah (Annette) Saati, whom he married on 1 July 1894 in Cairo at the Church of Notre-Dame-de-l'Assomption du Mousky. We are left to speculate on the reasons for such a representation.

The years leading up to 1897 had been difficult for Bernard. On 22 July 1896 Bernard and his family left Cairo, where they had been living, and travelled to Spain. Several reasons triggered their departure from Egypt, including the deaths of Bernard's sister and her fiancé in 1895 and the poor health of Bernard's son Otsy.[18]

At the end of the summer in 1896 they settled in Grenada. Bernard subsequently became very ill.[19] Hanénah had difficulties handling the situation, and Bernard had to call for his mother. She arrived in November of 1897 when Bernard was close to death. His mother cared for him and saved his life. By that time, Emile had realized that he had nothing in common with his wife; she was not interested in art, she was indifferent to his work and she regarded it only as a source of income. He likely blamed her for the family environment that undoubtedly became suffocating for him. Thus, the painting *Salome with the Platter*, in which Salome is portrayed as Hanénah and he as the Baptist, probably reflects Bernard's

Fig. II-5-5. Emile Bernard, *Salome with the Platter*

perception of his wife at that time. He seems to perceive her as a destroyer, a symbol of a "base nature," capable only of physical life and procreation, who annihilates everything creative, spiritual and heroic, thus destroying him, the artist.

Fig. II-5-6. Emile Bernard, *The Dancer or Salome*

After marrying an Egyptian woman who had no artistic interests or talents, Bernard was very much attracted to women-artists, including Armène Ohanian, a dancer of Iranian background, and Andrée Fort, a musician and the sister of his friend, the poet Paul Fort. When Bernard fell in love with Ohanian in 1912, he was already separated from his first wife, Hanénah, and was living with and had a family with Andrée Fort, though they were not officially married.[20]

In 1914 Bernard painted another work that involved Salome (Fig. II-5-6), *The Dancer or Salome* (*La Danseuse en Salomé*), and although it is not a direct self-portrait, it too is an autobiographical painting. As a model for his dancing Salome, he used the dancer, Armène, who was also his lover at that time.[21] The title of the work reflects Bernard's perception of Armène as a dancer, his perception of her personality and his views on their relationship.

Although he was attracted to women-artists, his tendency was to turn these women-artists into little more than servants who sacrificed their own ambitions for him. It worked with Andrée. She was fully devoted to him and was ready to accept anything to keep him by her side. But it was not the case with Armène. She was aware of the wealth of her own personality and her artistic talents and she wanted to be loved fully and exclusively, without having to share the man she loved with other women.[22]

Though they were passionately in love with each other, Bernard and Armène's love affair was tempestuous. During their affair, Armène was Emile's muse and he painted her over twenty times in the guise of different personalities. He wrote:

> Sometimes I painted her singing while playing the long Persian guitar, dressed in white with dreamy eyes; sometimes she was dancing or dreaming leaning on the large tambourine; she was dressed in sultan telling the marvellous stories . . . or Eve, naked and scary after committing the sin. Finally I painted her without her veils, as Salome.[23]

The image of Armène as the dancing Salome is likely the best reflection of her personality and profession, as well as of Bernard's perception of her. Sources reveal her to be a strong woman, unwilling to accept compromises. She was also beautiful and charming. Thus, in many ways she was the embodiment of the perfect image of Salome as perceived by artists, poets and writers of the second half of the nineteenth century. For Bernard, she was an enchantress; he was fully charmed by her dance, her beauty, her intelligence and her personality. At the same time, she was his executioner. She resisted him and his will and by doing so caused him a great deal of pain. The painting *Salome* foreshadows the evolution of their relationship and Bernard's symbolic beheading through Ohanian's book, *Les Rires d'une charmeuse de serpents (Laughs of a Serpent Charmer)*, published in 1915 after their affair ended. The book, in which she parodies Bernard and portrays him as a liar and a crook, was Ohanian's way of appearing in front of the world as the victorious Salome. Its publication was also a means of beheading Bernard, her beloved John, who in his way rejected her.[24]

As I mentioned in the previous chapter, "The Seducer-Destroyer Salome of Nineteenth-Century Art and Literature," the nineteenth century produced some 2,789 paintings of Salome, not only because of the new trend embodied in the cult of the beautiful woman but also because of men's fear of the new woman. The new woman was perceived as strong, independent, often beautiful and no longer interested solely in procreation. Instead, she wanted to study and work and was consequently admitted to universities and the work force. She became man's competitor, a woman who was asserting herself both in and outside the home, in realms that were traditionally the domain of men. Artists, who are often among the most perceptive members of society, sensed these changes and the associated fears. Thus, the nineteenth-century image of Salome became a symbol of men's perception of a new woman. Bernard's painting *The Dancer or Salome*, in which Salome was modelled after Armène Ohanian—herself an archetype of a new woman—reflects both Bernard's admiration for and fear of the new woman. On a more personal level, it foreshadows the evolution of his relationship with Armène and his symbolic beheading.

Gustave Moreau

Nivardus' twelfth-century legend of Salome's unrequited love for the Baptist never gained official recognition but it did influence some popular medieval songs. The story became especially important during the Feast of St. John. In 1833, Jacob Grimm published the tale of Nivardus in *German Mythology*. It then reappeared in a narrative poem by Heinrich Heine, *Atta Troll*. In his poem, Heine writes:

> For she loved the Prophet once,
> Though the Bible naught reveals,
> Yet her blood-stained love lives on
> Stories in her people's hearts.[25]

It is through that poem that the love story between Salome—whom Heine, like German medieval mysteries, names Herodias—and John the

Baptist reached an audience in nineteenth-century France.

Heine originally published the poem in German in 1841, but because he lived in France he subsequently translated it into French.[26] That version was published in 1847. The poem met with great success and popularity among French poets and writers, including Gérard de Nerval, Théophile Gautier and Charles Baudelaire—the precursors of French Symbolism. The poem's many literary digressions fascinated artists of the period, and though the poem is not primarily about Salome, one of its digressions is based on the legend of her love story.

In the poem, the narrator participates, as an observer, in the hunt for a symbolic bear named Atta Troll. On the night before *Johannestag* (Saint John's Day, named after John the Baptist) the poet opens the window and sees a nocturnal procession consisting of the ghosts of prominent sinners. As punishment, these sinners are deprived of eternal peace by being called every Saint John's Day night to redeem their crimes by participating in the procession until the day of final Judgment. Among the participants of the procession are three beauties: the Greek Goddess Diana, the virgin huntress, to whom Heine attributes the sin of betraying her chastity; Abunda, the "fairy queen," a seductress; and Herodias, "the third fair phantom." He relates her story thus:

> Of most royal blood was she,
> She the Queen of old Judea,
> She great Herod's lovely wife,
> She who craved the Baptist's head.
>
> For this crimson crime was she
> Banned and cursed. Now in this chase
> Must she ride, a wandering spook,
> Till the dawn of Judgment Day.
>
> Still within her hands she bears
> That deep charger with the head
> Of the Prophet, still she kisses—
> Kisses it with fiery lips.
>
> . . .
>
> How might else a man declare
> All the longing of this lady?
> Would a woman crave the head
> Of a man she did not love?

She perchance was slightly vexed
With her darling, and was moved
To behead him, but when she
On the trencher saw his head,

Then she wept and lost her wits,
Dying in love's madness straight.
(What! Love's madness? pleonasm!
Love itself is madness still!)

Rising nightly from her grave,
To this frenzied hunt she hies,
In her hands the gory head
Which with feline joy she flings

High into the air betimes,
Laughing like a wanton child,
Cleverly she catches it
Like some idle rubber ball.[27]

Ary Renan claims that Moreau was familiar with Heinrich Heine's poem of 1847; he certainly had it in his library. The poem's striking image of Herodias playing with the head of John the Baptist on the night before *Johannestag* affected the artist's imagination and contributed to his conception of two paintings exhibited at the 1876 Salon: the oil painting *Salomé dansant devant Hérode* (*Salome Dancing Before Herod,* Fig. II-5-7) and a watercolor, *L'Apparition* (*The Apparition,* Fig. II-5-8), with an image of the Baptist's head rising from the platter. Both works impressed the public and the critics for their originality of conception and stunning colors. The expressive, wordless exchange between Salome and the rising head of John the Baptist is strikingly unusual in *The Apparition*, although both cases are notable for their original characterization of Salome. In these paintings Moreau narrated his own myth, a story that corresponds to his own aesthetic philosophy.[28]

Both *Salome Dancing Before Herod* and *The Apparition* were also inspired by the innovative painting *Herodias* by Henri Regnault (Fig. I-4-7), a painter in whom Moreau was interested and who won a prize at the 1870 Salon for his *Salome*. Regnault's painting was the first work to represent Salome holding an empty platter in her lap. She is the center of attention and not merely an appendage to John the Baptist. In the Renaissance, when Salome's image started to supersede that of the Baptist's head in importance, the platter was never shown empty; the head was always included as a reminder of the fleeting vanity of life and the

Fig. II-5-7. Gustave Moreau, *Salome Dancing Before Herod*

Fig. II-5-8. Gustave Moreau, *The Apparition*

ever-present shadow of death. In Regnault's painting, John's head is on the platter only by implication, and it is Salome, a beautiful and sensual woman, who is the only center of attention. She appears as a young gypsy girl who holds a charger without the head but with the sword placed on it. If the title of the painting were absent, she could be any young and beautiful woman. From then on, painted alone either dancing or holding the (occasionally empty) charger, Salome became in her own right the main subject of works of art, a cult figure, and ceased being secondary to John.

In his writings, Moreau contends that when he created his *Salome Dancing Before Herod* he was

> obliged to invent everything. . . . In my head I first construct the personality that I want to give to my figure and then I dress her according to that first and dominant idea. Thus, I wanted to create my Salome as Sybil and the religious magician with a mysterious personality. Then I conceived her costume.[29]

Although his Salomes are very personal, Moreau borrowed ideas from both Raphael and Rembrandt as well as from his mentor, Chassériau, and from Oriental miniatures. He combined periods and religions; he mixed together symbols and ignored history, as Jules Kaplan shows in his book *The Art of Gustave Moreau*:

> Moreau scoured the history of art for visual ideas he could use in Salome. Especially struck by the elaborate decoration of Renaissance altarpieces, he developed a principle he designated 'necessary richness' and applied it to Salome. . . . The elaborate architectural setting with its complicated interplay of light and dark derives from Rembrandt, and the detail of the hanging lamp enframed by an arch may well have been taken from one of the Rembrandt reproductions Moreau owned. The Salome figure itself was initially inspired by Raphael, but another source was probably Delacroix's dramatically gesturing young oriental dancer in the *Jewish Wedding*, 1839. Thus, . . . Moreau integrated studies from nature—as the drawing from the model shows—with the elements borrowed from the Old Masters.[30]

Kaplan also suggests a connection between the notion of Salome as a *femme fatale* and Moreau's interest in Eastern Art.[31] This is based partly on the artist's interest in the French author Chateaubriand and partly on the fact that French literature of the period was saturated with images of destructive and beautiful Oriental women. Examples include Gautier's *Une Nuit de Cléopâtre* (1838) (*A Night of Cleopatra*), Flaubert's *Salammbô* (1862) and Mallarmé's poem *Hérodiade* (1871). These were the books with which Moreau was familiar. Moreau also collected the *Magasin pittoresque* and borrowed from it the elements that he would use to dress his dancing Salome and decorate the palace. Luisa Capodieci shows that on the body of the dancing Salome, Moreau, using *encre de Chine* (Chinese ink), designed hieroglyphs.[32] He drew on her breast the apotropaic eyes of Osiris; on her stomach he drew the lotus of immortality. These elements impart a new and special meaning to Salome. She is no longer the goddess of death. Rather, she becomes the goddess of life, Isis, able to resurrect through her magical powers. Two laughing monsters on her body, borrowed from Etruscan jewels, imply her ancient origins and eternal nature.

Moreau's watercolor *The Apparition* is of particular interest for the present study, since it depicts the head of John the Baptist floating in mid-air, having risen from its platter.[33] The haloed head looks at Salome with eyes that are kind and innocent. It does not seem to accuse Salome of anything, yet she is portrayed as filled with rage, and she points at the head as though hurling an accusation at the Baptist. The setting of this painting is similar to Moreau's other painting of Salome, although here the center of attention is not Salome dancing before Herod. Instead, the focus is now Salome dancing before the head of the Baptist and the striking exchange of glances between the two. Is John's "floating" head a suggestion that it is only present in Salome's imagination? Is she so shocked by it that she interrupts her dance and enters into communication with her vision?

If we look closely at John's face and compare it with Moreau's self-portraits or photographs, we can see that the face in *The Apparition* is that of the artist. Moreau lived for four years in Italy and studied Italian art. He was therefore familiar with the use of self-portraits by Renaissance artists. In *The Apparition* he follows the tradition of Renaissance artists who painted themselves as victims and in *decapité*, even while endowing this self-portrait with his own particular meaning.

Although Moreau received a level of appreciation by some collectors, such as Charles Hayem, he remained an independent painter throughout his life, never belonging to any of the schools of his time, such as Naturalism, Impressionism or Realism. Those movements were largely preoccupied with the representation of the external world, whether it be nature or society. Moreau, in contrast, did not believe that the role of the artist was to imitate or record any kind of physical reality. For him, the role of the artist was to create his own imaginary reality. "Art inspired by nature cannot be reduced to exact and servile imitation, because, in this case, it is not an art, and nature is preferable."[34] As a result, he was recognized neither by the artists of the major schools nor by the public at large, and he returned the compliment. Moreau believed that art has a

Fig. II-5-9. Gustave Moreau, *Dancing Salome*

spiritual mission, *un sacerdoce*. He was seeking, through his art, to give individual expression to universal meanings and to represent a reality more perfect than that which was merely physical. He saw himself as a messenger of truth through art.

Thus, it is not surprising that Moreau might easily identify himself with John the Baptist, the first lonely preacher of a future universal faith. Like John, Moreau felt himself a prophet, rejected by society and "executed" for his message. At the same time, the halo around John's head, the sign of posthumous fame and recognition, may be a symbol of Moreau's conviction of his own posthumous success, the recognition and acceptance which would eventually come to him after death.

In Moreau's works, women are usually an incarnation of nature, which Moreau perceived as mortal and chaotic and therefore destructive. Women destroyed everything heroic and spiritual.[35] Works such as *Oedipus and the Sphinx* (*Oedipe et le Sphinx*), *Les Chimères* and *Dalila* reflect this view of women.[36] Describing to his deaf mother the image of a beautiful feminine Sphinx in his *Oedipe et le Sphinx*, Moreau wrote:

> This is the earthly Chimera, vile and attractive as matter. She is represented by this charming head of a woman who has wings that are promising of an ideal, but her body is the body of a monster. She is a vamp who tears to pieces and destroys.[37]

He expressed similar sentiments about his Salome, writing:

> This woman [Salome] who represents the eternal woman, a light bird, often fatal, crossing life with a flower in her hand, in search of her vague ideal, often horrible. She always walks trampling on everyone, even the genius and the saints. That dance executed, this mysterious walk demonstrated in front of death that endlessly looks at her, yawning and attentive, and in front of the executioner who carries the sword that kills. This is the emblem of that horrible future reserved to those who search for an ideal... One saint, one severed head are at the end of her journey.[38]

For Moreau, Salome in *The Apparition* is a symbol of society and its passing fashions and tastes. Since Salome—through her dance—is herself an artist, for Moreau she might be an embodiment of the artistic trends that were fashionable at his time, such as Realism, Naturalism and Impressionism. This was the kind of art that was contrary to his since it focused on the physical world, either society (Naturalism and Realism) or nature (Impressionism). Moreau referred to Realism and Naturalism as "ras de caniveau" (the brim of the gutter), and viewed Impressionism and academic art as "art without any ideas."[39] Describing his attitude toward fashionable art and artists and the way they are perceived by society and his own place within it, Moreau writes:

> Now there is a false daring and there is a false artistic ardor, when there are all these disinherited jesters searching to attract by all means the attention and support of the crowd and of stupid connoisseurs; there is ... a reproach [a stone] that they throw endlessly at the head of the true artist, who is a modest conscientious worker, saying that such and such doctrine, such and such school, such and such genre must be followed because they are the future of art.[40]

Thus, Salome in *The Apparition* is a symbol of the artists that Moreau calls "disinherited jesters," as well as the art critics, whom he names "the stupid imbeciles of art connoisseurs," and the public that follows whatever the critics say. Such a society is unable to recognize "true" art, i.e., his art, and therefore rejects him. Since Moreau was convinced that true art and the true artist-prophet would eventually triumph over society, Salome has a vision of a John who will eventually rise over her. The head of the Baptist, a symbol of unrecognized art, will vanquish the art and the society Salome embodies, and in doing so it will be triumphant over her (and the critics') falsehoods. [41]

Salome was Moreau's favorite subject. His interest in this subject started after the Franco-Prussian war of 1870 and France's subsequent defeat. From a historical perspective, Salome might be a symbol of the German barbarism that aspired to destroy France, itself embodied in the noble figure of John the Baptist, whose beheading would bring him glory. Geneviève Lacambre suggests that in one version of the Salome theme, King Herod "has the mien of a feeble sovereign and features reminiscent of those of Napoléon III... Indeed, the king's empty gaze echoes that of the 1863 portrait of Napoléon by Hippolyte Flandrin."[42] This weak leader was the reason for France's defeat, for letting Salome (the Germans) behead John the Baptist (France).[43]

Moreau's first Salome was a small painting of *Salome in the Prison,* also called *Salome with a Rose* because this Salome holds a beautiful red rose in her left hand, the symbol of passion. It was sold to the dealer Brame in December of 1872. Then, probably in 1883, Moreau painted a watercolor of a *Dancing Salome* (Fig. II-5-9), in which her face is turned toward the viewer while she is standing on her toes. She holds in her right hand a white lotus, the mixed symbol of passion and purity. One of his most striking Salomes is the watercolor *Salomé au jardin* (*Salome in the Garden,* Fig. II-5-10), painted around 1878.[44] The poet Jean Lorrain was inspired by this work to write a poem entitled "Salome à la charmille,"

Fig. II-5-10. Gustave Moreau, *Salome in the Garden*

which he dedicated to Gustave Moreau. Moreau, writing about this Salome, expresses his sharp view of women and gives us a clear picture of his intentions:

> This woman . . . of an animal nature, gives pleasure to herself . . . by seeing her enemy vanquished. She is disgusted with all her other desires that have

been already satisfied. This woman who walks light-heartedly in a vegetal and bestial way in admirable gardens . . . , has just been dirtied by this horrible murder.
. . .
When I want bring out all these nuances, I do not find them in my mind, but in the nature itself of woman who searches for unhealthy emotions and who, stupidly does not understand the most horrible of situations.[45]

Many of Moreau's images of Salome show her dancing, and he explores the dance from a variety of perspectives. The unusual *The Apparition* and *Salome Dancing Before Herod* are his most striking Salomes; *The Apparition*, already touched on above, is, arguably, the most original and is loaded with dense meaning.

The fame of both paintings is partly due to their description and role in Joris-Karl Huysmans' novel *Against Nature (A Rebours)*. Huysmans brings these works alive by picturing them through the eyes of Des Esseintes, the main character of the novel and the owner of *The Apparition* and *Salome Dancing Before Herod*. Des Esseintes is an aesthete who has chosen to lead his life away from society, believing that he can create his own world, parallel to the disappointing physical world, by surrounding himself with objects that will make his inner life vibrate. He has a special relationship with both works. Of *Salome Dancing Before Herod*, he says:

> In Gustave Moreau's painting, which was conceived without any reference to the facts of the Gospel story, Des Esseintes could at last see realized that superhuman, strange Salome of whom he had dreamt. No longer was she just the dancer who by a shameless gyration of her hips wrests a lustful, ruttish cry from an old man, who destroys the resoluteness and breaks the will of a king with the thrusts of her breasts, undulations of her belly, and quiverings of her thighs; there she became, in a sense, the symbolic deity of indestructible Lechery, the goddess of immortal Hysteria, the accursed Beauty singled out from among all others by the cataleptic paroxysm that stiffens her flesh and hardens her muscles; the monstrous, indiscriminate, irresponsible, unfeeling Beast who, like the Helen of Antiquity, poisons everything that comes near her, everything that sees her, everything that she touches.
>
> Perceived in that light, she belonged to Far Eastern theogonies; she could no longer be associated with biblical tradition, could no longer even be likened to the living symbol of Babylon, the royal Harlot of the Apocalypse who, like her, is draped in jewels and purple, who like her is powdered and rouged . . .[46]

Des Esseintes' perception of *The Apparition*, which involves John the Baptist's floating head, is even more striking, and we can do no better to close our discussion of Moreau's Salome than to quote Huysmans/Des Esseintes' description of that picture and its effect.

> ... but the watercolour entitled *The Apparition* was perhaps even more disturbing. ...
> The decapitated head of the saint had risen from the charger lying upon the flagstones, and he was staring, his countenance livid, his open mouth waxen, his neck scarlet and dripping tears of blood. Mosaics framed the face from which emanated a halo radiating out into shafts of light beneath the porticos, illuminating the horrifying levitation of the head, igniting the glassy orbs of the pupils which remained fixed, almost riveted, on the dancer.
> With a terror-stricken gesture, Salome wards off the ghastly vision, which keeps her standing there, motionless, on tiptoe; her eyes widen, her hand clutches convulsively at the throat. She is almost naked; in the heat of the dance, the veils have come undone, the brocaded draperies have fallen; now she is clad only in the creations of goldsmiths and silversmiths, and in pellucid precious stones. ...
> In the blazing shafts of light emanating from the head of the Baptist, all the facets of the jewels catch fire. ... The dreadful head blazes with light and continues to drip with blood, which forms clots of deep purple on the ends of the beard and hair. Visible to Salome alone, it embraces in its bleak gaze neither Herodias who sits brooding over her hatred, now finally appeased, nor the Tetrarch who, leaning forward slightly with his hands upon his knees, still pants with desire, driven wild by this woman's nakedness which has been soaked in musky scents, drenched in sweet-smelling balms, and steeped in the fumes of incense and of myrrh.
> Des Esseintes, like the old king, was overwhelmed, stunned, unhinged by this dancer, who was less majestic, less haughty, but more unsettling than the Salome of the oil painting.[47]

Thanks to that "dreadful head" blazing with light and dripping with blood, this image of Salome is surely one of the most meaningful and complex self-portraits ever created. It is a stunning reflection of Moreau's glory and pain, in which the artist—in the guise of the beheaded saint—confronts with a glance all at once pure, innocent and firm his terrified enemy, whom he has already forgiven.

Notes

[1] Pascal Bonafoux, *Portraits of the Artists. The Self-Portrait in Painting* (New York: Skira, Rizolli, 1985), 36 and 38.

[2] The most famous self-portraits of antiquity were by Phidias and Theodorus. Phidias was one of the greatest sculptors of antiquity. He created his self-portrait as

a part of the Amazonian battle-scene carved on the shield of his statue of Athena Parthenos on the Acropolis. This self-portrait was mentioned in a number of literary sources, such as *De Mundo* (a work ascribed to Aristotle), Cicero's *Tusculan Disputations* and Plutarch's biography of Pericles.

Each source described the self-portrait from a different point of view. In *De Mundo*, the role of Phidias's self-portrait on the shield is compared to "the position of God in the universe." (Luba Freedman, *Titian's Independent Self-Portrait* [Leo S. Olshki Editore: Pocket Library of "Studies" in Art, 1990], 12). The author of *De Mundo* stated that the divine is entirely dependent on the artist's portrait; if the portrait disappears, the statue will be destroyed. Thus, the work of art is inseparable from its creator. Without a creator, there is no work of art. Without God, there is no life. Cicero asserted that it was Phidias's way to "become famous after death." He wrote: "Artists wish to become famous after death, or why did Phidias insert his likeness on the shield of Minerva though not allowed to inscribe his name on it?" (in Freedman, *Titian*, 12). Plutarch sees Phidias's self-portrait in the composition of the sacred statue as a challenge to the gods, which led later to his imprisonment and death from illness.

Theodorus was an architect, known for his famous labyrinth on the island of Samos. We only know of this self-portrait from Pliny's *Natural History*. Allegedly, "the architect represented himself in a bronze statue of a sculptor holding a tiny team of four horses." (Freedman, *Titian*, 14)

In the Middle ages, as Pascal Bonafoux points out, self-portraits were done "In the margins of homilies, psalms and prayers. . . . But these veiled nuns and tonsured monks are only portraits because they are near the names with which the work is signed." (Bonafoux, *Portraits of the Artists*, 19.) These self-portraits do not reflect the likeness of the painter. We know that it is a self-portrait only because of a signature attached to it. This is the case of Herrade de Landsberg, the mother superior of the Convent of Hohenburg, who directed the creation of the illuminated manuscript *Hortus Deliciarum (The Garden of Delights*, 1160-1170) and who painted her portrait in the margin. It is also the case of a nun known as Guda, who wrote and painted a *Book of Homilies* (twelfth century) and who drew her self-portrait within the curving stem of an ornamental letter in the margin. We can find a similar representation in the case of a nun named Claricia, who painted her body as a part of the illuminated orb of a letter that she holds with her outspread hands.

Some examples of early self-portraits of artists include: artists portraying themselves on sets of bronze doors in the Middle Ages (on which see Ursula Mende, *Die Bronzetüren des Mittelalters, 800-1200* [Munich: Hirmer, 1983], figs. 95, 100, 157, and 163), with examples at the Cathedral of San Zeno, Verona, c. 1130s (the sculptor shown with his tools); the Cathedral at Novgorod, (the sculptor with his tools); the Cathedral at Trani, c. 1180/90 (the sculptor kneeling to patron saint); the Cathedral at Monreale, 1185-89 (the sculptor kneeling to patron saint); Nicolo di Montefonte's pulpit in Benevento Cathedral, dated 1311, in which Nicolo kneels by the crucifix (see A. Venturi, *Storia dell'arte Italiana*, iv [*La Scultura del Trecento e le sue origini*] [Milan, 1906], 250-253); Francesco da Milano's Reliqury of St. Simeon, in San Simeone, Zara, dated 1377-80, in which Francesco works at a metal column (C. Cecchielli, *Zara* [Rome, 1932], 107ff); Matteo di Ser Cambio's self-portrait with compasses on his illumination of statues of Matricola del Cambio, fol. 1r, Perugia, Collegio del Cambio, dated 1377 (P. d'Ancona, *La miniature italienne du Xe au Xve siècle* [Paris, 1925], 44, plate xl: 'Io Mateo di ser Cambio orfo, che quie col sesto in mano me fegurai Quisto libro scrisse, dipinse et miniae'); Neri da Rimini, in Antiphonary I, fol. 1v, Faenza Cathedral, dated c. 1300, in which the artist is shown kneeling (A. Corbara, "Due Antifonari miniati dal riminese Neri" *La Bibliofilia* xxxvii (1935), 40ff; fig. 1); Pietro di Pavia shows himself seated in his study in Pliny's *Historia naturalis*, MS E24, fol 332r, Bibliotheca Ambrosiana, Milan, dated 1389 (Virginia Wylie Egbert, *The Medieval Artist at Work* [Princeton: Princeton University Press, 1967], plate xxx, 81). The preceding examples and associated bibliography are taken from Catherine King, "Filarete's Portrait Signature on the Bronze Doors of St Peter's" *Journal of the Warburg and Courtauld Institutes* 53 (1990), 296-299.

[3] For more information about those self-portraits and the meaning of the self-portrait associated with the representation of the Virgin, see Joanna Woods-Marsden, *Renaissance Self-Portraiture* (New Haven & London: Yale University Press, 1998), 48.

[4] Bonafoux, *Portraits*, 8.

[5] For more on the categories of self-portraits and how to determine the image of the artist, see Freedman, *Titian's Independent Self-Portraits*, 41-72.

[6] In this category, there is Artemisia Gentileschi's portrait of herself as Judith in her *Judith with the Head of Holofernes* from the early seventeenth century. Another example is Giorgione's *David*, painted in 1650, in which the artist depicted himself as David and portrayed his master, Bellini, as the severed head of Goliath.

[7] Erwin Panofsky, *Problems in Titian, Mostly Iconographic* (New York: New York University Press, 1969), 42-43.

[8] Ibid., 43.

[9] Ibid., 44.

[10] Ibid., 44-45.

[11] Ibid., 45.

[12] Nivardus of Ghent, *Ysengrimus*, quoted and summarized (with the Latin) in ibid., 45.

[13] "Toujours, le visage du décapité est d'une beauté romanesque, tendre, fatale, qui attendrirait un cœur de tigresse. Ces saint Jean à belle barbe sont des portraits comme les Salomé qui les portent. A Berlin, dans un tableau attribué à Romanino, un grand seigneur assiste au supplice de saint Jean et la tête que l'on présente à Salomé est si pareille à la sienne qu'il ne peut y avoir du doute ; ce beau seigneur témoigne qu'il est prêt à offrir sa vie aux beaux yeux de sa dame." Louis Hourticq, *La jeunesse de Titien* (Paris: Librairie Hachette, 1919), 139.

[14] Bonafoux, *Portraits*, 27.

[15] Titian used his daughter Lavinia as a model for his works on numerous occasions. There are three works—*Lavinia with a Tray of Fruit* (1555, Berlin-Dahlem, Staatcliche Gemaldegalerie), *Lavinia with a Casket* (Sixteenth century, London, Mrs. Abbott, variant 1), and *Lavinia as Salome* (About 1550-1555,

Madrid, Prado Museum, variant 3)—that are the same in composition. They all represent a young girl with her face turned toward the viewer, apparently dancing and holding the same platter but with different attributes: a platter with fruits, a platter with a jewelry box and a platter with the head of John the Baptist. In each painting the girl is dressed differently and her facial expressions and features vary slightly. Among the three works the most impressive is *Salome*. Salome's face, her gaze and her lips are striking for their sensual flavor. She does not wear a necklace, which makes her shoulders and her neck more open and suggestive. Titian also painted *Lavinia as Bride* (About 1555, Dresden, Staatliche Gemaldegalerie) and *Lavinia as Matron* (About 1560, Dresden, Staatliche Gemaldegalerie).

[16] Given that Titian was a Venetian painter, the figure of Salome holding a platter over her head while dancing may have been inspired by the *Dancing Salome* in Venice's San Marco.

[17] The servant, although present in Titian's *Salome*, was never an attribute of works representing Salome holding the head of John the Baptist on a platter. Usually the servant is present next to Judith in Judith's beheadings of Holofernes. Titian's painting is an exception. We can still recognize the painting as a Salome image because in the case of Judith and Holofernes the head of Holofernes is never represented on a platter. Bernard eliminated the servant, probably to emphasize that his work is a painting of Salome holding the head of John the Baptist and not of Judith and Holofernes.

[18] Bernard's sister, Madeleine, came to visit Emile in Cairo. Before her arrival, she lost her fiancé, Charles Laval, who died of tuberculosis. Soon after her arrival, Madeleine began to feel very weak, and on 20 November of 1895 she also died of tuberculosis. She was only twenty four. The loss of Madeleine was a very painful trauma for Bernard and his wife. In addition, they were concerned with the weak health of their son Pierre-François-Laurent, called Otsy, who probably became contaminated with tuberculosis from his mother, Hanénah. She had cared for Madeleine and unknowingly transmitted the illness to her children, three of whom eventually died. At that time, however, the family hoped that a change in the environment would lead to an improvement in their son's overall condition and would help them to recover from Madeleine's death. The decision to go to Spain in particular was a result of Bernard's interest in Spanish art and a desire to learn more about it. During the summer of 1896, the family traveled in Italy to Naples and then in Spain to Malaga, Barcelona and Valencia.

[19] During the winter the situation became difficult. The weather was very cold and the family had serious financial problems. In addition, Hanénah was pregnant.

[20] Only at the very end of his life did Bernard marry Andrée.

[21] This work is located in the collection of Mme Katia Granoff, in Paris.

[22] Bernard met Armène Ohanian in 1912 at a banquet of people connected to the Orient. Her true name was Astinée Aravian. Of Iranian origin, she had been educated in Iran and Russia. Bernard was fascinated by her. He describes that meeting and Ohanian's personality in his unpublished manuscript, *Aventure de ma vie* (*My Life Adventure*): "I had met her [Armène Ohanian] at the Banquet of the Orientalists. . . . After the Banquet, there was a theater performance that was

followed by Armène Ohanian's dances. Her grace, the originality of her nature, her personality both devilish and affectionate, conquered me. I put myself at her service and was successful in obtaining her agreement to model for me at my studio at the Quai de Bourbon. She was a distinguished, cultured and fragile person. . . . Her complicated nature touched all the cultures; she knew French, English, Iranian, Russian, and she traveled widely. She seemed to be the summary of all the civilizations, a soul of all times. With all that, she was the most stunning artist in her own right and an insightful and talented judge in all other arts. Armène was truly not a woman, but Woman; not a stranger, but the civilization itself with all its aspects and instances. She possessed the most exquisite charms: large deep black eyes, an elegance of conversation and of manners; she was a perfect aristocrat in her feelings and taste. We met . . . in that Paris where we both were reacting against vulgarity and stupidity, often surrounding us." (Emile Bernard, *L'Aventure de ma vie*, 237-238, unpublished manuscript located in the archives of the Musée du Louvre, MS 374.) Soon after their first meeting, they became lovers. Their affair lasted from 1912 until the fall of 1915. Emile Bernard writes that these were very happy moments of his life (*My Life Adventure*, 240), and would have continued to be if "she [Armène] had not been taken by jealousy for Andrée who, as a matter of fact, put up with my infidelity with a true grandeur. She had been writing to me, and I, myself, tried to persuade her by all means open to me, that despite my attachment to Armène, I had preserved for her the purest part of my heart." (*My Life Adventure,* 241). The affair between Bernard and Armène ended when Armène refused to continue to accept his relationship with his life partner, Andrée Fort. In *L'Aventure de ma vie,* Bernard writes that in the fall of 1915, "Armène, outraged by my constant correspondence with Andrée and by my unwillingness to leave her, decided to escape from my house. When I came home, I found on my table a short poem which expressed her 'eternal love' and told me farewell. I was saddened by that departure. I did not sleep for a number of nights, but I took a resolution to be firm and not to give in to Armène even for her new caresses. This way it was easier for me to break off completely, and I managed at least to free my body from her conquest. As far as the charms of her personality are concerned, it was not the same. I missed them for a long time. I described in *La Danseuse Persane* the anguish that the separation cost me. Very quickly Andrée retook her position next to me; it was not that difficult. Finding in her the permanence and the forgiveness of my error, I started over our life together. . . . She bore with angelical patience the worst wounds that her true love had to suffer. She re-conquered me fully." (*My Life Adventure,* 247)

Emile Bernard spent many years of his life in the Orient and may have unknowingly assimilated its mentality and the attitude of Eastern men toward women. The idea of a harem, even on a small scale, was not foreign to him. For instance, after meeting Andrée Fort she followed Bernard from France to Egypt, where she, Bernard and his wife, Hanénah, lived together in the same house. Bernard was a lover of both women, although his wife for a while was not aware of that. When she realized that Fort was Bernard's lover she became very upset; Bernard considered his actions perfectly natural and felt no remorse (for more information, see *My Life Adventure*). Moreover, for a while, before the exposé, Andrée was on very good terms with Bernard's wife and helped her with domestic chores, including caring for Bernard and his wife's children. Bernard left his home only because his wife refused to accept the situation.

After Bernard left Hanénah, he settled in France with Andrée Fort. There was little change in his pattern of behavior. After meeting Armène, he wanted her to befriend Andrée. For a while the three of them lived together, although he was constantly and falsely trying to convince Armène that his relationship with Andrée was over. When Armène became tired of it and left Bernard's house he followed her, and while living with Armène away from Andrée he regularly corresponded with Andrée, trying to persuade her that he was almost fully devoted to her.

[23] Bernard, *My Life Adventure*, 240.

[24] Later in life, Ohanian became a writer and received world recognition. Her letter to her friend, Monsieur Bénédite, the curator of the Luxembourg museum, written in January of 1923, reflects the strengths of her personality but also her bitter attitude towards the way Europe perceived women and especially working women like herself. Her letter shows her to be the strong, independent, beautiful and working woman that Europe was afraid of, the woman whose rise was so threatening to nineteenth-century European men. Ohanian writes about her perception of the European attitude toward working women like herself in relation to her forthcoming marriage: "I am sure that you and all your family . . . will be glad to know me happy. I deserve it for the frequent pain I endured through my 'independent' life in Europe. I do not renounce either dance, or literature, or my travels. But the fact that I can do them for my pleasure and not by necessity, changes everything. Also in the European world, I would like to say 'civilized,' where only women supported by their husbands, are appreciated and paid attention to, and not those who support themselves, I will have an advantage of being easily respected without making efforts of an independent woman. All that is ridiculous, very ridiculous, Monsieur Benedicte: in our society we acclaim 'feminism' and 'equality' of a woman that 'belongs' to a man, and treat like dogs those who work!" (letter written by Ohanian from Mexico, 10a caillé, Medelin 151, Mexique D.F., on 18.I.23, 5).

[25] Heinrich Heine, *Atta Troll*, trans. Herman Scheffauer (New York: B.W. Huebsche, 1914), 114.

[26] Heine lived in France for political reasons.

[27] Heine, *Atta Troll*, 113-115.

[28] *La Décollation de saint Jean-Baptiste (Saint John the Baptist's Beheading)*, painted by Moreau's good friend Pierre Puvis de Chavannes, could have added to his desire to create his own story of Salome.

[29] "Je suis obligée de tout inventer.... Je construit d'abord dans ma tête le caractère que je veux donner à ma figure et je l'habille ensuite en me conformant à cette idée première et dominante.

Ainsi, dans ma Salome, je voulais rendre une figure de sibylle et d'enchanteresse religieuse avec un caractère de mystère. J'ai alors conçu le costume qui est comme une chasse. . . . » *Ecrits sur l'art par Gustave Moreau,*

Sur ses oeurvres et sur lui-même, préfacé de Geneviève Lacambre, textes établis, présentés et annotés par Peter Cooke, vol. I (Fontfroide : Bibliothèque artistique et littéraires, 2002), 99.

[30] Julius Kaplan, *The Art of Gustave Moreau* (Ann Arbor: UMI Research Press, 1982), 34.

[31] Ibid., 34.

[32] See Luisa Capodieci, "Gli ornamenti simbolici: l'uso degli elementi decorativi nella *Salome tatuata* di Gustave Moreau" *Ricerche di Storia dell'Arte* 57 (1995), 5-22, and "Salome" in *Moreau's Watercolors*.

[33] The head of John the Baptist, as a head of Orpheus, and the head of Goliath, were the part of the 19th century fascination with decapitated floating heads. Odilon Redon and Gauguin were very much enticed by the representations of the floating heads, and numerous times Redon painted a floating head of Orpheus as his self-portrait in martyr who, similar to Moreau, is convinced of the survival of his works and of eventually being recognized and appreciated. One of the interesting examples is Redon's 1881 drawing *Fallen Glory* in which he identifies himself with the floating head of John the Baptist and about which he writes that "It returns to life."

[34] "L'art s'appuyant sur la nature ne peut être réduit a en être l'imitation exacte et servile car, a ce compte, il n'est pas l'art, et la nature est préférable." Peter Cooke, ed., *Ecrits sur l'art par Gustave Moreau*, 2 volumes (Paris: Fata Morgana, 2002), 252.

[35] In contrast, the images of men, especially of heroes or prophets, symbolize artists and poets. Usually his ideal men, his poets and artists, are androgynous, because the ideal human being is above any kind of gender. He is both a man and a woman. An example of it is the painting entitled *Dead Poet Borne by a Centaur*.

[36] An interesting article to consult is Pierre-Louis Mathieu, "Femmes damnées: Sphinx, Chimères, Sirènes, Pasiphaé, Dalila, Messaline, Salomé" in *Monographie et Nouveau Catalogue de l'oeuvre achevé* (Paris: ACR Edition Internationale, 1998).

[37] "C'est la chimère terrestre, vile comme la matière, attractive comme elle, représentée par cette tête charmante de la femme, avec ces ailes prometteuses de l'idéal, mais le corps du monstre, du carnassier qui déchire et anéantit," Cooke, *Ecrits*, vol. I, 73.

[38] Ibid., 97-98. Of his image of Salome, he writes that "Cette femme [Salome] qui représente la femme éternelle, oiseau léger, souvent funeste, traversant la vie une fleur à la main, à la recherche de son idéal vague, souvent terrible, et marchant toujours, foulant tous aux pieds, même des génies et des saints. Cette danse s'exécute, cette promenade mystérieuse s'accomplit davant la mort qui la regarde incessamment, béante et attentive, et devant le bourreau à l'épée qui frappe. C'est l'emblème de cet avenir terrible réservé aux chercheurs d'idéal sans nom de sensualité et de curiosité malsaine."

[39] Elisabeth Lièvre-Crosson, *Du Réalisme au symbolisme* (Les Essentiels Milan, 2000), 36.

[40] Cooke, *Ecrits*, vol. II, 224-225.

[41] As for Michelangelo, art for Moreau was both a struggle and a spiritual mission. For Michelangelo, the pain of the artist was similar to the flaying of St. Bartholomew. For Moreau, the pain of the artist was similar to the decapitated head of John the Baptist, the head that, despite its painful separation from the body, remains alive and eventually attains a halo, the symbol of glory and recognition.

[42] Geneviève Lacambre, *Gustave Moreau: Magic and Symbols* (Harry N. Abrams, 1999), 57.

[43] For more on this topic and the interpretations of Moreau's *Salome Dancing Before Herod*, see Peter Cooke, "Gustave Moreau's 'Salome': the poetics and politics of history painting," *The Burlington Magazine* 149 (August 2007), 528-536.

[44] *Salomé au jardin* was presented at the Exposition universelle of 1878. Then it entered the collection of the Countess Greffulhe, and in 1886 was presented at the Goupil Gallery. In 1885, a second version was painted for Charles Hayem, a collector and admirer of Gustave Moreau.

[45] Cooke, *Ecrits*, vol. 1, 101-102.

[46] Joris-Karl Huysmans, *Against Nature (A Rebours)*:

> Besides, the artist seemed to have wanted to assert his intention of remaining outside the passing centuries, of not specifying either race, country, or period, by placing his Salome within this extraordinary palace built in a grandiose mixture of styles, by dressing her in sumptuous, fanciful garments, by crowning her with a kind of diadem shaped like a Phoenician tower, like that worn by Salammbô, and finally by placing in her hand the scepter of Isis, the sacred flower of Egypt and India, the great lotus.
>
> Des Esseintes speculated about the meaning of this emblem. Did it have the phallic significance with which it is endowed by the primeval religions of India; did it promise the ageing Herod an oblation of virginity, an exchange of blood, an impure penetration solicited and tendered under the express condition of a murder; or did it represent the allegory of fertility, the Hindu myth of life, an existence held between a woman's palms whence it is torn and crushed by the quivering grasp of men overpowered by madness, deranged by a frenzy of the flesh?
>
> Perhaps, also, by arming his enigmatic goddess with the venerated lotus, the artist had thought of the dancer, the mortal woman, the sullied Vessel, the source of every sin and every crime; perhaps he had called to mind the rites of ancient Egypt, the funereal ceremonies of embalmment, when the chemists and the priests lay out the corpse of the deceased on a bench of jasper, use curved needles to extract her brains through her nasal fossae, her entrails through an incision made in her left side, then before gilding her nails and her teeth, before anointing her with tars and essences, insert into her genitals, to purify them, the chaste petals of the divine flower." (46-47)

[47] Ibid., 47-48.

CHAPTER SIX

POETRY: STÉPHANE MALLARMÉ

Mallarmé's poem *Hérodiade* was the poet's life work. He started it at the age of twenty two, in 1864, and died while working on it, in 1898, at the age of fifty six. Jean-Luc Steinmetz, in *Stéphane Mallarmé: L'absolu au jour le jour* (*Stéphane Mallarmé: The Absolute from Day to Day*), writes:

> Even if there is a question in appearance of a woman, would Mallarmé similar to Flaubert state: 'Hérodiade is me,' or should we understand that in the risky place of Saint John the Baptist, it is appropriate to see him, Mallarmé, as a herald in a desert of the new poetry?[1]

Bertrand Marchal asserts that "*Hérodiade* is first of all a drama of spiritual mutation, a drama in which those who wish will recognize Mallarmé."[2] Helen Zagona believes that "*Hérodiade* is the first major effort in which Mallarmé attempted to project himself into a work in terms of an extraordinary symbol."[3] Is this fatal poem Mallarmé's self-portrait and, if so, in what way?

The finished version of the poem *Hérodiade* consists of three parts: "Overture" ("Ouverture ancienne"), the Nurse's monologue at dawn; "Scene" ("Scène"), a dialogue between Hérodiade and her Nurse, which is the main part of the poem; and a short poem, "The Song of Saint John" ("Le Cantique de saint Jean"), spoken by the decapitated head of John the Baptist. During Mallarmé's lifetime, only "Scène" was published, first in the 1871 collection of poetry *Le Parnasse contemporain* (*The Contemporary Parnassus*) and then in 1887 in the collection *Poetry (Poésie)*. "Ouverture ancienne" and the third part, "Le Cantique de saint Jean," were published in 1913 and 1926, respectively, long after Mallarmé's death. However, these parts are inseparably connected and they represent one story painted in three panels—a triptych. They are also part of the unfinished larger poem, *Hérodiade's Wedding (Les Noces d'Hérodiade)*, that was intended to encompass them. In 1898, when Mallarmé was reworking *Hérodiade* into *Les Noces d'Hérodiade*, he changed the structure of his poem and clarified his message.[4] In the final, unfinished version of the poem, Mallarmé introduced the notion of *viol occulaire* (visual rape), which corresponded to the metaphorical "love affair" between Hérodiade and John the Baptist. The clearer structure of this version conveyed best Mallarmé's message and the abstract nature of his philosophy of creativity. *Les Noces d'Hérodiade* was also designed to be the first part, or "Overture," to Mallarmé's *Livre, Grande Oeuvre*, the book that he dreamt of but did not have a chance to bring to life.

* * *

In one of the letters to his friend Henri Cazalis, in 1864, before he began to write *Hérodiade*, Mallarmé explained that he had encountered the Void (*Néant*). For him the Void meant the loss of faith in God and the loss of faith in the typical romantic role of the poet, in which the poet was perceived as a herald of divine reality on earth. But the Void, for him, also meant the encounter with the Absolute, the perfect but not divine world whose mystical experience and earthly loss led toward the feeling of Nothingness (*Néant*).

In his book *Mallarmé and the Language of Mysticism*, Thomas Williams depicts a mystical experience, explaining that the mystic and mystical experience can be determined by a sense of the loss of a primeval wholeness.[5] This seems to be the experience that Mallarmé went through when he began to write his *Hérodiade*.

While writing, Mallarmé decided that although God did not exist and the poet did not represent God on earth, the poet was still a herald. The question for him was, then, the herald of what? Through his mystical experience, Mallarmé came to the conclusion that the poet was a herald of the Absolute. The Absolute then became for him an embodiment of ideal Beauty, the incarnation of the sublime through poetry. Mallarmé wrote in July of 1866 that after he found Nothingness, he found Beauty.[6] On 14 May 1867, he reaffirmed his ideas:

> I made a quite long descent to Nothingness to be able to talk with certainty. There is only Beauty and only It has a perfect expression, Poetry. Everything else is a lie.[7]

Thus for Mallarmé the work of art, the poem, must be beautiful in order to represent the Absolute, or at least to aspire to doing so. The poem then becomes a symbol of Beauty, which—when it is in its ideal state—in turn becomes the symbol of the Absolute.

Mallarmé believed that poetry's role is "To paint not the object, but the effect it produces,"[8] and that "The verse should not be composed of words, but of intentions, and all the words are wiped out by the sensation."[9] From 1864 on, Mallarmé searched for artistic ways to express these ideas. *Hérodiade* is the work that is destined to bring to life his philosophy. At the same time, through that poem Mallarmé aspires to create a metaphorical self-portrait of his poetic soul, an image of his inner world that is involved in the process of creating, separating from, and then reuniting with his work of poetic art.[10] As Wallace Fowlie points out:

> *Hérodiade* is not only an early poem which Mallarmé recast at the end of his life. It is a poem he lived with or rather struggled with all his life, and it illustrates perhaps better than any other piece Mallarmé's intense love for a poem and the desperate difficulty he underwent in achieving it, in finding for it a form or expression suitable to translate the idea. On one level of interpretation, Hérodiade is a cold virginal princess who stands aloof from the world of men, but she may also represent the poem itself, so difficult to seize and possess that the poet ultimately despairs of knowing it. Hérodiade is therefore both a character whom Mallarmé tried to subdue, and a mythical character whose meaning goes far beyond the comprehension of the poet. She presides over Mallarmé's life as poet in a dual role of princess and myth, of character and symbol.[11]

The main character in "Scène," the central part of the poem, is a beautiful young blond princess, Hérodiade. Mallarmé explains in his preface that by renaming Salomé he hoped to set his character apart from the biblical story and the legends built around the biblical Salomé.

> I left the name of Hérodiade to be able to make her clearly different from Salomé whom I would call modern or exhumed with her archaic crime—the dance etc., to isolate her from the solitary paintings, expressing the event, horrible and mysterious, and to help reflect what probably followed—appearing with its attribute—the head of the Saint—the demoiselle represents the monster of vulgar lovers of life—that adornment was disturbing.[12]

Robert Cohn believes, though, that the pronunciation of *Hérodiade* sounds like the French words *rose*, *Eros*, and *héros*,[13] which could be one of the reasons why Mallarmé preferred that name to Salomé.

The images and stories of Hérodiade/Salomé that Mallarmé describes became widespread only in nineteenth-century art. As mentioned earlier, in the Middle Ages there was confusion about the roles of the mother and the daughter in the Baptist's execution story. The daughter would often be identified by the mother's name and vice versa.[14] The painter Henry

Regnault, a friend of Mallarmé who was killed during the Prussian war in 1870, was the first in the nineteenth century to paint his Salomé, whom he called Hérodiade, as a young gypsy girl (Fig. I-4-7), the central and the only figure in his painting. As we have seen in the previous chapter, although she holds the plate with the sword her plate does not contain the head. It makes the girl, Hérodiade/Salomé, rather than the head of the Baptist, the center of attention in Regnault's painting. This painting, in which Hérodiade/Salomé is represented for her own sake and not simply as a supporting character in John the Baptist's story, starts a new tradition in the history of the *femme fatale* in art.

Mallarmé, however, follows that tradition only in appearance, since in reality his purpose is to bring another, more important and more personal meaning to the image of his Hérodiade. His intention is to stress not her fatal dance and the role she played in John the Baptist's beheading, but rather her character as he paints her in his poem. It is her character as a metaphor that becomes essential in Mallarmé's poem. Under the guise of a *femme fatale*, Mallarmé creates a vivid picture of Hérodiade's unusual beauty and of her inner being in order to make her the metaphor for his philosophy of creation, the double symbol of the work of art, embracing both the poem and the poet.

At the same time, the purpose of the unfinished *Les Noces d'Hérodiade* was to metaphorically reflect the artist's inner search for the poetic image of the creation of the perfect work of art. That perfect work of art, the perfect poem, the symbol of perfect Beauty, would be the embodiment of the Absolute.[15] *Les Noces* was aimed at symbolically expressing the moment when the artist merges with the Absolute and becomes inseparable from it.[16] How can the character of Hérodiade be a reflection of both the poet and the poem, and in what way is *Les Noces*, metaphorically speaking, a spiritual path of the poet toward the achievement of the Absolute?

In "Ouverture ancienne" and "Scène," Mallarmé creates the metaphor of a poet through an image of Hérodiade as a young, beautiful and unusual princess who rejects the outside world and feels at home only in her own world. That image is painted through Hérodiade's monologues and her dialogues with the Nurse and through the contrast in the personalities of both women.

The Nurse symbolizes the ideas of the past. Her age is an implication of her inability to belong to the new era and the new perception of the world. She represents the older generation, the generation of "fathers" who are often unable to understand their "sons." But she is also a metaphor for both the traditional religion and the traditional art that Mallarmé rejected when "he discovered the Void while 'digging' the verse" (*il a trouvé le Néant en creusant le ver*).[17] For the Nurse, Hérodiade has been a mystery from a very young age, and the Nurse does not understand her and her world.[18] Hérodiade, in contrast to the Nurse, becomes a symbol of the new religion that Mallarmé discovered, the religion of Beauty aspiring toward the Absolute, incarnated in mystery and created through the special sounds of poetic music. Like Mallarmé, Hérodiade belongs to the new generation, to new ideas and new art. She is an embodiment of a new era and of times to come.

Hérodiade, as a metaphor for a poet, fits within Mallarmé's philosophy, which he states in his article "Hérésies artistiques: L'Art pour tous" ("Artistic Heresies: Art for Everybody"). In that article, Mallarmé expands on his concept of art. He writes, "Everything sacred and that would like to remain sacred wraps itself in mystery."[19] Mallarmé despised crowds and popularity, because for him true art could not be exposed to "profane minds incapable of disinterested contemplation of its deepest significance." His princess, already inaccessible to the mind of a common person, personified in her Nurse, is Mallarmé himself, a poet and "the admirer of beauty inaccessible to vulgarity."[20]

If in "Ouverture" Mallarmé depicts Hérodiade as a person predisposed toward the unusual—a metaphor for the poet who is in the process of growing and becoming aware of who he is—in the second part, "Scène," through the character of Hérodiade, Mallarmé creates the next stage of the creative process. He creates the image of the poet in the process of creating his work of art, the poem, before he gives birth to it and releases it to the world of readers.

Hérodiade's withdrawal into herself, her aspiration to live in solitude, her contempt for the outside world and for everything banal in that world, are metaphors for the poet, Mallarmé. He believes that in order to be creative and independent of the influences of the world, in order to be the herald and creator of supreme and pure Beauty, he has to endure a solitary path of withdrawal within himself. In a way, his path should be the path of Narcissism, because only then, when he looks into himself, can he find the right words to create the images of the Beautiful.

Like the poet whose work of art is constantly in the process of becoming, Hérodiade's aspiration is toward the horizons that vanish upon approach, because for the poet complete and total fulfillment is not possible on earth. In earthly existence the Absolute is inaccessible.[21] That is why in the poem Beauty is identified with Death: "One kiss would kill / if beauty were not death."[22]

Death in this case represents the Ideal, the world beyond, inaccessible to the earthly world; it is the only world where perfect and ideal Beauty can exist or be achieved. It is toward that world that Hérodiade, the symbol of the poet, aspires, and it is that world that constantly escapes her.[23] Thomas Williams points out:

> When Hérodiade said that beauty was death, she recognized that to maintain a perfect vision of beauty involved dying to oneself as an artist, that the role of mystic and maker are irreconcilable in any absolute sense. Even in the purest work there must always remain the barest tincture of failure.[24]

Hérodiade belongs to some "unknown era." That is why the Nurse, at the beginning of "Scène," tells her:

> You are alive! Or do I see the ghost of a princess?
> Cease walking in some unknown era; let me press
> your fingers and their rings to my lips . . . .[25]

This "unknown era" is the symbol of a world open to only a few selected and initiated, the so-called spiritual aristocrats. It is unremembered by the common and the uninitiated, like the Nurse, herself a symbol of the banality of life with its everyday preoccupations and commonplace aspirations.

Like the poet who constantly struggles with the constraints of worldly existence and easily accepted traditional art forms, Hérodiade constantly struggles with her Nurse and constantly strives to escape from the world that the Nurse wants to impose on her. The Nurse tempts the princess with the banal existence of a commonplace life, much as the world tempts the poet. That existence is embodied in a union with a common man, an existence unacceptable to the princess.[26] The princess, like the poet, rejects those impositions and remains faithful to herself, her nature and her aspirations.

In "Ouverture" and in "Scène," Hérodiade is also a metaphor for a poem. While constructing the image of his princess as a poem, Mallarmé loosely follows the Hegelian dialectic of thesis, antithesis, and synthesis, with which he was clearly familiar through the literature that popularized Hegelian ideas. For example, Scherer, in his article "Hegel and Hegelianism," explains that the Hegelian dialectic of thesis, antithesis, and synthesis is based on the dialectical movement of three stages.[27]

Austin quotes a letter in which Mallarmé describes the thesis, antithesis, and synthesis of the transformation of Beauty throughout the centuries. It metaphorically depicts the three stages undergone by Beauty (and then the poem) in order to achieve synthesis.[28]

At first, in "Ouverture," when Hérodiade as a poem is still part of the "unknown era," she is "The Serene Beauty" (*la Beauté sereine*), a poem that has not yet been born but that already lives in the soul of the poet as an idea. This is the thesis. Then, in "Scène," when metaphorically the poem is in the process of being created but has not yet been born and separated from its creator, it loses its stage of serenity. It becomes "troubled" Beauty. This is the antithesis. Finally in the third part, "Cantique de Saint Jean," Beauty goes through synthesis and becomes the perfect Beauty.

* * *

In "Scène," Hérodiade has a virginal and pure nature. Her invisibility to the outside world, her stunning beauty, and her constant expectation of something that would lead her to another state of existence, which would liberate her from her self-imposed isolation, make her a symbol of a poem. She is awaiting and at the same time apprehensive of being released into the world. When the Nurse asks her:

> For whom would you, consumed by pangs, keep the unknown
> splendour and the vain mystery of your being?

Hérodiade answers:

> For myself alone.
> . . .
> Besides, I long for nothing human; if you see
> me like a statue with eyes lost in paradise,
> that is when I recall the milk you gave me formerly.
> . . .
> Yes, for myself alone I bloom, in isolation!
> . . .
> I love the horror of being virgin.
> . . .
> I wait an unknown thing.[29]

Hérodiade's subconscious expectation of "an unknown thing" (*une chose inconnue*), of the possible passage from one state of existence to another, is a symbol of the maturation of the work of art. The next stage, after the work's creation, is separation from its creator, the poet, in order to be exposed to the world of readers.

On a literal level, Hérodiade is troubled by her Nurse, who is both a symbol of a common life and the one who nurses the princess, the poem, and helps her reach maturity. Metaphorically, Hérodiade is troubled because, as a poem, she is in the process of being born and maturing, and she is waiting to be released to the world and separated from her creator. It is a frightening and painful process.

In a later unfinished version of *Les Noces d'Hérodiade,* Mallarmé explored the encounter of Hérodiade with John the Baptist, which is depicted as a *viol occulaire*, as well as her reaction to this encounter and then her passage from one state of being to another. As with everything in Mallarmé's work, this encounter bears a double meaning. On the one hand, it is an intrusion into Hérodiade's mystery, and even a rape, figuratively speaking, at least from her perspective. This is why the character of Hérodiade wishes John's execution. On the other hand, it is an initiation of Hérodiade into the world of John the Baptist's mystery, which would eventually initiate her into the world of the Absolute. This can occur only when John the Baptist reaches the appropriate state, the state beyond physical existence.

For Hérodiade, a symbol of a poem, John's execution is necessary. It is only in the ideal transcendental world, the symbol of the Absolute, that the free and total initiation into each other's supreme mystery—the *Noces*, the synthesis, the perfect work of art—is possible. That encounter, that *viol occulaire*, transforms Hérodiade, as a character and as a poem undergoing constant change, into "The Troubled Beauty" (*la Beauté troublée*). That Beauty embodies the poem, a work of art, which has not yet achieved its supreme state of purity, since it is still in a state of constant change and evolution as it undergoes the creative process. Nonetheless, that encounter is Hérodiade's first stage of being initiated as a character and as a poem into the world of John the Baptist, the mystery that belongs to the Absolute.

* * *

In the finished version of "Scène," Mallarmé suggests that although the ideal work of art does not exist on earth and is only in the process of being created, it still could become visible as a reflection through the perfect mirror. The imagery used to convey this message is hair, specifically Hérodiade's hair.

The symbolism of hair was widely used in the nineteenth century by both poets and painters. Baudelaire, for example, who was the idol of Mallarmé when Mallarmé wrote his "Scène," wrote the poem "Head of Hair" (La Chevelure). In that poem, Baudelaire glorifies hair as an embodiment of beauty that takes the lyrical hero to the exotic world of unreal beauty, sensuality and passion.[30] The English Pre-Raphaelite painters, especially Dante Gabrielle Rossetti, painted most of their *femmes fatales* with long seductive hair, often red in color. The English poet Robert Browning used the image of hair in his poem "Porphyria's Lover," in which he describes a lover who strangles his beloved with her own long hair, the symbol of his torturous lust for her. Hair is a symbol of the destructive beauty of woman, of earthly lust that is often mistakenly taken by the seduced to be a symbol of perfect beauty.

But in Mallarmé's case, hair has a different meaning. He attributes the qualities of a perfect mirror to Hérodiade's beautiful hair and uses extensively the symbolism of hair, metals and precious stones to convey this idea. In "Scène," there is constant reference to Hérodiade's hair, which is described like the metals and gems that create reflections. It makes her a beautiful reflection of the ideal Beauty, the beauty that on earth can be only reflected, just as the earthly work of art is only a reflection of the poet's search for the Absolute.

Hérodiade's hair is long, immaculate and immortal. It reflects the beauty of the infinite and is the symbol of the immortal, because hair "does not partake of the transient, mortal character of the rest of the body."[31] The immaculate aspect of Hérodiade's hair is a symbol of the purity of art. These are the reasons for which Hérodiade is ready to endure being wrapped in her blond hair. She wishes it to remain immaculate and immortal, although there is a sensation of horror when her body is wrapped in that "blond torrent" ("white stream").

> Stand back there!
> Even the strong blond stream of my unspotted hair
> bathing my solitary body freezes it
> with terror, woman, and my hair entwined and knit
> with bright light are immortal.[32]

For Mallarmé, the ideal woman's hair is almost always blond, like Hérodiade's. When Mallarmé commented on the poetry of his friend Emmanuel des Essartes, he explained the importance of blond hair for him: "the ideal of a woman—I mean that facet of the beauty, that diamond—is not the brunette. . . . The blondness, which means gold, light, richness, dream, shining."[33] Thus, for Mallarmé, blond is associated with light and the color of precious metals, such as gold, and with precious stones, such as diamonds. These images and associations are used extensively in his poem in order to create the magic of the work of art and the beauty that he knits through the words of his poem. The imagery of precious stones in the poem is a reminder that the work of art is itself a precious stone, and the poem is a "divine gem capable of seizing and reflecting the elusive light of eternal truth."[34] The ideal work of art has the pure beauty of a diamond, to which one might compare the image of Hérodiade and her hair. As a symbol of a poem, however, Hérodiade endures the torturous process of finding a way of reaching the reflection of the ideal work of art, and her hair is a symbol and a tool that helps her in the endeavor of reflecting that ideal.

* * *

"The Song of Saint John" (Le Cantique de Saint Jean), the third part of the finished version of the poem, although very different from "Scène" in terms of style, structure and color, is the panel of the triptych most closely corresponding and linked to "Scène." "Le Cantique" is a final, short, finished poem, and it is a path toward the third stage of the Hegelian dialectic of thesis, antithesis, and synthesis, a metaphorical path taken toward the achievement of the "perfect" Beauty.[35]

"Le Cantique de Saint Jean," like *Hérodiade*, is a metaphor. At the most obvious level, the John the Baptist figure mirrors Mallarmé's perception of who the poet is. Through the image of John the Baptist, Mallarmé describes his own mission as a poet.

Historically, John the Baptist was a prophet and an embodiment of the martyr. He was the precursor of a new religion and of Christ himself. Like John, Mallarmé, in his turn, was a founder of a new style of poetry, of a new poetic language and a new poetic philosophy; like John, his ideas at that time could be adapted and understood by only a few. Nonetheless, Mallarmé knew that his time would come and his ideas would find followers and would bring him the halo of recognition, as they did to John.

Like the character of Hérodiade in "Scène," in "Cantique" John is also a double metaphor for the poet and the poem during the creative process, but at a stage different from the one of "Scène." In "Cantique," Mallarmé metaphorically portrays his relationship to the poem when the poem is already completed and is ready to start its independent existence in the world of readers. Once it is released and its earthly mission of being read and recognized is fulfilled, the poem is ready to merge with the poet again to become a perfect harmonious unity, this time in the world of the Absolute. In "Cantique," Mallarmé's poem becomes the voice of a poet, singing his prophetic truth about the Absolute.

Mallarmé conveys this through the striking and skillfully painted imagery of the beheading of John the Baptist, which is a metaphor for the separation of the poem from the poet. The first stanza of "Cantique" sets up the time of decapitation and the connection between "Scène" and "Cantique," which in appearance seem to be disconnected. In "Cantique,"

The sun that was exalted
when it miraculously halted
is once more sinking low
brightly aglow[36]

In this stanza we see the sun interrupted in its course and the head of John the Baptist at the moment of decollation. The beheading takes place at the solstice, when the sun reaches its peak, seems to stop for a moment, and then descends in an incandescent light. The feast of John the Baptist takes place on June 24, which is very close in date to the solstice. That feast is directly associated with the "love affair" legend,[37] which presumes Salomé was in love with John and requested his beheading for his failure to respond to her advances. It places the reader within that context and implies that John in the poem is beheaded because of the encounter he had with Hérodiade and the feelings that he inspired in her.[38] Thus, by giving the time of John's execution, Mallarmé establishes the connection between the "love story" of Salomé and John's beheading, or between Hérodiade and John.

The second and third stanzas of "Cantique" paint, in a metaphorical way, the relationship between the poet and the poem. They state the following:

I seem to feel shadowy
wings unfurl in my vertebrae
which are shuddering one
and all in unison

and my head now full-blown
a watchman on its own
in the victory flights made
by the scythe's blade[39]

The imagery in these stanzas is a metaphor for the creative process at the point when the poet and the poem are "severed" from each other. The head is a poem, severed from the whole body, which formerly united the poet and the poem. That process of separation is very painful, although necessary. Once severed from the body, the head—the poem—will have to exist on its own and be exposed to the world of readers until it meets the poet again and becomes one with him in the ideal realm of the Absolute.

In the poem, the hymn is spoken by the head of John the Baptist while it is severed from the body. It is this act that ends "the primordial clash with the flesh." When the body and the head were connected, the harmony between these two did not exist, just as there is no harmony between the poet and his poem while the poet gives birth to his work of art. The separation of the head—the bearer of the mind and creativity—and the body brings some peace, but at the same time it is painful. It is, after all, a beheading.[40]

* * *

In "Cantique," Mallarmé depicts not only the separation of John's severed head, the poem, from his body, but he also metaphorically paints the process of recognition and initiation of John's severed head, of a metaphorical poem, into the world of the Absolute. As we saw in the earlier stanza, when the head is severed it is thrown upward. Once that occurs, the saint expresses a wish:

rather than drunk with fasting
commit itself to lasting
pursuit of its pure sight
in some wild flight

on high where the perpetual
coldness cannot endure that all
of you O frozen glaciers
are its superiors[41]

He wishes to continue to look up toward eternity and the coldness of the sky and to search for the perfect, the Absolute. At the end of the poem, John the Baptist's head sings:

but as an act of baptism my
head was illuminated by
the principle of my salvation
and bows in salutation.[42]

It is through beheading, through metaphorical separation of the poem from the poet and the poem's subsequent exposure to the world, the second baptism, that salvation comes. Right at the moment when the saint's head expresses his wish, the head acquires a halo, the sign of holiness and recognition. That head then has a double meaning: It is a poem and the poet at the same time.

For John the Baptist the body had been always an obstacle. St. Paul says:

but I see in my members another law at war with the law of my mind and making me captive to the law of sin which dwells in my members. Wretched man that I am! Who will deliver me from this body of death?[43]

Hence, the liberation from the body is the Baptist's and the poem's freedom.

In the unfinished *Noces d'Hérodiade*, the connection between "Scène" and "Cantique" is much clearer than in the finished version of the triptych, which is difficult to understand without knowing Mallarmé's intentions. Sylviane Huot, Lloyd James Austin and other scholars demonstrate that "Scène" and "Le Cantique" in *Les Noces d'Hérodiade* are linked through the glance of John the Baptist, *le viol occulaire*. The following quote from Robert de Montesquiou seems to be central in understanding the idea of the Mallarméen synthesis.

> The secret . . . that was shared with me by the poet himself, is of the future violation of the mystery of her being through the glance of John who would notice her, and would pay by his death that only sacrilege, since that savage virgin would feel herself intact again and fully reconstructed to her integrity only at the moment when she would hold between her hands the decapitated head in which dared to be perpetuated the memory of the momentarily seen virgin.[44]

The importance of the glance becomes apparent in the final unfinished versions of *Les Noces*. By his glance, John the Baptist in a way "fertilizes" Hérodiade. That glance troubles Hérodiade because she perceives his glance as an attack on her virginity and purity—as a rape.[45] Austin calls it the violation of Hérodiade's Mystery, but it can also be perceived as an encounter of Hérodiade with Mystery, embodied in the glance of John the Baptist. That glance—and Hérodiade's reaction to it—is the "love affair" between her and John the Baptist. It eventually leads to John's execution and later to the purification of Hérodiade through the glance of the beheaded John, who, liberated from the chains of physical existence, becomes the symbol of the Ideal.

Hérodiade's perception of being violated through a glance can also be seen as the first encounter of the poem and the poet—both embodied in her—with a reader. It is that encounter that transforms Hérodiade into the troubled Beauty. Eventually, the encounter leads toward the union, toward *Les Noces*, of the "unpolished" Beauty, Hérodiade, with the Mystery of John the Baptist's head. The final result of this union is a Perfect Beauty, the embodiment of the Absolute. *Les Noces* take place in the world to which both aspire. John aspires toward

> The sparkling cold of your pale clarity
> You who die, you who burn of chastity,
> White night of ice and of cruel snow![46]

which is also the image of Hérodiade. Hérodiade aspires to something similar, to something that is also elsewhere but at the same time represents the image of John the Baptist, the Mystery:

> Mild seas
> are swaying and, beyond, you may know some terrain
> where the sinister sky's glances are hated by
> Venus who burns among the leaves at evening:
> there I would go.[47]

That perfect Beauty, the result of the union of Beauty and Mystery, was supposed to be achieved in Mallarmé's *Grand Oeuvre*. For him "the entire universe exists to achieve a Book,"[48] and his Final Book (*Livre definitif*) that he dreamt of was meant to be "the hymn . . . harmony and joy . . . of the relationships between everything."[49]

In his poem, through a very complex metaphor, Mallarmé attempts to convey the idea that he expressed earlier in life:

> Since the spirit is absolute and since nothing can exist outside of the Absolute, the object thought will make one with the being who thinks; that object is the shape of the thought itself, the action through which the thought is produced. That idea . . . is above all. . . . In its essence it is what thinking is.[50]

That idea was Mallarmé's spiritual path throughout his entire life, and he chose to fulfill it using the characters from the story of the dance of Salomé and the beheading of John the Baptist. The story, in which the characters have been endowed with personal meaning, mirrors Mallarmé's soul, his creative search, and his philosophy of creativity. He was at the point to fulfill his path as a poet when he died.

Gustave Moreau and Stéphane Mallarmé

There are striking similarities between Mallarme's poem "Le Cantique de Saint Jean" (The Song of John the Baptist) and Moreau's watercolor *The Apparition* (Fig. II-5-8). Both artists use the beheading of John the Baptist to portray themselves—or more precisely their souls—and thus depict the deepest aspects of their worldviews and their artistic philosophies. The French poet Paul Valéry described "Le Cantique" in his correspondence as the chant of the disembodied head that flies toward the divine light.[51] Similarly, Geneviève Lacambre, the curator of the exhibit "Gustave Moreau," which took place in 1998 at the Grand Palais, states that *The Apparition* greatly surprised the audience "primarily because of the iconographic novelty of its depiction of the head of Saint John the Baptist levitating in the palace of Herod."[52] Both the painting and the poem place the head of John the Baptist in a very unusual position—in the air, levitating, surrounded by a halo—and both the painter and the poet use the head as their respective self-portraits. In both cases, the levitating head and its halo are inseparable from the idea and presence of Salome/Hérodiade and are therefore linked to the philosophical idea of the relationship between the artist and his art.

Mallarmé had a keen interest in art. He visited all the yearly art exhibits at the Salon, was friends with many painters—including Claude Monet, Edouard Manet, Berthe Morisot, James McNeill Whistler and Odilon Redon—and even wrote a number of articles on the art of Manet. Gustave Moreau, although a few years older, was a contemporary of these painters, and his works were an inspiration for the painter Odilon Redon. Huysmans' novel *Against Nature* made them both known to a larger public and linked them together as representatives of the same type of art, and of the same artistic movement, the movement of Symbolism. In addition, Moreau and Mallarmé both lived in the same neighborhood in Paris, the area of *gare Saint Lazare* (the Saint Lazare Train Station), and at the same time. Nonetheless, Mallarmé only mentions Moreau once in his published correspondence and diaries, and then it is only to state that Moreau's art is part of the past. Moreau never mentions Mallarmé in any of his published documents.

Both men were obsessed with the theme of Salome/Hérodiade and John the Baptist, to a degree that is surprising even for the nineteenth century. Moreau created around one hundred paintings on the theme, and Mallarmé spent all his life writing his *Noces d'Hérodiade*, never finishing it and eventually dying at his table while working on it. Most interestingly, Mallarmé used the same image of the floating head in his "Le Cantique de Saint Jean" as was used by Moreau in his watercolor, *The Apparition*, twenty years earlier. Even more interesting: Moreau reworked *The Apparition* in 1896, the year Mallarmé was writing "Le Cantique de Saint Jean."

Despite Mallarmé's disparaging comment on Moreau, he was familiar with the latter's works and seemed to have liked them. Indeed, one of Moreau's lithographs—which had been a gift—was located in Mallarmé's summer home, where it still hangs on the wall in his study.

Mallarme undoubtedly saw Moreau's *The Apparition* at the Salon of 1876 and at the Exposition Universelle in Paris, in 1878. The image probably had at least a subconscious effect on the poet, such that twenty years later it came out in his own poetry as a means of expressing his own philosophy. Similarly, Moreau read Mallarmé's *Hérodiade* when it was published in *Parnasse contemporaire* and, although he did not own any of his books, Mallarmé was on his list of authors to read. Nonetheless, for all of the amazing similarities in thought and education, in artistic philosophies and in the themes they worked on and even in physical closeness, their paths never crossed. They belonged to different circles. Yet it is clear that their works affected each other. Thus, Moreau painted his most famous *Salome*s after he read Mallarmé's poem *Hérodiade*, whereas Mallarmé created his image of John's rising head surrounded by a halo after seeing Moreau's *The Apparition*.

Notes

[1] "Même S'il est question, en apparence, d'une femme, Mallarmé serait-il fondé à dire, à l'instar de Flaubert: 'Hérodiade c'est moi', ou bien devons-nous pressentir qu'à la place risquée de saint Jean-Baptiste, il convient de le voir, annonciateur dans le désert de la poèsie nouvelle?" Jean-Luc Steinmetz, *Stéphane Mallarmé: L'absolu au jour le jour* (Paris: Librairie Arthème Fayard, 1998), 108-109. All translations from French are mine unless otherwise noted.

[2] "*Hérodiade*, c'est d'abord le drame d'une mutation spirituelle, drame où reconnaitra qui veut celui de Mallarmé." Bertrand Marchal, *Lecture de Mallarmé* (Paris: José Corti, 1985), 56.

[3] Helen G. Zagona, *The Legend of Salome and the Principle of Art for Art's Sake* (Genève: Droz, 1960), 49.

[4] The final structure of the work was intended to be the following: "Prélude" (instead of *Ouverture*), "Cantique de saint Jean," "Scène," "Scène intermédiaire," "Finale" (I: *Finale/monologue*; II: *Finale/nourrice*). Of these pieces only *Cantique de saint Jean* was finished. It was probably written in 1896. At the final version of *Les Noces*, Mallarmé planned to place *Cantique* in the beginning of the poem, before the *Finale*, as if *Cantique* were a vision that Hérodiade had, before John's decapitation occurred. The new location of *Cantique* within the poem and its premonitory meaning might make us think of Gustave Moreau's watercolor and then oil painting, *The Apparition*, in which the head of John the Baptist appears to Salomé, possibly as a premonition.

[5] Thomas A. Williams, *Mallarmé and the Language of Mysticism* (Athens: University of Georgia Press), 1970. Brent Judd, in his thesis writing about Mallarmé, cites Williams to note that:

The mystic is one who has had an intense personal experience of the actual Oneness of all things, leading to an acute awareness of the fractured nature of reality in its present state. As Adam and Eve were driven out of the garden of Eden and lost their ideal (whole) relationship with God, the mystic, through an extraordinary personal encounter, experiences the wholeness of this Ideal state of life before losing it again and returning to the everyday world with an awareness of what has been lost. . . .

The mystic returning from his mystical experience, experiences a tremendous sense of loss. What he or she is left with is reduced to nothing in comparison to the infinite. So the mystic comes to encounter the Nothing, and by living in this Nothing, however excruciating such an encounter may be, the mystic emerges with a new identity. The spiritual masters of the past spoke of such an encounter with the Nothing as being in a state of desolation. It is the feeling that one has been completely abandoned by God. One feels as if everything that used to give life meaning has been suddenly and violently ripped away.

Brent Ronald Judd, *William Faulkner and the Symbolist Movement: Absalom, Abasalom! as a reflection of Stéphane Mallarmé's L'Après-midi d'un faune* (Springfield: University of Illinois at Springfield, 2007), 20-21.

One can imagine that this may have been the experience that Mallarmé went through when he began his *Hérodiade*.

[6] "Après avoir trouvé le Néant," il avait "trouvé le Beau." Lloyd James Austin, "Mallarmé et le rêve du livre," in *Essais sur Mallarmé* (Manchester and New York: Manchester University Press, 1995), 77.

[7] "J'ai fait une assez longue descente au Néant pour pouvoir parler avec certitude. *Il n'y a que la Beauté*—et elle n'a qu'une expression parfaite: la Poésie. Tout le reste est mensonge." Ibid.

[8] "Peindre, non la chose, mais l'effet qu'elle produit." Paul Bénichou, *Selon Mallarmé* (Paris: Gallimard, 1995), 38.

[9] "Le vers ne doit ... pas ... se composer de mots, mais d'intentions, et toutes les paroles s'effacent devant la sensation." Ibid.

[10] As Charles Mauron wrote, "*Herodiade*, despite its verbal wealth, seems to be the most strange, the most clumsy poem, and if I can use that term, the most 'submarine' of the French language. It can be understood fully only when we understand that the poet is in communication with the depths of his subconscious." Henry Nicolas, *Mallarmé et le symbolism* (Paris: Librairie Larousse, 1986), 35.

[11] Wallace Fowlie, *Mallarmé* (Chicago: The University of Chicago Press, 1953), 125-126.

[12] "J'ai lassé le nom d'Hérodiade pour bien la différencier de la Salomé je dirai moderne ou exhumée avec son fait divers archaïque—la danse etc., l'isoler comme l'ont fait des tableaux solitaires dans le fait même terrible, mystérieux—et faire miroiter ce qui probablement hanta—en apparue avec son attribut—le chef du saint —dût la demoiselle constituer un monstre aux amants vulgaires de la vie—parure gênait." Mallarmé, *Poesies* (Paris: GF Flammarion, 1989), 151.

[13] Judd, *William Faulkner*, 24.
[14] See Part II, Chapter 5.
[15] Lloyd James Austin writes: "Mais quel est cet Absolu que Mallarmé croyait incarner? Scherer, dans sa critique de la philosophie de Hegel, affirme que l'Absolu de Hegel équivaut au Néant. Vraie ou fausse, cette interprétation semble bien avoir été celle de Mallarmé. Scherer écrit en effet:

> "L'absolu est donc une *notion purement négative*; seulement, cette notion négative est conçue comme une affirmation, présentée comme une réalité et une substance. *L'absolu*, pour qui le regard regarde derrière les mots, *c'est le néant personnifié*, c'est-à-dire la contradiction même. Or l'hégélianisme n'est pas autre chose que la philosophie de ce néant." Austin, *Essais sur Mallarmé*, 77.

[16] For Mallarmé, he and his poem are one in the ideal world. In his letters to Cazalis he writes:

> Since our spirit is absolute, and since nothing can exist outside of the Absolute, what is thought will make unity with the being who thinks; that object is the shape of the thought itself, the action through which the thought is produced. The idea . . . is above all. . . . In its essence it is what the thinking is.
> The goal to which the Absolute aspires, going from one state to another is to arrive to the state, in which it will be identical to itself, the state in which . . . the being would make one with the thought, the idea with the reality, in which . . . the Absolute will recognize itself as an Absolute, because it will know itself as such, and because to know itself as an Absolute, means to be an Absolute. . . . The consciousness, says Hegel, is aware of itself, and the consciousness that is aware of itself is the Absolute.
> The original French reads:
> Puisque l'esprit est absolu, et qu'il ne peut rien y avoir en dehors de l'absolu, la chose pensée ne fera qu'un avec l'être qui pense, elle sera la forme même de la pensée, l'acte par lequel la pensée se produit. . . . L'idée . . . est antérieure à tout . . . c'est elle au fond qui se pense.
> Le but auquel tend l'absolu est d'arriver, de manifestation en manifestation, à une forme dans laquelle . . . l'être ne fasse plus qu'un avec la pensée, l'idée avec la réalité, dans laquelle l'absolu, parce qu'il se connaîtra comme tel et parce que se savoir absolu, c'est être absolu. . . . La conscience, dit Hegel, a conscience de soi, et la conscience ayant conscience de soi, c'est l'absolu. (Ibid., 76–77.)

[17] See endnote 6. Bertrand Marchal points out that "The first period of the drama ["Overture"] is dedicated to the abandonment of the religious aspirations, symbolized by the fires of the dawn and the decoration by the magicians in the room of a shape of the Church." The Nurse is depicted as a personification of the

ghost of Sybille, who comes out of the tapestry to play the role of birds who predict evil when they encounter things they do not understand. Bertrand Marchal writes: "From the abolished Nurse whose dress melts with the decoration of the tapestry, there is only the ghost of the dead religion who is left." (Austin, *Essais sur Mallarmé*, 56.)

[18] Stéphane Mallarmé, *Collected Poems and Other Verse*, trans E.H. and A.M. Blackmore (Oxford: Oxford University Press, 2006), 196-197:

> The princess is an unusual child, she is
> the child exiled in her own precious heart
> like a swan veiling its eyes in its plumage
> as the old swan plunged them there, and passed through
> from the perturbed quills into the timeless avenue
> leaving all hope, to see the diamond prize
> of a star that no longer shines, but dies.

> l'enfant, exilée en son coeur précieux,
> Comme un cygne cachant en sa plume ses yeux,
> Comme les mit le vieux cygne en sa plume, allée,
> De la plume détresse, en l'éternelle allée
> De ses espoirs, pour voir les diamants élus
> D'une étoile, mourante, et qui ne brille plus!

As is often the case, that lack of understanding makes one—in this case, the Nurse—see a dark cloud in Hérodiade's future. "Will he [Herodiade's father] return some day from the Cisalpine lands! Soon enough? For all things are bad dreams and ill omens!" ("Reviendra-t-il un jour des pays cisalpins! Assez tôt? car tout est présage et mauvais rêve!") Ibid., 196.

[19] Cited in Zagona, *The Legend of Salome*, 47. "Toute chose sacrée et qui veut demeurer sacrée s'enveloppe de mystère. Les religions se retranchent à l'abri d'arcanes dévoilés au seul prédestiné: l'art a les siens."

[20] He wrote: "That a philosopher searches for popularity . . . but that a poet—the admirer of beauty inaccessible to vulgarity—does not limit himself for the suffrages of the Sanhedrin of art, irritates me, and I do not understand it. A man can be a democrat, but the artist doubles himself and must remain an aristocrat."

"Qu'un philosophe ambitionne la popularité . . . mais qu'un poète, un adorateur du beau inaccessible au vulgaire,—ne se contente pas des suffrages du sanhédrin de l'art, cela m'irrite, et je ne le comprends pas. L'homme peut être démocrate, l'artiste se dédouble et doit rester aristocrate." Ibid., 47.

[21] The passage from Scherer's article "Hegel and Hegelianisme," published in *la Revue des deux mondes* (cited in Austin, *Essais sur Mallarmé*, 80), which Mallarmé read, states: "C'est dire que rien n'existe, ou que l'existence est un simple devenir. *La chose, le fait, n'ont qu'une réalité fugitive, une réalité qui consiste dans leur disparition aussi bien que dans leur apparition, une réalité qui se produit pour être niée aussitôt qu'affirmée.* Tout n'est que relatif, disions-nous

tout à l'heure; il faut ajouter maintenant: *tout n'est que relation.*" This passage certainly expresses the idea of becoming in the process of creativity that we can find in the character of Hérodiade and that Mallarmé was able to express metaphorically.
[22] Mallarmé, *Collected Poems and Other Verse*, 28-29. "O femme, un baiser me tuerait / Si la beauté n'était la mort."
[23] Judd observes: "In conflating beauty with death, Mallarmé articulates the central paradox of the poet. Only in death can one escape the physical world, the source of all corruption. Such an escape is what the mystic desires. Yet the poet must invoke physical objects as a means of representing Beauty." Judd, *William Faulkner*, 25.
[24] For Thomas Williams' citation, see *Mallarmé and The Language of Mysticism* (Athens: The University of Georgia Press, 1970), 71.
[25] Mallarmé, *Collected Poems and Other Verse*, 29.

> Tu vis! Ou vois-je ici l'ombre d'une princesse?
> A mes lèvres tes doigts et leurs bagues, et cesse
> De marcher dans un âge ignoré ...

[26]
> N. Will he be here some time?
> H. O you pure
> stars, do not listen!
> N. How, except among obscure
> terrors, can we envisage the divinity
> still more implacable and like a suppliant
> whom all the treasures of your beauty must await!
> For whom would you, consumed by pangs, keep the unknown
> splendour and the vain mystery of your being?
> . . .
> H. Go, spare your pity and your irony.
> N. Yet tell me this: oh! no, your triumphal disdain,
> your poor innocent child, will some day surely wane.
> H. But when lions respect me, who would dare touch me?
> Besides, I long for nothing human; if you see
> me like a statue with eyes lost in paradise,
> that is when I recall the milk you gave me formerly.
> —Ibid., 33, 35. See French version on pages 32, 34.

[27] He writes: "According to the law of dialectical movement, every affirmation expects a negation, as any existence has a limit. To say what one thing would mean that it is not any other thing. On the other hand, the result is that the negation will not negate the previous affirmation; the negation would simply limit it; it will modify the previous affirmation and would force us to embrace one and the other in its unity, to reconcile them. . . . The reconciliation occurs by the intermediary of the third notion which contains two previous notions, combined and absorbed. Nonetheless, that new notion goes through the same experience as the experience

of the previous phenomena: it will not be affirmed until the contradiction that it carries within itself is cleared up. The contradiction will push this notion in its turn, toward the transformation. That is, according to Hegel, the law of the movement. . . . The affirmation, negation, conciliation—thesis, antithesis, synthesis—here is a succession of stages through which the idea realizes itself through transformation." Austin, *Essais sur Mallarmé*, 78.

[28] "The Beauty, complete and unconscious, unique and unchanging, or the Venus of Phidias, the Beauty which was bitten in the heart by the Chimera since Christianity, and coming back to life in pangs with the smile full of mystery, but with the forced mystery that she *feels* being the condition of its being. Finally, the Beauty, which through the man's science, fount in the entire Universe its *correlative phases*, having had the supreme word from it, remembered the secret horror which forced it to smile—at the time of Vinci, and to smile with mystery—but now it smiles with mystery from happiness and the eternal tranquility of the Venus of Milo who knew the idea of mystery of which only Jaconda knew the fatal feeling." Ibid., 78-79.

"La Beauté complète et inconsciente, unique et immuable, ou la Vénus de Phidias, la Beauté ayant été mordue au coeur depuis le christianisme par la Chimère, et douloureusement renaissant avec un sourire remplie de mystère, mais de mystère forcé et qu'elle *sent* être la condition de son être. La Beauté, enfin, ayant par la science de l'homme, retrouvé dans l'Univers entier ses *phases corrélatives*, ayant eu le suprême mot d'elle, s'étant rappelé l'horreur secrète qui la forçait à sourire—du temps du Vinci, et à sourire mystérieusement—souriant mystérieusement maintenant, mais de bonheur et avec la quiétude éternelle de la Vénus de Milo retrouvée ayant su l'idée du mystère dont la Jaconde ne savait que la sensation fatale."

[29] Mallarmé, *Collected Poems and Other Verse,* 35, 37, 39. For the French version see pages 34, 36, 38.

[30] Charles Baudelaire, *The Flowers of Evil*, trans. James McGowan (Oxford: Oxford University Press, 1998), 51, 53. For the French version see pages 50, 52.

[31] Zagona, *The Legend of Salome*, 51.

[32] Mallarmé, *Collected Poems and Other Verse*, 28–29.

> Reculez.
> Le blond torrent de mes cheveux immaculés
> Quand il baigne mon corps solitaire le glace
> D'horreur, et mes cheveux que la lumière enlace
> Sont immortels.

[33] Zagona, *The Legend of Salome*, 51. "l'idéal de la femme—c'est-à-dire d'une des facettes de la beauté, ce diamant, —n'est pas la brune. . . . La blondeur, c'est l'or, la lumière, la richesse, le rêve, le nimbe."

[34] Ibid., 51.

[35] Mallarmé's unfinished version of *Les Noces* attempts to convey that Hérodiade, the poem, through discovering the mystery by the intermediary of the *viol occulaire*—the encounter with John the Baptist—and later through her union with

him, becomes "Perfect Beauty" (la Beauté parfaite), which finds its state of serenity. Austin, *Essais sur Mallarmé*, 161.
[36] Mallarmé, *Collected Poems and Other Verse*, 213.

> Le soleil que se halte
> Surnaturelle exalte
> Aussitôt redescend
> Incandescent

[37] See Chapter 5.
[38] See Chapter 5.
[39] Mallarmé, *Collected Poems and Other Verse*, 215.

> Je sens comme aux vertèbres
> J'éployer des ténèbres
> Toutes dans un frisson
> A l'unisson
>
> Et ma tête surgie
> Solitaire vigie
> Dans les vols triomphaux
> De cette faux

[40] Already in 1865, in Mallarmé's poem "Gift of the Poem" (Don du poème), he depicts his theory of the creative process that we encounter in "Cantique." "Gift of the Poem" (Don du poème) could be perceived as a preface to *Hérodiade*, especially because it was written in 1865, when Mallarmé began working on *Hérodiade* and was thinking about imagery that could metaphorically express the birth of a poem.

The title "Gift of the Poem" refers to the birth of a poem. The poem begins with the stanza: "I bring you this child of an Idumean night!" (Ibid., 27. "Je t'apporte l'enfant d'une nuit d'Idumée!") In this stanza, Mallarmé, by calling the child "the child of an Idumean night," alludes to Cabal's story, in which Idume is the country of Edom, the country of monstrous Esau, who ruled over the pre-Adamite people. There all inhabitants were asexual and reproduced without women. See Wallace Follie, *Mallarmé* (Chicago: University of Chicago Press, 1953), 146, note 9. In this note Follie cites the article by Denis Saurat, *Perspectives* (Paris: Stock, 1935), 113-116. That article emphasizes the Cabalistic tendencies of the poem. Saurat says that the kings of Edom were sexless and reproduced without women. The poet also produces his poem alone.

The child in the poem, thus, is a creation of one person, of a poet. At its birth, this child is ugly and covered with blood. Mallarmé describes it as a bleeding bird: "black, with featherless wings bleeding and nearly white."(Mallarmé, *Collected Poems and Other Verse*, 27: "Noire; à l'aile saignante et pâle, déplumée.") When the father, the poet, sees his child, a "relic," his poem, his feeling of sterile solitude, induced by a long and lonely night, when he tried to write his poem, trembles:

> ... and when it [dawn] showed that relic
> to this father attempting to unfriendly smile,
> the blue and sterile solitude shivered all the while.

> ... et quand elle [aurore] a montré cette relique
> A ce père essayant un sourire ennemi
> La solitude bleue et stérile a frémi. (Ibid., 27, 29)

At first, the poet sees in his creation an enemy, because the process of creativity, a birth, is very painful. But it is also a loss and in a way a betrayal, since through its birth the poem separates itself from its creator, with whom it lived for a long time until its birth, and now it leaves him alone, abandoned. Once the birth is complete, the child is given to a nurse (to readers) and she (a reader) nurses it with her milk (care) and songs (recitations). The poem, like a child, begins its own life, separate and independent from the poet: "Woman lulling your little daughter, greet / a cruel birth, with the innocence of your cold feet." (Ibid., 29: "O la berceuse, avec ta fille et l'innocence / De vos pieds froids, accueille une horrible naissance.")

The poem needs an audience, a reader. The singer, the woman lulling, *la berceuse*, the nurse (a reader) will warm up the child (the poem) by reciting it (by bringing it to the world). The poet expresses the hope that the child, the poem, will be nursed and will acquire its own life through the reading and recognition, the nourishment of the poem.

> And your voice which both viol and harpsichord invest,
> will you with shriveled fingers press the breast
> from which flows woman, Sibylline and white,
> for lips starved of the virgin azure light?

> Et ta voix rappelant viole et clavecin,
> Avec le doigt fané presseras-tu le sein
> Par qui coule en blancheur sibylline la femme
> Pour des lèvres que l'air du vierge azur affame? (Ibid., 29.)

[41] Ibid., 215.

> Qu'elle de jeûnes ivre
> S'opiniâtre à suivre
> En quelque bond hagard
> Son pur regard

> Là-haut où la froidure
> Eternelle n'endure
> Que vous le surpassiez
> Tout ô glaciers

[42] Ibid., 215.

> Mais selon un baptême
> Illuminée au même
> Principe qui m'élut
> Penche un salut.

[43] Saint Paul's Letter to the Romans, VII, 23-4. *The Holy Bible* (Cleveland and New York: The World Publishing Company, 1961), 147.
[44] Austin, *Essais sur Mallarmé*, 151. "Le secret . . . que je tiens du poète lui-même, n'est autre que la future violation du mystère de son être par le regard de Jean qui va l'apercevoir, et payer de la mort ce seul sacrilège; car la farouche vierge ne se sentira de nouveau intacte et restituée tout entière à son intégralité, qu'au moment où elle tiendra entre ses mains la tête tranchée en laquelle osait se perpétuer le souvenir de la vierge entrevue."
[45] For more about the power of a glance see Theophile Gautier, *Le Roi Candaule* (Paris: Librairie des amateurs, A. Perroud, Libraire-editeur, 1893), and Theophile Gautier, *Jettatura* (Boston: D.C. Heath and Co., Publishers, 1904).
[46] Austin, *Essais sur Mallarmé*, 158.

> Le froid scintillement de ta pale clarté
> Toi qui te meurs, toi qui brules de chasteté,
> Nuit blanche de glaçons et de neige cruelle!

[47] Mallarmé, *Collected Poems and Other Verse,* 38-39.

> Des ondes
> Se bercent et, là-bas, sais-tu pas un pays
> Ou le sinistre ciel ait les regards hais
> De Venus qui, le soir, brule dans le feuillage:
> J'y partirais.

[48] Austin, *Essais sur Mallarmé*, 81: "tout univers existe pour aboutir à un livre."
[49] Ibid. "l'hymne . . . harmonie et joie . . . *des relations entre tout.*"
[50] Ibid., 76. "Puisque l'esprit est absolu, et qu'il ne peut rien y avoir en dehors de l'absolu, *la chose pensée ne fera qu'un avec l'être qui pense,* elle sera la forme même de la pensée, l'acte par lequel la pensée se produit. . . . L'idée . . . est antérieure à tout . . . c'est elle au fond qui se pense."
[51] Austin, *Essais sur Mallarmé*, 161.
[52] Geneviève Lacambre, *Gustave Moreau: Between Epic and Dream* (Chicago: The Art Institute of Chicago, 1999), 167.

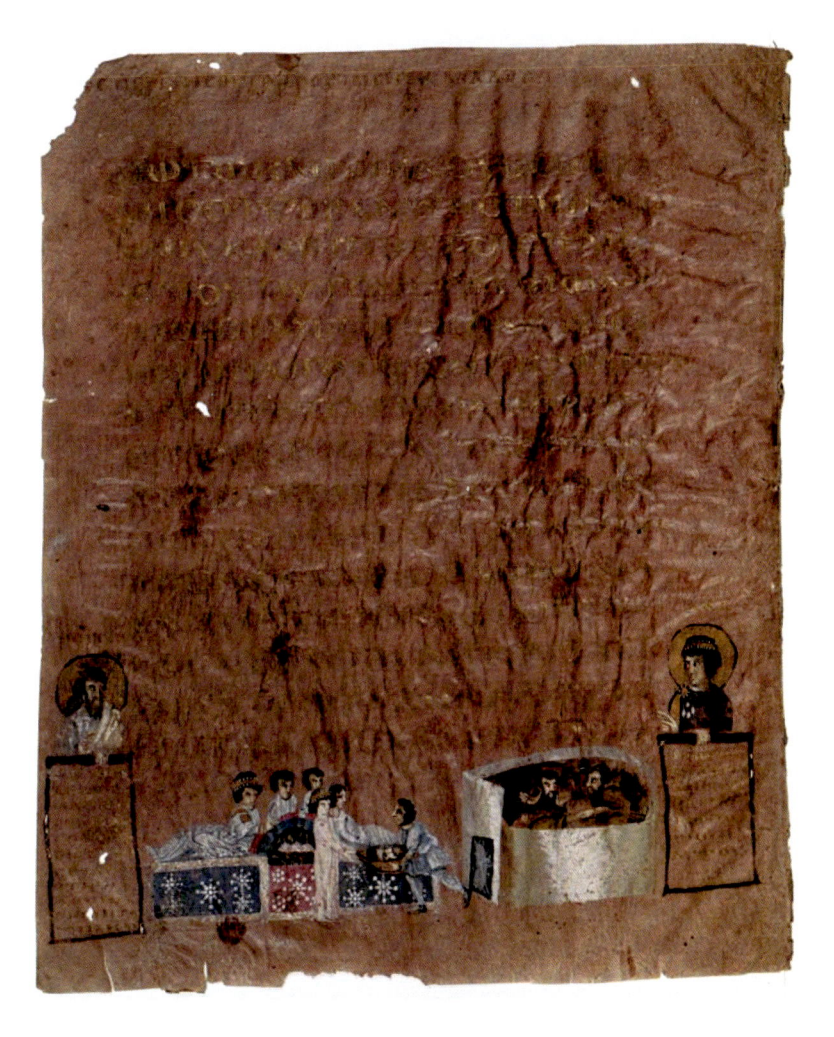

Fig. I-2-1. *Herod's Banquet and John the Baptist's Decapitation,* a sixth-century miniature in the *Codex Sinopensis,* BNF, France

Fig. I-2-2. *Dancing Salome* in the *Évangéliaire de Chartres*, the first part of the ninth century, BNF, France

Fig. I-2-3. *Dancing Salome*, mosaic, fourteenth century, San Marco, Venice, Italy, Scala/Art Resource, New York

Fig. I-2-4. Giovanni di Paolo, *The Head of John the Baptist brought to Herod*, tempera on panel, 68.5 x 40.2 cm, 1455/60, The Art Institute of Chicago

Fig. I-2-7. Andrea Solario, *Salome with the Head of John the Baptist*, wood, 58.5 x 57.5 cm, sixteenth century, Kunsthistorisches Museum, Gemaeldegalerie, Vienna, Austria

Fig. I-2-8. *Decapitation of John the Baptist*, mosaic, thirteenth century, Florence Baptistery, Scala/Art Resources, New York

Fig. I-2-9. Bernardino Luini, *Salome Receiving the Head of John the Baptist*, oil on canvas, 62.5 x 55 cm, sixteenth century, Louvre, Departement des Peintures, Scala/Art Resource, New York

Fig. I-2-11. *Salome Presenting the Head of John the Baptist to Herodias*, mosaic, thirteenth century, Florence Baptistery, Scala/Art Resources, New York

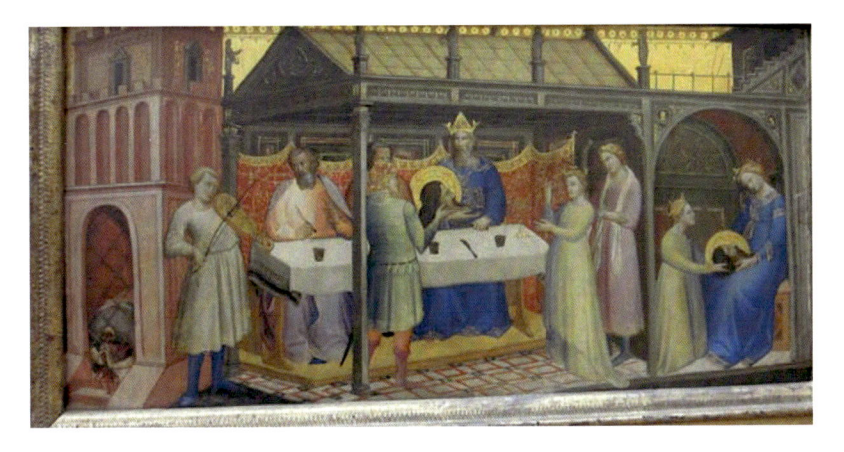

Fig. I-2-13. Lorenzo Monaco, *Herod's Feast, Salome with the head of the Baptist*, left wing of a predella for an altar in Santa Maria degli Angeli, Florence. Tempera on wood, 33.8 x 67.7 cm, 1387-1388, Louvre, Departement des Peintures

Fig. I-3-2. Filippo Lippi, *The Banquet of Herod*, fresco, 1465, Capella Maggiore of Santo Stefano Cathedral, Prato, Italy, Scala/Art Resource, New York

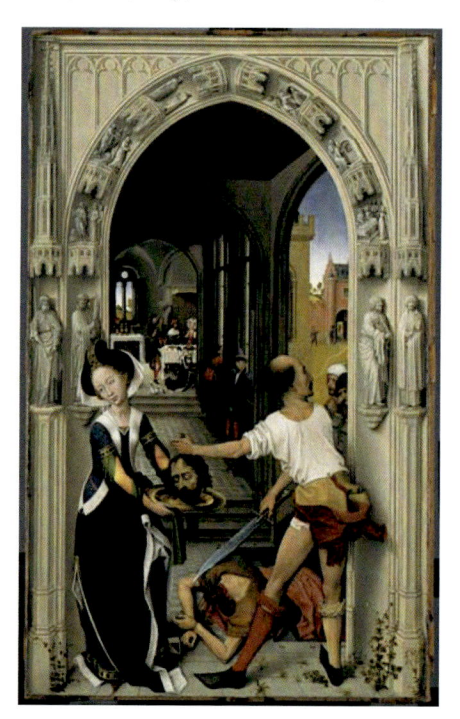

Fig. I-3-3. Rogier van der Weyden, *Saint John Altarpiece*, *The Beheading of John the Baptist,* rightmost panel, oil on oak panel, 77 x 48 cm, 1455-1460, Staatliche Museen, Berlin, Scala/Art Resource, New York

Fig. I-3-10. Guido Reni, *Salome with the Head of John the Baptist*, oil on canvas, 248.5 x 174 cm, 1639/42, The Art Institute of Chicago

Fig. I-4-3. Gustav-Adolf Mossa, *Salome,* 1906, Musée des Beaux Arts, Nice, France

Fig. I-4-5. Franz Von Stuck, *Salome Dancing*, oil, 45.7 x 24.7 cm, 1906, private collection, Scala/Art Resource, New York

Fig. I-4-7. Henri Regnault, *Salome*, Oil on canvas, 160 x 102.9 cm, 1870, Metropolitan Museum of Art, New York, Scala/Art Resource, New York

Fig. I-4-8. Jean-Sylvain Bieth, *Salome*, three pieces, 1985-88, private collection

Fig. I-4-9. Sergei Chepik, *Salome*, oil on canvas, circa 1980, private collection

Fig. II-5-1. Michelangelo, *Last Judgment*, detail, fresco, 1340 x 1200 cm, 1537-1541, Sistine Chapel, Vatican City, Scala/Art Resource, New York

Fig. II-5-3. Titian, *Salome*, oil on canvas, 90 x 72 cm, 1515, Galleria Doria Pamphilj, Rome, Scala/Art Resource, New York

Fig. II-5-4. Titian, *Lavinia as Salome*, oil on canvas, 87 x 80 cm, 1549, Museo del Prado, Madrid, Scala/Art Resource, New York

Fig. II-5-6. Emile Bernard, *The Dancer or Salome*, oil on canvas, 1914, Galerie Larock-Granoff, Paris, France

Fig. II-5-8. Gustave Moreau, *The Apparition*, watercolor on paper, 106 x 72 cm, 1876, Cabinet des dessins, Louvre, Scala/Art Resource, New York

Fig. App 1-1. Lovis Corinth, *Salome*, oil on canvas, 127 x 147 cm, 1900, Museum der Bildenden Künste Leipzig, Germany, Scala/Art Resource, New York

Fig. App 2-1. Valentin Serov, *Ida Rubenstein as Salome*, oil and charcoal on canvas, 147 x 233 cm, 1910, Russian Museum, Saint Petersburg, Russia. Photo: www.abcgallery.com

Fig. II-5-8. Gustave Moreau, *The Apparition*, watercolor on paper, 106 x 72 cm, 1876, Cabinet des dessins, Louvre, Scala/Art Resource, New York

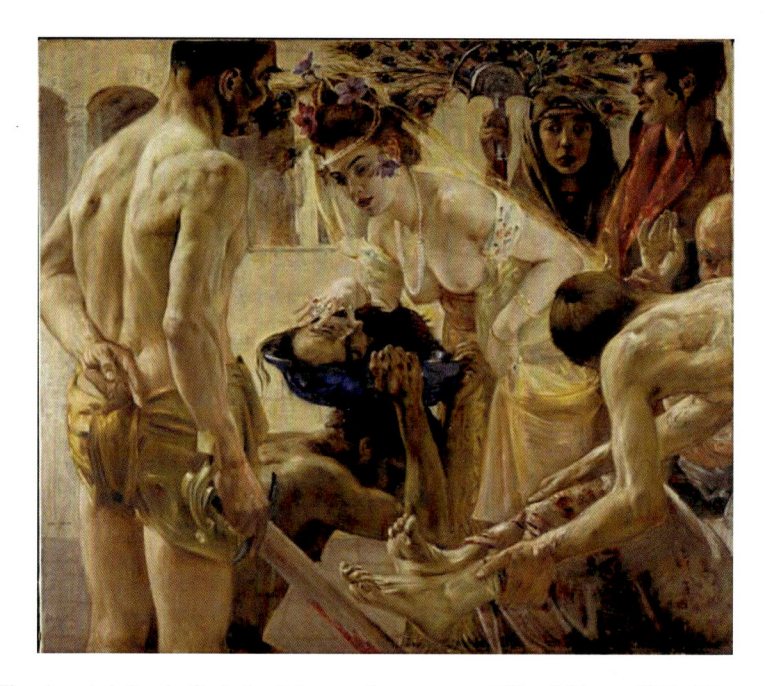

Fig. App 1-1. Lovis Corinth, *Salome*, oil on canvas, 127 x 147 cm, 1900, Museum der Bildenden Künste Leipzig, Germany, Scala/Art Resource, New York

Fig. App 2-1. Valentin Serov, *Ida Rubenstein as Salome*, oil and charcoal on canvas, 147 x 233 cm, 1910, Russian Museum, Saint Petersburg, Russia. Photo: www.abcgallery.com

Fig. App 2-2. Marianna Werefkina, 1911, *Salome with a Head of John the Baptist*. Photo: http://www.liveinternet.ru/journalshowcomments.php?journalid=3259969 &jpostid=109962196

Part III

Salome in Story, Drama, Music

CHAPTER SEVEN

SALOME'S DANCE IN FLAUBERT'S "HERODIAS": PICTORIAL OR EKPHRASTIC?

Gustave Flaubert's "Herodias" is one of the many renderings of the story of John the Baptist's beheading as a result of Salome's dance. Huysmans' novel *Against Nature (A Rebours)* contains an ekphrasis of Salome's dance as portrayed in two of Gustave Moreau's works, *Salome Dancing before Herod (Salome dansant devant Herod)* and *The Apparition (L'Apparition),* both of which were exhibited at the Salon of 1876. In contrast, Flaubert's description of Salome's dance is an example of a "pictorial" image, that is, a cumulative and associative image, in which, as P-M de Biasi puts it, "the ways of plastic and literary expressions mutually enhance each other without being able to stand alongside each other."[1] According to James Heffernan,

> picturalism is the generation in language of effects similar to those created by pictures, as opposed to ekphrasis (the depiction in language of a real work of art) or 'notional ekphrasis' (the depiction of an imaginary art work).[2]

In "Herodias," Flaubert has created a striking literary picture of a dancing Salome who hypnotizes her audience, makes Herod Antipas lose control in his desire for her, and causes the death of John the Baptist. Images, according to Roland Barthes, are the focus of desires:

> Images are also a snare and a delusion. The mistake is to think that images embody what they represent. . . . Images are the signs of madness and death. . . . The contents of images are often less important than their associations or connotations.[3]

What does Flaubert's image of the dancing Salome signify? Does that image embody what it represents? What are the possible associations evoked by Flaubert's image of the dancing Salome? If this image is pictorial and results in associative and cumulative effects, then what are its origins and how can it affect our reading of the tale? Such are the questions that I shall address in this chapter.

Adrianne Tooke contends that Flaubert, like Victor Cousin and unlike Lessing, believed that "art was constrained by its own formal requirements."[4] She asserts:

> It is certain that Flaubert was highly dubious about what was usually understood in his time to be pictorialist writing, whether in the form of the *transposition d'art*, as practised by Hugo, Gautier, and others, and to which Huysmans later remained faithful, or in the form of highly descriptive, Parnassian writing. Flaubert was particularly critical of the latter, and remarked of Leconte de Lisle that, for all the latter's plasticity, crucially "he is lacking the ability to see." (*Correspondance*, Gallimard, Pléiade, 1973-98, 298.) Flaubert shares with certain other writers, not only Symbolists but also people like Diderot, Stendhal, and Turgenev, the sense that exhaustive description is not necessarily the most effective way to evoke an object.[5]

Tooke observes that Flaubert perceived

> visual art not quite as a sister, not quite as a rival but above all as a foil. . . . Some of the finest and most original effects in Flaubert's writing are produced by the never-resolved tension between image and text, between all that Flaubert personally associated with the pictorial and the status of his own art.[6]

Flaubert was very sensitive to the visual in general and painting in particular,[7] and his writing was often inspired by art that he indirectly incorporated in his work. Thus, Flaubert's writing becomes an embodiment of "the generation in language of effects similar to those created by pictures." It is this writing of the visual (*écriture du visuel*) which "constitutes a true work of rewriting and integration . . . when the ways of plastic and literary expressions mutually enhance each other without being able to stand alongside each other."[8] Flaubert's description of the dancing Salome in "Herodias" is a striking example of that *écriture du visuel*.

"Herodias" is the last in a collection of three tales that also contains "St. Julien l'hospitalier" and "Un coeur simple." The collection was published in 1877, a year after Gustave Moreau presented *Salome Dancing Before Herod* (Fig. II-5-7) and *The Apparition* (Fig. II-5-8) at the Salon of 1876. Flaubert is known to have visited that exhibition and to have seen Moreau's works. He mentioned this visit in a letter to Ivan Turgenev, explaining that, as a result of it, he planed to write a story about Ioakanann, the Hebraic name of John the Baptist. Nonetheless, it is quite possible that the idea of writing "Herodias" had been maturing in Flaubert's mind for some time before he saw Moreau's works, and that seeing *The Apparition,* in particular, fully confirmed his intention. In March-April 1876, Flaubert was traveling to Normandy to collect the material for "Un coeur simple" and took with him a notebook containing many earlier notes, the bulk of which were made in 1871-1872 for *The Temptation of Saint Anthony.* Among those notes there were some on John the Baptist, Vitellius and Pontius Pilate. It is possible that while traveling in Normandy and looking through those notes Flaubert began to think about his past trips to the Orient and to remember the dances of Egyptian courtesans that had once inflamed him.

In "Herodias" the description of the dancing Salome is the culmination of the story. Flaubert depicts her dance in an unusual way. Although it is sensual, and it makes her desirable and strikingly attractive to her audience, it is more of an acrobatic exercise than a mere dance. Salome shocks the spectators with her erotic movements and her ability to stand on her hands and create the figure of a bridge while dancing:

> And now the graceful dancer appeared transported with the very delirium of love and passion. She danced like the priestesses of India, like the Nubians of the cataracts, or like the Bacchantes of Lydia. She whirled about like a flower blown by the tempest. . . . Her arms, her feet, her clothing even, seemed to emit streams of magnetism, that set the spectators' blood on fire.
>
> Suddenly the thrilling chords of a harp rang through the hall, and the throng burst into loud acclamations. All eyes were fixed on Salome, who paused in her rhythmic dance, placed her feet wide apart, and without bending her knees, suddenly swayed her lithe body downward, so that her chin touched the floor; and her whole audience,—the nomads, accustomed to a life of privation and abstinence; the Roman soldiers, expert in debaucheries; the avaricious publicans; and even the crabbed, elderly priests—gazed upon her with dilated nostrils.
>
> Next she began to whirl frantically around the table where Antipas the tetrarch was seated. He leaned towards the flying figure, and in a voice half choked with the voluptuous sighs of mad desire, he sighed: "Come to me! Come!" But she whirled on, while the music of dulcimers swelled louder and the excited spectators roared their applause. . . .
>
> Again the dancer paused; then, like a flash, she threw herself upon the palms of her hands, while her feet rose straight up into the air. In this bizarre pose she moved about upon the floor like a gigantic beetle; then stood motionless.
>
> The nape of her neck formed a right angle with her vertebrae. The full silken skirts of pale hues that enveloped her limbs when she stood erect, now fell to her shoulders and surrounded her face like a rainbow. Her lips were tinted a deep crimson, her arched eyebrows were black as jet, her

glowing eyes had an almost terrible radiance; and the tiny drops of perspiration on her forehead looked like dew upon white marble.

She made no sound; and the burning gaze of that multitude of men was concentrated upon her.[9]

It is well known that Rouen, Flaubert's native city, has a thirteenth-century Gothic cathedral that Flaubert had visited since his childhood and revisited during his adult years. His tale "St. Julien l'hospitalier" was inspired by windows in that cathedral that narrate St. Julien's life. This cathedral also has a tympanum on the northern door of the facade, called *La Porte de St. Jean*. In his introduction to "Herodias," René Dumesnil suggests:

> one day, walking into the cathedral of Rouen, Flaubert . . . looked with particular attention at the tympanum of the northern door of the facade of the cathedral, where, since the beginning of the thirteenth century, Salome has danced before Herod in order to obtain John's head. . . . The posture of the young girl is strange: she is dancing on her hands, her feet are raised, and her heels are in the air. These are the exact words that Flaubert uses to describe the dance of Salome before Herod.[10]

This unusual representation of Salome's dance has a long history. We first find Salome dancing in that position in the twelfth-century manuscript *Hortus deliciarum*, an encyclopedia of the period illustrated and compiled by Herrad de Landsberg, the prioress of the Sainte-Odile convent in Alsace. Herrad was known for her great erudition and culture, and her manuscript displays a high level of imaginative imagery. Here Herrad has painted Salome standing on her hands, making a "bridge" before Herod's assembled banquet; perhaps this is the seminal instance of Salome pictured more as an acrobat rather than as a dancer.[11]

Interestingly, in Herrad's manuscript Salome is not the only figure represented in that posture. The pose is also seen in "The Whore of Babylon Inverted" (Fig. III-7-1), "The Whore of Babylon Falling" (Fig. III-7-2), "Lucifer Falling" (Fig. III-7-3), (*Hortus Deliciarum*, images 321, 351, 352), and, in the famous "Stairs that lead toward the skies" (Fig. III-7-4), in the figure of the Priest of the People. The last figure is depicted in the manuscript as representing those clerics who had fallen prey to "the extremes of eating and drinking, of lust . . . and other vices; . . . falling upside-down and . . . never [reaching] the crown of life,"[12] virtue, which is at the top of the ladder. It is clear that in the *Hortus Deliciarum* the bridge or the upside-down position is associated with evil, sin and vice. The Whore of Babylon, Lucifer, the vicious Priest and Salome are all figures that will never achieve virtue.

Fig. III-7-1. Herrad de Landsberg, *The Whore of Babylon Inverted*

Fig. III-7-2. Herrad de Landsberg, *The Whore of Babylon Falling*

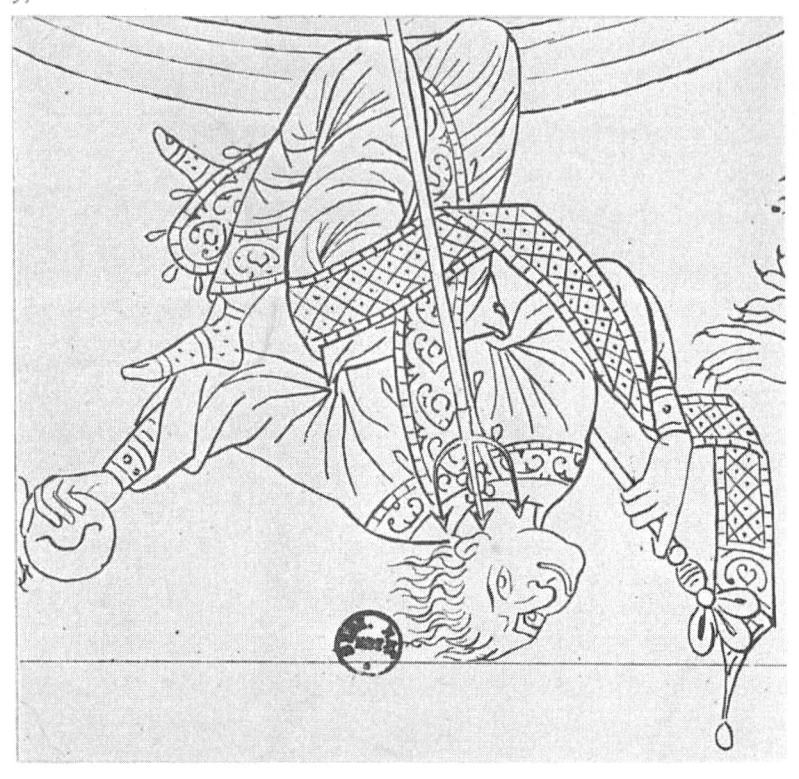

Fig. III-7-3. Herrad de Landsberg, *Lucifer Falling*

The highly learned Herrad de Landsberg incorporated in her manuscript knowledge derived from Arabian writings that had recently reached Northern Europe. Arabian scholars had a great interest in the philosophy and sciences of the ancient Greeks. Since 800 AD, Arabian caliphs had been purchasing Greek classics and having them translated into Arabic. At the European point of entrance, which for such works was the college of translators at Toledo, in Spain, the manuscripts were translated into Latin and Hebrew and from there spread to Western and Northern Europe. Arabian, Greek and Byzantine ideas and culture were propagated via these translations.

Salome's Dance in Flaubert's "Herodias": Pictorial or Ekphrastic? 157

L'échelle du paradis, le salut difficile à gagner

(D'après l'*Hortus Deliciarum*, manuscrit de Herrade de Landsberg, abbesse de Hohenbourg – original détruit pendant la guerre de 1870 – Munich, Allemagne.)

Fig. III-7-4. Herrad de Landsberg, *Stairs that lead toward the skies*

Similarly, ancient Egypt exerted a strong influence on Greek, Byzantine and Roman art and culture. Egypt was the first civilization in which we find evidence of a cult of resurrection. It is manifested in the cult of Isis, the goddess of resurrection, fertility, life and the changing seasons, the sister-wife who resurrected her brother-husband Osiris. The cult of Isis was expressed in ritual dances, which in ancient Egypt were a widespread form of art and which later became a part of traditional Egyptian dance and, arguably, even the foundation of modern dance.

The art of ritual dancing was so important that some hieroglyphs have specific names for dance-figures. For example, the goddess Isis was associated with the acrobatic position known as the "bridge" (Fig. III-7-5), in which the hands and the feet are on the ground, with the navel pointing to the zenith.[13] This position was also associated with the overarching night sky and, when the feet were off the ground, was the expression of the wind swaying the reeds and grain of the Nile,[14] an important symbol of the worship of Isis. That "bridge" can also be found in visual representations of Greek and Roman acrobats. Thus, it is reasonable to assume that Herrad de Landsberg might have seen the image of the "bridge" when she came into contact with Byzantine, Greek or Arabic manuscripts, most likely in the library of Gandersheim. The image was subsequently used in her encyclopedia, where she endowed the image with her connotations of evil, sin and vice. Her way of interpreting this acrobatic image, which is the polar opposite of the Egyptian interpretation, may well be associated with the Church's struggle against the traveling acrobats with whom Herrad could easily associate that image. Alternately, if Herrad knew the origin of the image it could have been associated with the Church's struggle against paganism.

Herrad de Landsberg's manuscript was well known in the Middle Ages. Theatrical companies or troupes often looked to similar manuscripts to find the images and texts that they wanted to employ and imitate in their performances.

Naturally, many medieval theater performances, including the morality plays that were the most popular form of medieval theater, were based on biblical stories. They were performed all over Western Europe and appeared at various times over a 600-year period from the middle of the tenth to the middle of the sixteenth century. Medieval theater groups must have seen Herrad de Landsberg's manuscript and been impressed by the image of the dancing Salome, because they adopted that image for their morality plays.

Salome's Dance in Flaubert's "Herodias": Pictorial or Ekphrastic? 159

Fig. III-7-5. The goddess Isis in the acrobatic position known as the "bridge"

Often the morality plays were performed in the squares in front of cathedrals, even when the cathedrals were in the process of being constructed. It is possible, therefore, that performances of Salome dancing on her hands took place in front of Rouen Cathedral at the time of its construction, and that the Salome of the morality plays, standing on her hands, inspired a medieval sculptor to represent her in that acrobatic position on the tympanum of the cathedral. If that were the case, the theater performance could be perceived as a reflection of Landsberg's Salome, and Rouen's representation of a dancing Salome would then be an illustration of that reflection.

Leaving aside these suppositions, it should be noted that despite its similarities Flaubert's image of the dancing Salome is not derived directly from the *Hortus Delicarum*, since Flaubert probably did not even know of Herrad de Landsberg's manuscript. The immediate roots of Flaubert's dancing Salome are found in the sculpture of Salome on the north tympanum of Rouen Cathedral (Fig. III-7-6).

Flaubert's Salome probably also reflects his travels in Egypt. While traveling in Egypt in 1849, Flaubert met a living version of the dancing Salome, similar to the one he had seen on the tympanum of Rouen Cathedral. The dance he saw was the same dance that is to be found in visual representations of Greek and Roman acrobats. For Flaubert, the acrobatic dance of Salome in a "bridge" pose—in which she stands on her hands and head, as on the tympanum of Rouen Cathedral—found its counterpart in the Egyptian dancers Kuchiouk-Hanem and Azizeh. After observing the dance of the Egyptian courtesan Kuchiouk-Hanem, Flaubert even noted: "I saw this dance on the old Greek vases."[15]

Fig. III-7-6. Dancing Salome on the north tympanum of Rouen Cathedral

Flaubert met Kuchiouk-Hanem in Esneh, a small but well-known town on a bend of the Nile, halfway between Luxor and Aswan. All of Cairo's professional prostitutes had been exiled there by edict since 1834. Flaubert gives a very detailed description of the different dances that Kuchiouk-Hanem performed before him. They were all sensual, and some of the movements were similar to the dance that Flaubert's Salome was later to perform. Nonetheless, none of Kuchiouk-Hanem's dances were fully the dance of Isis, the "bridge" dance, although they contained some elements of a "bridge."

A little later in his voyage, Flaubert encountered another dancer, Azizeh. Her dance seemed to him more sophisticated than Kuchiouk-Hanem's, and it was a true "bridge" dance, a dance of Isis. In his eyes this dance looked similar to the dance of Salome represented on Rouen Cathedral. He wrote: "She began—her neck slid toward the back vertebrae and more often to the side, to make one believe that her head would fall."[16]

Flaubert most probably knew the meaning of the "bridge" dance and was able to recognize it since he had an extraordinary knowledge of and passion for oriental culture in general and Egyptian culture in particular. Indeed, from a very early age he had been interested in the Orient. His first version of *L'Education sentimentale*, for example, contains many passages about the Orient. In 1846, Flaubert decided to write a *Conte oriental*, and he plunged into reading about the Orient. He subsequently abandoned this plan in order to write *La Tentation de saint Antoine*. To prepare for this work he studied oriental religions and read extensively about the Orient in general. In 1849, Flaubert and his friend Maxime du Camp decided to travel together to the Orient, where they intended to visit Egypt, Palestine, Syria, Baghdad and Babylon. Flaubert engaged in an impressive intellectual preparation for this journey, reading books on Egypt and the Orient, many of which he mentions in his works, letters, papers and notebooks.[17]

In his accounts of his trip to Egypt, Flaubert mentions a number of visits to the temples of Isis. For example, during his visit to a small Egyptian village called Edfou, he describes a dilapidated temple where there is a representation of Isis nurturing Horus.[18] Later, when preparing to rewrite *The Temptation of Saint Anthony* in 1872, he embarked on additional studies that included Champollion-Figeac's *Egypte ancienne* and Strabon's *Egypte et Alexandrie*, the two works that most enriched his knowledge of Egyptian rituals, traditions and culture. There can be no doubt, therefore, that he was familiar with the significance of the goddess Isis and the symbols associated with her, including the bridge/arch figure. While in Egypt, watching the Egyptian dancers who fascinated him, he may well have connected their dances to their ancient origins, even if he does not explicitly mention them in his *Voyage en Egypte*. Indeed, he is very discrete about his erudition concerning Egyptian and oriental cultures, unlike earlier memoirs and diaries by other travelers to exotic countries.

Flaubert returned to the study of ancient cultures while working on "Herodias," but this time he did so in order to create an image that seemed to have pursued him for years. As Pierre-Mark de Biase points out:

> The idea of describing the dance of a woman-child, presented almost naked to the gaze of the entire crowd, could only have inflamed Flaubert's imagination. He also saw in it a way of revisiting the Orient that he had known in 1850 . . . the landscape and the erotic memories.[19]

This notion of experience and expression appears in a letter to Turgenev, in which Flaubert wrote: "It is not only a question of seeing. It is important to arrange and to fuse what we see. Reality, in my opinion, should only be a springboard."[20] De Biase adds that this same kind of synthesis also absorbs the material that Flaubert drew from his reading. Flaubert loved historical information and documentary sources for their own sake, but from an artistic point of view he used that material to feed his imagination and create images. Most importantly, he transformed his source material into a finished literary product through a complex creative and integrative process.[21]

All of the preceding source material merges in Flaubert's description of Salome. The image of the young daughter of Herodias draws from the dancing figure of Salome on Rouen Cathedral, the dances associated with the ritual of Isis and the dancing Egyptian women who elicited Flaubert's excitement and admiration and whose dances he described in detail in his *Voyage en orient*. Through the collection and arrangement of these sources Flaubert creates a Salome who arouses the senses of all the spectators present at the banquet and whose dance of lust and death ultimately leads to the beheading of John the Baptist.

The image of the dancing Salome in "Herodias" is reflected in the eyes and reactions of those who look at her, and her audience includes the reader as much as it includes the spectators Flaubert describes. Flaubert's dancing Salome is an image that awakens desire in the reader, though the object of that desire is a representation rather than a real person. One cannot touch Salome, but only imagine and fantasize about her. The spectator/reader is constantly caught between the desire to embrace the image of the dancing Salome and the necessity of staying at a distance. Thus, like Herod, we are readers and spectators who can see but cannot touch, although we desire to touch, even as the dancing Salome herself sees us and touches us through her dance. This image of Salome as the focus of desire is highly erotic.[22] Furthermore, it could be perceived as an image of madness and death, for the desire awakened by the image of the dancing Salome drives Herod Antipas to destruction and leads to the death of the Baptist.

For Flaubert, however, this was not the only meaning of the image. Indeed, a suggestive reading was very important for him. On the surface the meaning of what he describes might seem obvious, but in reality it is much more subtle, and his image certainly does not embody only what it seems to represent. As Roland Barthes notes: "The mistake is to think that images embody what they represent. . . . The content of images is often less important than their associations or connotations."[23]

At the end of Flaubert's story, the severed head of the Baptist is illuminated by candelabra and is then carried to Jesus. From a visual perspective, the idea of the illuminated head was undoubtedly inspired by Flaubert's visit to the salon of 1876 and his encounter with Moreau's watercolor *The Apparition*. As de Biasi writes,

> Flaubert's use of the striking image of the radiant, levitating head is much more than a coincidence. Flaubert's project of writing "Herodias" was probably already in place by 1876, but it is clear that the encounter with Moreau's works confirmed him in his idea. An explicit reference to the Salon is not absent from Flaubert's drafts, and it seems that Flaubert intended to introduce Moreau's famous "shining" head in association with the sun myth in the final sentences of the tale.[24]

The visual image of the illuminated head fully reveals the profound meaning of the story hidden behind the appearance of an image of Salome dancing. As Margaret Lowe and Colin Burns write in their article "Flaubert's 'Herodias' – a New Evaluation":

> In medieval Celtic and Icelandic myth . . . the head of the great leader sometimes lived on after his death, giving advice and comfort to his followers. . . . it seems clear that the head of Ioakanann takes on something of the same symbolic value as this ancient mythical conception. . . . The method used to execute the Prophet was, significantly, decapitation, that is to say, the familiar 'cutting off the ideas at their source.' But his ideas continue to live in the severed head and can be passed on.[25]

The image of Salome seems to kill the Word in Ioakanann, since with earthly death he seems to lose his ability to propagate his faith and his ideas. Yet his Word survives and in "Herodias" Flaubert stresses its survival, because John the Baptist's head, the symbol of his ideas, continues to live in its severed form. Flaubert, in describing the illuminated head of the Baptist, draws attention to the Baptist's life after death. The light thus becomes an aureole of eternity, a symbol of eternal life and of an eternal Word that survives to propagate itself throughout the centuries. So too does John's Word survive through Jesus, for it is to him that the Baptist's head is carried after decapitation. The survival and propagation of John's Word underscores his role as a prophet.

We know that Flaubert believed in the idea of "spontaneous evocation" ("évocation spontanée"). He always aspired to create a text that would not be static. Rather, his aim was a text filled with suggestive meanings that would flow between the author and the reader, permitting an associative reading and allowing the reader to create his own interpretation of the text. In the present case, the image of the dancing Salome that Flaubert created has a double meaning. She is not only an image of madness and desire, the image of a destroyer, but her image also contains a less obvious idea: She is a creator who leads toward resurrection. Flaubert's Salome signifies resurrection and new life much in the same way that death in a pack of tarot cards can signify life after death or the notion of resurrection. Salome is the means to the end that leads to a new beginning. How can that be?

As we have seen, one of Flaubert's sources for Salome's "bridge" dance is ultimately the goddess Isis, the goddess of new life, whose dance is performed at the time of harvest.[26] Thus, if we were to link Flaubert's image of Salome to its original source, Isis, Salome's dance would also become a dance of life and resurrection. Yet Flaubert's Salome is also the Salome who performs her dance on the tympanum of Rouen Cathedral. This image originates from a different source, and here the dance is a symbol of a desire that leads to madness and death. The fact that the image of Flaubert's Salome was born out of two contradictory associative phenomena—the dance of Isis and the dance of Salome on the tympanum of Rouen Cathedral—can give Flaubert's dancing Salome an ambivalent meaning. It is an image that both ends and resurrects the Word. If Salome is partly Isis, then Salome's dance in Flaubert's story could also be taken to symbolize the cycle of life, in which transformation and reconciliation lead to new life. John, through Salome's dance and his own physical death, attains eternity, divine worship and earthly glory, in essence passing from temporal to eternal life. Salome is thus a catalyst, since her dance, like that of Isis, becomes a reconciliation of life and death. This intimacy of life and death, typical of the late nineteenth century, brings to Salome's image a possible double meaning: that of an executioner and a reconciler. She becomes a cult figure, which is one of her new roles in the art and literature of the second part of the nineteenth century.

The way in which Flaubert created his dancing Salome is a striking example of his "évocation spontanée," his way of creating a special relationship between the reader and the author through the possibility of an associative interpretation of the tale. Salome's inverted dance could be a symbolic reference to an "inverted" interpretation of her, provided via the associations with Isis, through which Salome is both a catalyst and a reconciler as well as a seducer and destroyer.

Notes

[1] "où les modes d'expression plastique et littéraire s'enrichissent mutuellement, mais sans pouvoir se juxtaposer." This quotation is taken from P-M de Biasi's postface to Flaubert, *Trois contes* (Paris: Seuil, 1993), 269.
[2] Quoted in Adrianne Tooke, *Flaubert and the Pictorial Arts. From Image to Text* (Oxford: Oxford University Press, 2000), 3. For that definition, she has used James Heffernam's book *The Museum of Words: The Poetics of Ekphrasis from Homer to Ashbery* (Chicago: University of Chicago Press, 1993).

[3] Quoted in Tooke, *Flaubert and the Pictorial Arts*, 228-230.
[4] Ibid., 73.
[5] Ibid., 73.
[6] Ibid., 3-4.
[7] Ibid., 4.
[8] "un vrai travail de réécriture et d'intégration. . . . où les modes d'expression plastique et littéraire s'enrichissent mutuellement, mais sans pouvoir se juxtaposer." Ibid., 3.
[9] Gustave Flaubert, *Trois Contes* (Paris: Booking International, 1994), 122-123. English translation from Gustave Flaubert, *Trois Contes*, ed. Raymond Decesse (Paris: Bordas, 1965), 47-48.

> Ce fut l'emportement de l'amour qui veut être assouvi. Elle dansa comme les prêtresses des Indes, comme les Nubiennes des cataractes, comme les bacchantes de Lydie. Elle se renversait de tous les côtés, pareille à une fleur que la tempête agite. . . . de ses bras, de ses pieds, de ses vêtements jaillissaient d'invisibles étincelles qui enflammaient les hommes. Un harpe chanta ; la multitude y répondit par des acclamations. Sans fléchir ses genoux en écartant les jambes, elle se courba si bien que son menton frôlait le plancher ; et les nomades habitués à l'abstinence , les soldats de Rome experts en débauches, les avares publicains, les vieux prêtres aigris par les disputes, tous, dilatant leurs narines, palpitaient de convoitise. . . .
> Elle se jeta sur les mains, les talons en l'air, parcourant ainsi l'estrade comme un grand scarabée; et s'arrêtant, brusquement.
> Sa nuque et ses vertèbres faisaient un angle droit. Les fourreaux de couleur qui enveloppaient ses jambes, lui passant par-dessus l'épaule, comme des arcs-en-ciel, accompagnaient sa figure, à une coudée du sol. Ses lèvres étaient peintes, ses sourcils très noirs, ses yeux presque terribles, et des gouttelettes à son front semblaient une vapeur sur du marbre blanc.
> Elle ne parlait pas. Ils se regardaient.

[10] René Dumesnil, "Introduction" (Paris: Editions Gallimard, 1952), 583. The tympanum was sculpted in the thirteenth century in the Parisian Gothic style.
[11] This image, located in a copy of the Strasbourg manuscript (the original was destroyed by fire in 1870, during the Franco-Prussian War), was not allowed to be reproduced, despite my efforts.
[12] Rosalie Green, ed., *The Hortus Deliciarum of Herrad of Hohenbourg (Landsberg, 1176-96): A Reconstruction* (London: Warburg Institute/Brill, 1979), images 321, 351, 352.
[13] Kirstein Lincoln, *Dance. A Short History of Classic Theatrical Dancing* (Princeton: Princeton Book Co., 1987), 14.
[14] Ibid., 15.
[15] "J'ai vu cette danse sur vieux vases grecs." Gustave Flaubert, *Voyage en Orient*, Préface de Claudine Gothot-Mersch (Paris: Gallimard, 2006), 133.

[16] "Elle s'y met—son col glisse sur les vertèbres d'arrière en avant et plus souvent de côté, de manière à croire que la tête va tomber." Ibid., 141.

[17] Flaubert's readings include *Livres sacrés de l'Orient,* translated by Guillaume Pauthier in 1840; *Le Recueil d'Antiquités égyptiennes, étrusques, grecques et romaines* in two volumes, published by Desaint et Saillant in 1761; *An Account of Manners and Customs of the Modern Egyptians*, published in London at Knight in 1837; and *Le Voyage en Egypte et en Syrie de Volney*. Flaubert took with him a Bible, Homer, Herodotus and *The Manual of the Archeology of Art* in three volumes by Edward W. Lane.

[18] Gustave Flaubert, *Voyage en Orient*, 177.

[19] "L'idée de décrire la danse de la femme-enfant, offerte presque nue aux regards de toute une foule, ne pouvait qu'enflammer l'imagination de Flaubert. Il y voit aussi une façon de revenir en esprit vers cet Orient qu'il avait connu en 1850—la Palestine, l'Egypte—paysage et souvenirs érotiques." *Postface et notes de Pierre-Marc de Biasi*, L'école des lettres (Paris: Seuil, 1993), 258.

[20] "Il ne s'agit seulement de voir, il faut arranger et fondre ce que l'on a vu. La Réalité, selon moi, ne doit être qu'un tremplin." Ibid., 260.

[21] Ibid., 260.

[22] See Daniel Arasse, *On n'y voit rien* (Paris: Editions Denoel, 2000).

[23] Quoted in Tooke, *Flaubert and the Pictorial Arts*, 228-229.

[24] This citation is taken from P-M de Biasi, *Trois contes / Postface et notes de Pierre-Marc de Biasi*, 268.

[25] Margaret Lowe and Colin Burns, "Flaubert's 'Herodias' – a New Evaluation" *Montjoie* I (May 1953), 14.

[26] Salome is also depicted dancing on her hands on the stained glass of the cathedral of Bourges and on a miniature in an English psalter with which Flaubert was not familiar.

CHAPTER EIGHT

WILDE'S *SALOME*

In February 1893 the Librarie de l'Art Indépendant in Paris, along with the joint publishers Elkin Mathews and John Lane in London, published in French Oscar Wilde's play *Salome*. When the play appeared, Wilde received a number of laudatory letters from his French-speaking fellow writers, including French symbolist poet Stéphane Mallarmé, whose poem *Noces de Hérodiade* was discussed earlier; Belgian symbolist playwright Maurice Maeterlinck, who had a strong impact on turn-of-the-century European theater (including Wilde's *Salome*); and French writer Pierre Loti. After Mallarmé read Wilde's *Salome*, he wrote:

> My dear Poet
> I marvel that, while everything in your *Salome* is expressed in constant, dazzling strokes, there also arises, on each page, the unutterable and the Dream.
> So the innumerable and precise jewels can serve only as an accompaniment to the gown for the supernatural gesture of that young Princess whom you definitely evoked.
>
> Friendly greetings from
> Stéphane Mallarmé

Maurice Maeterlinck in his letter to Wilde also expressed his admiration of *Salome*:

> Pray excuse me, dear sir, if my circumstances have not permitted me to thank you sooner for the gift of your mysterious, strange, and admirable *Salome*. I expressed my thanks to you today as I emerged, for the third time, from this dream whose power I have not yet explained to myself. I assure you of my great admiration.

Pierre Loti's reaction was similar to Mallarmé's and Maeterlinck's: "Thank you, sir, for having introduced me to your *Salome*—it is fine and somber like a chapter of the Apocalypse—I admire it deeply."[1]

Wilde wrote *Salome* in French in 1891 during his extended visit to

Paris. According to his friend Gomez Carrillo, a young Guatemalan diplomat and writer, Wilde at first wrote some pages in prose, and then he changed his mind and decided to write a poem. But gradually he came to the conclusion that it was a play that he was interested in writing. One evening he told his version of the Salome story to a group of friends, mainly young French writers. When he returned to his rooms he saw the blank notebook sitting on the table and it inspired him to write down the Salome story that he had just told to his friends. Later he pretended that "If the book had not been there I should never have dreamed of doing it."[2] He spent the evening writing before going out to the Grand Café, then located at the corner of the boulevard des Capucines and the rue Scribe. In that cafe there was a concert of the orchestra of Tziganes, directed by a man named Rigo who was known for having run away with the Princesse de Chimay, Clara Ward. Wilde called him over and told him "he was writing a play about a woman dancing with her bare feet in the blood of a man she has craved for and slain." He then added, "I want you to play something in harmony with my thoughts." Apparently Rigo played such wild and terrible music that those who were there stopped talking and looked at each other with blanched faces. Following this performance, Wilde went home and finished *Salome*.[3]

Although the writing of *Salome* might seem impressively fast, Wilde had been thinking of Salome for a long time and he was well familiar with Salome's iconography. He had seen Titian's *Salome* (Fig. II-5-4), located in the Prado Museum in Madrid, and knew the Salome images of Veronese, Rubens, Bernardino Luini (Fig. I-2-9), Ghirlandaio, Dürer and Callisto Piazza. He had seen Henri Regnault's famous *Salome* (Fig. I-4-7). Yet for Wilde none of those images captured the spirit of Salome as he imagined her. The only one that truly inspired him was Gustave Moreau's, a description of which he first encountered in Chapter V of J-K Huysmans' novel *A Rebours* (*Against Nature*) in June of 1884 during his honeymoon in Paris. Apparently Wilde liked to quote Huysmans' almost diabolic description of Moreau's *Salome*:

> She is almost naked! In the heat of the dance her veils have become loosened, the brocaded robes have fallen away, and only the jewels protect her naked body. A slender belt binds her waist, a superb jewel shines like a star between her breasts; below, a band of garnets covers her thighs and two shining emeralds hide her sex.[4]

It is said that it was after reading *A Rebours* that Wilde began to think of writing his play. Apparently there were periods in his life when he was simply obsessed with Salome. His young friend Gomez Carrillo recalls:

Wilde never ceased to speak of Salomé. Women passing in the street would remind him of her and he would wander through the Parisian streets, looking in jewelers' windows and imagining the perfect jewellery for the adornment of her body.

One evening after a long empty silence, he suddenly said to me right in the middle of the street:

–   Don't you think she would be better completely naked?

At once I understood we were talking about Her.

–   Yes, he continued, utterly naked. But with jewels, many jewels, interlacing strands of jewels; the gems flashing, tinkling and jingling at her ankles, her wrists, her arms, about her neck, around her waist; their reflection making the utter shamelessness of that warm flesh even more shocking . . . Her lust must be an abyss, her corruptness, an ocean. The very pearls must die of love upon her bosom. The fragrance of her maidenhood must make the emeralds dim, and inflame the rubies' fire. On that burning flesh even the sapphire must lose the unstained purity of its azure blue.[5]

Wilde was also familiar with various literary manifestations of Salome. He had read Heine's famous poem *Atta Troll*, inspired by German medieval mysteries, in which a ghost of Salome/Hérodiade is in love with John the Baptist.[6] The ghost of Salome/Hérodiade plays with and repeatedly kisses the severed head of the Baptist. Wilde also read Flaubert's short story "Herodias,"[7] Mallarmé's poem "Hérodiade,"[8] Laforgue's story "Salome," and basically all other writings, including minor works, dedicated to Salome in late nineteenth-century literature. It is possible that he was particularly influenced by the book of the American writer J.C. Heywood, whose poem *Salome* he reviewed in the *Pall Mall Gazette* in February 1888. The poem was first published in the 1860s and then republished in 1888. Like Heine, Heywood uses the image of Salome/Hérodiade kissing the head of the Baptist, but in Heywood's version she is a real person rather than a ghost. Wilde, in expanding this scene, made it the pinnacle of his play.

In 1890 Wilde told his friends that he was planning to write *Salome*. Richard Ellmann tells us:

[Wilde] had dinner at a Piccadilly restaurant with [the American writer] Edgar Saltus, and afterwards they visited Lord Francis Hope in his rooms across the street. The decor of the rooms was generally sober, an exception being an engraving of Herodias dancing on her hands, as she is pictured doing in Flaubert's 'Hérodias.' Wilde went up to the picture, and said, '*La bella donna della mia mente.*' According to Mrs Saltus, Wilde said he would write about her, and Saltus, who planned to write about Mary Magdalene, replied, 'Do so. We will pursue the wantons together.' Saltus's book came out first, and Wilde praised it as 'so pessimistic, so poisonous, and so perfect.'. . . Saltus returned the compliment when he read *Salome*, saying that the last line had made him shudder.[9]

When Wilde visited the home of the poet Jean Lorrain, who in 1883 had also published a poem about Salome, Wilde saw the sculpted head of a decapitated woman. That sculpture reminded Wilde of a story apparently taken from a Nubian gospel discovered by Boissière. It relates the tale of a young philosopher to whom Salome sent the severed head of John the Baptist as a token of her love. In recognition of the gift the philosopher bowed and said:

> "What I really want, beloved, is your head.". . . The afternoon of the same day a slave presents the philosopher with his darling's head on a gold platter. And the philosopher asks, "Why are they bringing this bloody thing to me?" and goes on reading Plato. Doesn't it seem to you that this princess is Salome? Yes, and—pointing to the bust—'this marble is her head. With this execution John the Baptist had his revenge'[10]

Seeing this sculpture gave Wilde the idea of writing a play called *The Decapitation of Salome*. In this play he wanted to combine the punishment of Salome for John the Baptist's decapitation with her becoming a saint. Following in the tradition of folklore, he planned to link two different stories together: the story of Magdalene—and her wanderings in the desert—and the medieval mysteries in which Salome is decapitated by ice. Wilde told Maurice Maeterlinck that

> Herod, incensed at her kissing the decapitated head, wanted to have her crushed, but at the pleas of Herodias contented himself with banishing her. She went off to the desert, where for years she lived on, maligned, solitary, clothed in animal skins, . . . When Jesus passed by, she recognized him whom the dead voice had heralded and she believed in him. But, feeling unworthy of living in his shadow, she went off again, with the intention of carrying the Word. Having passed over rivers and seas, she encountered, after the fiery deserts, the deserts of snow. One day she was crossing a frozen lake near the Rhône when the ice broke under her feet. She fell into the water and the jagged ice cut into her flesh and decapitated her, though not before she managed to utter the names of Jesus and John. And those who later went by saw, on the silver plate of the re-formed ice, showing like the stamen of a flower with rubies, a severed head on which gleamed the crown of a golden nimbus.[11]

As we know, Wilde did not pursue this idea. But in his final version he remained faithful to his conviction that "All excess, as well as all renunciation, brings its own punishment."[12]

While Wilde was considering his Salome, he saw at the Moulin Rouge in Paris a Romanian acrobat dancing on her hands, like Salome in Flaubert's short story "Herodias." Wilde was very impressed by her, even going so far as to write her a note inviting her to dance the part of Salome in his future work if it were staged. She never replied to his invitation but his encounter with her dance added to his motivation to create his own dancer.

Although Wilde's *Salome* had many sources of influence, its interest lies in its originality. One could consider his play a kind of summation of all existing Salomes created before his. The Salome of Wilde has features from Moreau's painting *Salome Dancing in Front of Herod*—features that had been described and perceived through the eyes of Des Esseintes in Huysmans' novel *A Rebours*. Moreover, Wilde attributes to his heroine the masculine role of a Lover as opposed to the feminine role of the Beloved, and brings to the reader a number of striking messages about his views on women, religion and art. Wilde's play might also be a kind of dialogue with Mallarmé's unfinished poem *Hérodiade* or a homage to it. Some aspects of the play, like Mallarmé's poem, address Wilde's aesthetics and philosophy of creativity. Finally, on a more basic level, the play is an illustration of Wilde's belief that the successful work of art should be profoundly dramatic, because "the world will never weary of watching the troubled soul in its progress from darkness to darkness."[13]

As we have seen, Chapter V of *A Rebours* has Huysmans describe two *Salomes* by Gustave Moreau through the eyes of Des Esseintes: the oil painting *Salome Dancing in Front of Herod* and a watercolor, *The Apparition*. It is Des Esseintes' perception of *Salome Dancing in Front of Herod* that served as an inspiration for Wilde:

> No longer was she just the dancer who by a shameless gyration of her hips wrests a lustful, ruttish cry from an old man, who destroys the resoluteness and breaks the will of a king with thrusts of her breasts, undulations of her belly, and quivering of her thighs; there she became, in a sense, the symbolic deity of indestructible Lechery, the goddess of immortal Hysteria, the accursed Beauty . . . the monstrous, indiscriminate, irresponsible, unfeeling Beast who, like the Helen of Antiquity, poisons everything that comes near her, everything that sees her, everything that she touches.[14]

Wilde's Salome seems to be a perfect illustration of this description. In the play, Salome, "like the Helen of Antiquity, poisons everything that comes near her." She manipulates the Young Syrian into opening the cistern where Jokanaan is locked, despite Herod's interdiction:

Thou wilt do this thing for me, Narraboth. Thou knowest that thou wilt do this thing for me. And on the morrow when I shall pass in my litter by the bridge of the idol-buyers, I will look at thee through the muslin veils, I will look at thee, Narraboth, it may be I will smile at thee. Look at me, Narraboth, look at me. Ah! thou knowest that thou wilt do what I ask of thee. Thou knowest it. . . . . I know that thou wilt do this thing.[15]

The moment the Young Syrian fulfills her wish she forgets about him. When he commits suicide for not being able to bear his beautiful Princess humiliating herself, she is absolutely oblivious to it. Her only answer is "Suffer me to kiss thy mouth, Jokanaan."[16]

In Wilde's play, Salome is determined to fulfill her hidden plan to get the head of John the Baptist in order to kiss his mouth.[17] She manipulates Herod's lust for her in order to get what she wishes. Thus she brings death, pain or imbalance to everybody who is attracted to her or to whom she is attracted. Her behavior undoubtedly fits Huysmans' description. She is "the monstrous, indiscriminate, irresponsible, unfeeling Beast who, like the Helen of Antiquity, poisons everything that comes near her, everything that sees her, everything that she touches."[18] As we saw earlier, this description is typical of the male description of women, especially toward the end of the nineteenth century.[19]

Wilde's Salome dance is highly sensual. It is the dance of Seven Veils, an invention of Wilde, and the effect that Salome produces while dancing is the same as that found in *A Rebours*. But Wilde's Salome, unlike Salome in Huysmans' novel, is not "draped in jewels and purple, . . . powdered and rouged."[20] Seen through the eyes of the Young Syrian, she resembles Maeterlinck's feminine characters, who are fragile, pure and innocent: "She is like the shadow of a white rose in a mirror of silver. . . . She is like a dove that has strayed. . . . She is like a narcissus trembling in the wind.... She is like a silver flower."[21] Salome, while looking at her reflection in the moon, describes the moon in ways that suggest her perception of herself, a pure and severe virgin: She is "cold and chaste," a virgin who "never defiled herself; never abandoned herself to men."[22] It is a description nearly akin to that of Mallarmé's Hérodiade.

By creating a striking contrast between Salome's innocence, purity and fragility and her "monstrous, indiscriminate, irresponsible, unfeeling" personality, Wilde constructs a quite standard nineteenth-century image of *a femme fatale*, a dangerous and destructive woman, beautiful in appearance and dreadful in her essence.

At the same time, Wilde uses Salome's behavior to portray a more complex character than the typical nineteenth-century *femme fatale*. Salome is a tragic hero whose *hubris* is her pride in a Shakespearian sense, because it is her pride that dictates her actions and which eventually destroys her. She is a spoiled, willful, proud princess, who wants everything to be her own way. She is determined to kiss John's mouth at any price, and John's rejection of her only reinforces her determination. For her, it becomes an issue of pride. By adding to Salome the features of a tragic hero, Wilde shapes his character on a more multidimensional scale, a scale that is more human and more complex than Huysmans' Salome and the usual nineteenth-century *femme fatale*.

* * *

Much of the language used by Wilde throughout *Salome* is rooted in the *Song of Songs*, and through the language he permeates the play with the spirit of androgyny. Yet Wilde's *Song of Songs* is quite different from the biblical version. The biblical *Songs of Songs* is a love poem, and its title uses the Hebrew superlative to suggest it is the loveliest of all songs.[23] It consists of a number of poems depicting the passionate and affectionate love between a Lover and a Beloved who are meeting and parting and who are seeking and finding each other. The poetry is filled with striking images and colors. The Lover is a man, called king, and the beloved is a woman, called "the girl of Shulam." Wilde reverses the roles of the Lover and the Beloved by making Salome the bearer of the language of the Lover and John the Baptist the bearer of the language of the Beloved. The Lover is the one who courts the Beloved, and that is what Salome does in Wilde's play: She courts John the Baptist, Jokanaan. The Beloved is the one who is courted, and in the play John the Baptist is the one whom Salome courts. But in the conversations between Salome and John the Baptist (Jokanaan) there are no exchanges of mutual love; rather, it is an exchange of unrequited love and passion, a dialogue of hate and rejection. For example, in the Second Poem of the *Song of Songs,* the Beloved sings:

> My love lifts up his voice,
> he says to me,
> "Come then, my beloved,
> my lovely one, come." (2:10)

Jokanaan, in comparison, the moment he sees Salome, yells, "Back! Daughter of Babylon! *Come not*[24] near the chosen of the Lord." The essence of this is repeated a number of times in the play, almost as a refrain: "Daughter of Sodom, *come not near me!*"[25]

In this inversion of the characters' genders Wilde refashions both Salome and John the Baptist as androgynous beings. This allows Wilde to mock them and to infuse the play with the spirit of parody. Androgyny, in earlier times and at the end of the nineteenth century, was associated with a kind of universality and perfection. It takes us back to Plato's *Symposium* and Aristophanes' tale about the origins of humanity, before human beings were divided in two by the gods. Thus the original human was androgynous, in possession of the perfect love, since the two halves were united. At the turn of the twentieth century some writers perceived androgyny as the state of an ideal being, a result of the fulfillment of earthly evolution and growth. If deserved, this earthly evolution, at the moment of death, would culminate in the initiation to the ideal eternal world, in which gender does not exist and the ideal being is therefore androgynous.

As in Aristophanes, neither John nor Salome, as two separate halves of one whole, represent an ideal. However, as a unified whole they represent an ideal—but an ideal maleficence. They complement each other's ill-tempered qualities and are thus more than the sum of their parts—they are a united couple that is perfect through their imperfections. John is a cranky, intolerant, unloving and nasty prophet, and Salome is a spoiled, proud, stubborn and vengeful young girl, obsessed with her selfish desires. Furthermore, by making each character separately androgynous, Wilde mockingly conveys the idea that each of them is perfect, but once again he stresses the issue of their perfection in their perfect imperfection. This is Wilde's way of parodying his characters, the idea of paradise, the story of Salome's dance and John the Baptist's beheading resulting from it.

In the play, although the language is that of the *Song of Songs*, Wilde endows the exchange between John and Salome not only with new gender roles but he also gives his own meaning to the *Song of Songs'* colors. Among other things, this new color attribution shapes the masculine and feminine images of the two characters. When Salome sees John the Baptist for the first time, her first observation, like the observations of the Lover in the *Songs of Songs*, is about the Baptist's eyes. In the *Song of Songs* the eyes are compared to doves:

> How beautiful you are, my beloved,
> how beautiful you are!
> Your eyes are doves. (1:15)

Salome, in contrast, finds Jokanaan's eyes terrifying. She perceives them as black holes:

> It is his eyes above all that are terrible. They are like black holes burned by torches in a tapestry of Tyre. They are like the black caverns of Egypt in

which the dragons make their lairs. They are like black lakes troubled by fantastic moons.[26]

When Salome first speaks to John the Baptist she begins by expressing her admiration for his body, like the Lover in the *Songs of Songs*:

> The curve of your thighs is like the curve of a necklace,
> work of a master hand.
> Your navel is a bowl well rounded
> with no lack of wine,
> your belly a head of wheat
> surrounded with lilies.
> Your two breasts are two fawns,
> twins of a gazelle. (7:1-3)

The Lover in the *Song of Songs* concentrates especially on the shape of his Beloved's body and calls attention to her belly, the symbol of fertility and procreation. He also endows her form with color by bringing in the red of wine and the white of lilies, the colors of passion and purity. Salome, by comparison, mentions nothing of the shape of John's body, stressing only her admiration of its whiteness:

> I am amorous of thy body, Jokanaan! Thy body is white like the lilies of a field that the mower hath never mowed. Thy body is white like the snows that lie on the mountains of Judaea, and come down into the valleys. The roses in the garden of the Queen of Arabia are not so white as thy body. Neither the roses of the garden of the Queen of Arabia, the garden of spices of the Queen of Arabia, nor the feet of the dawn when they light on the leaves, nor the breast of the moon when she lies on the breast of the sea…. There is nothing in the world as white as thy body. Suffer me to touch thy body.[27]

Then, as in the *Songs of Songs*, Salome moves to praising Jokanaan's hair, though in the *Song of Songs* the Lover only compares his Beloved's hair with a flock of goats:

> Your hair is like a flock of goats
> surging down Mount Gilead. (6:5)

Salome compares the Baptist's hair to "clusters of grapes" and she especially stresses the hair's blackness:

> Thy hair is like clusters of grapes, like the clusters of black grapes that hang from the vine-trees of Edom in the land of the Edomites. Thy hair is

like the cedars of Lebanon. . . . The long black nights, when the moon hides her face, when the stars are afraid, are not so black as thy hair. The silence that dwells in the forest is not so black. There is nothing in the world that is so black as thy hair.[28]

Both Salome and the Lover in the *Song of Songs* praise the lips of their Beloveds. The biblical Lover notes both the appearance and the utterances of his Beloved: "Your lips are a scarlet thread," which utter "enchanting words." (4:3) Salome gives particular attention to the scarlet color of the Baptist's lips but says nothing of what the lips utter:

Thy mouth is like a band of scarlet on a tower of ivory. It is like a pomegranate cut in twain with a knife of ivory. . . . The red blasts of trumpets that herald the approach of kings, and make afraid the enemy, are not so red. Thy mouth is redder than the beet of the doves who inhabit the temples and are fed by the priests. . . . Thy mouth is like a branch of coral that fishers have found in the twilight of the sea, the coral that they keep for the kings! . . . There is nothing in the world so red as thy mouth.[29]

Wilde's own palette of colors and his usage of the *Song of Songs*' language bring a particular meaning to the play. His colors—black, white, again black and then red—allow the reader to "hear with his eyes,"[30] and to see the thread of the story, "watching the troubled soul in its progress from darkness to darkness."[31] The colors confirm the masculine role of Salome in the play. When Salome sees Jokanaan's eyes they are "black holes." Eyes can function as a mirror, and they are often considered to be the mirror of one's soul. John's eyes mirror the terrifying precipice into which one might fall to find one's death, because black is a color of the end and of death, pain and failure. Thus from the start Salome's encounter with John and her first impressions of him foreshadow the catastrophic end. Both the language of the play and the black color of John's terrifying eyes seem to hint at this tragic outcome and at Salome's masculine role in it. Perhaps Salome sees herself mirrored in those eyes in the guise of John's executioner.

The foreboding presence of the color black is repeated in the description of Jokanaan's hair. Hair carries connotations of power and—especially at the turn of the nineteenth century—of femininity. Both the hair of Samson in the Bible and the hair of Medusa in Greek mythology are symbols of power. Hair is also a feminine attribute. The Pre-Raphaelite artists, especially Dante Gabriel Rossetti, with whose works Wilde was well familiar, created an image of a *femme fatale* whose primary and most attractive attribute was often long seductive hair. Hair at the turn of the nineteenth century is a trope of feminine power, and black hair—and

Salome stresses its blackness—might be seen as a symbol of a black, destructive power. Hence, Salome as a Lover compliments John as the Beloved on the beauty of his hair while she sees in his hair the foreshadowing of the power that will eventually destroy both of them.

The colors white and red also factor prominently in Wilde's evocative verbal palette. White is the color of virginity and innocence, attributed to females and praised by males. Yet it is Salome who praises John and attributes to him and his body the white color, highlighting his femininity and his holiness. The lack of Salome's praise or even mention of John's body, in particular of his "belly," seems to symbolize Salome's and John's union, complementary in all their negative traits, unable to procreate and deprived of any future. Red, the color of John's lips, the color of passion and blood, represents the essence of the story and foreshadows the future developments: Salome's passion—the passion of a Lover—for her Beloved John, John's passionate rejection of her and ultimately his bloody death by decapitation and her death on the orders of Herod.

Wilde's play departs further from the *Song of Songs* when Salome's advances are spurned by the Baptist. After being rejected, Salome begins her speeches to John by saying how much she hates what she has just praised: "Thy body is hideous,"[32] and then: "Thy hair is horrible."[33] The only time Salome does not express a disgust for what she previously praised is when she talks about Jokanaan's mouth. Even after her rejection she still seems to be attracted to his mouth and finds it beautiful, since she tells him, "I will kiss your mouth, Jokanaan. I will kiss your mouth."[34] As we previously saw in the *Song of Songs*, when the Lover praises the beauty of the lips of his Beloved he adds that they utter enchanting words. The mouth, contrary to the body and hair, is a symbol of an expression of thoughts, of something within and of something intangible. Thus, on a symbolic level, it is possible to see that through the kiss Salome hopes to be initiated to Jokanaan's thoughts, his mind, his life and his religion—in short to his world. The kiss is a symbol of love. Thus it is through love that Salome hopes to enter that new and unknown world that she perceives in Jokanaan and that so fascinates her.

It seems that at this point Wilde goes further than parody and introduces the elements of satire. John is a prophet who is supposed to prophesy love, the symbol of Christianity and the essence of the teachings of Christ, and in doing so to attract newcomers to the religion of Jesus. Instead, his behavior is filled with hatred, intolerance, fanaticism and repulsion. In the character of Salome he has potentially found a new convert, but instead of noticing it he does everything to push her away. Since Salome is determined to enter John's world at any cost, she enters it through his hate and her revenge. It is these destructive and negative emotions that eventually lead to the death of both of them. Hence, it seems that through the story of Salome and John the Baptist Wilde satirizes Christianity as an institution; he mocks its blind and often cruel fanaticism and the intolerance of its servants of God.

A consideration of Plato's love dialogue *Symposium* and *Phaedrus* will further strengthen the notion that Wilde's play was meant partly as Christian satire and partly as a parody of the relationship between John the Baptist and Salome. Literary classics such as Plato were part of Wilde's cultural milieu, and such a line of inquiry is thus a fruitful area of research. In Plato's love dialogues, the Lover was usually an older man and the Beloved was a young boy whom the older man courted. Through the love affair with the Lover, the Beloved would receive not only a sexual education but an intellectual and political one, as well. According to Plato, the most important and the ultimate role of the Lover was to lead the Beloved toward the highest spheres of existence, toward perfection and the eventual union with God.[35]

In the Bible, John the Baptist is supposed to play the role of the teacher and to lead toward this perfection and union with God. But in Wilde's play there is an inversion, and the Baptist is the Beloved, whose role is to learn a lesson; Salome is then the Lover, the one whose role is to give the lesson. Thus, on some basic literal level, we can interpret the relationship between Salome and the Baptist as one of her imparting a lesson: Essentially, you rejected me and you have to pay for it by losing your head, since figuratively I lost mine over you. By inverting the situation—making John the pupil and Salome his teacher—Wilde mocks it, as well: The supposedly fervent Christian becomes the pupil of an uncontrollable pagan. Her lesson, though, is striking in its pettiness, primitivism and lack of true substance.

Wilde mocks John in the role of the Beloved who, as a precursor of Christianity, fully fails his leading role. But he also mocks Salome and her status as a woman in the position of a Lover. For Wilde, a woman in the position of leadership can be concerned only with base, primitive and petty issues. Since a woman lives not by the power of the mind and rationality but by the destructive and uncontrollable power of emotions she is a symbol of a creature that is fully human. Hence, by attributing to Salome the male role of the Lover and to the Baptist the female role of the Beloved, Wilde once again satirizes the legend. Such an inversion also conveys typical nineteenth-century fears of a new woman, a *femme fatale* who, although primitive and mindless, is gaining social power and eventually might take a leading male role in society, pushing man to take her female place and, if refused, destroying him. He reinforces the message in the words of the Young Syrian, who uses the language of the Lover from the *Song of Songs* and treats Salome as his Beloved. The Young Syrian uselessly perishes, without any recognition or gratitude, because of his love for her. Wilde's message thus implies that a woman in any role, either as Lover or Beloved, would find a way to use man and lead him to his perdition. "Gentlemen! Beware of women!" Oscar seems to cry, echoing the words of his contemporaries.

Richard Ellmann, in his article "Overtures to Salome," suggests that Wilde's *Salome* in a way represents the author's philosophy of art and life. Wilde, while a student, was very much influenced by two major figures in the field of art criticism and philosophy: John Ruskin and Walter Pater, both of whom were his teachers at Oxford. Ruskin's philosophy of art is mainly based on Christian morality; Pater's is rooted in a pagan view of the world. Pater celebrates the sensation of pleasure that comes from the beauty of art, which often hides the perversity and evil. Ruskin celebrates the pleasure of Christian morality that, according to him, is conveyed in art. Wilde vacillated for a while between the arguments of Ruskin and Pater, but eventually he came to the conclusion that those extremes were not essential. In his view there was something in between and it was okay to be a Ruskinian at one moment and a Paterian at another. Thus, in his play, Wilde seems to apply his own view of art. Salome, the pagan princess who lives by instinct and the sensation of the moment, can be taken as a symbol of the Paterian philosophy of art, with John serving as a symbol of Ruskin's views. Since both perish by the end of the play it seems that Wilde's execution of his characters is also the annihilation of both extreme points of view.

There are two characters in the play who represent a constantly changing point of view: one is the moon, a symbol of eternity and of the eternal necessity to change and to adapt oneself to new circumstances, and the other is Herod, the character who has the ability to change and to adapt himself to the situation and to his own needs of the moment. By attributing to those characters the winning position in the play, Wilde may be commenting on the flexibility of art. Art, in this view, survives because of its ability to change, and it is not bound to follow the inflexible philosophies of either Pater or Ruskin. Aubrey Beardsley captured Wilde's inclination to make Herod and the moon his heroes, and for that reason he portrayed the moon and Herod with Wilde's face, to be read as a symbol of constant change, flexibility and adaptability.

Wilde believed that art is more powerful than life, that art does not imitate life and that the life one leads should be a reflection of one's creative impulses and imaginative perception. His view is typical for the turn-of-the-century Symbolist movement. It seems that his character of Salome epitomizes this view. As Rodney Shewan points out: "In 'The Critic as Artist,' Wilde had developed a theory about the relationship between form and feeling,"[36] in which Wilde talks about some kind of self-hypnosis through language. Wilde states that the form one uses might influence the evolution of one's feelings. If one uses powerful metaphorical descriptions/expressions—as Salome does in creating aesthetic images of John while talking to him—those metaphors might become so convincing that the speaker himself will eventually believe in them. Thus will his feelings be shaped by the images and the metaphors he creates. It is a sort of self-hypnosis. Wilde writes:

> Yes; Form is everything. It is the secret of life. . . . Find expression for a joy and you will intensify its ecstasy. Do you wish to love? Use Love's Litany, and the words will create the yearning from which the world fancies that they spring. Have you a grief that corrodes your heart? Steep yourself in the language of grief, learn its utterance from Prince Hamlet and Queen Constance, and you will find that Form, which is the birth of passion, is also the death of pain.[37]

Salome's way of speaking to John as she tries to seduce him but is consistently rejected becomes a proof of this theory. She comes up with newly formed images while talking to him. As the play proceeds, Salome begins to believe in what she is saying. Initially, her metaphorical speech is the reflection of her desire to be noticed and appreciated for her beauty, charm and royalty—a desire for attention—but then it begins to reflect her stubborn determination to get what she thinks she is entitled to: John's attention and his attraction to her. John's rejection of her makes her language increasingly passionate and irrational. As Shewan contends, "The third speech is almost pure stream-of-consciousness, the images becoming progressively less concrete and more subjective."[38] Everything that happens in her is reflected in her language, and the language is so real to her that it culminates in her being convinced that she had been John's lover, although in reality he never even looked at her. "I was a virgin, and thou didst take my virginity from me," she claims.[39] Thus, in a way she reflects Wilde's theory of art: She is like an artist who, through her imagination, creates her own reality which, in the process of its creation, becomes more real and more powerful than the physical reality surrounding her. Like a work of art it has become independent of its creator and just as real. However, the tragic ending of the play, with Salome's death as well as the death of John the Baptist, does not necessarily look favorably upon such turn-of-the-century aesthetic philosophies. Could it be that in using the character of Salome, a *femme fatale*, as the epitome of this philosophy Wilde was perhaps parodying it?

* * *

As we saw earlier, the notion of the glance was very important in the second part of the nineteenth century and it plays a symbolic role of initiation in Mallarmé's unfinished poem *Les Noces d'Hérodiade*.[40] Interestingly, Wilde introduces the idea of the glance and makes it essential in his play. In his case, the pinnacle of the glance is John's inability to look at Salome and Salome's ability to look at him and to "see" him. "To look at the thing is very different from seeing a thing. One does not see anything until one sees its beauty. Then, and then only, does it come into existence," wrote Wilde.[41] The destruction comes from those inharmonious relationships between looking and seeing.

Wilde never denied that he was a literary thief. He even stated: "When I see a monstrous tulip with *four* petals in someone else's garden, I am impelled to grow a monstrous tulip with *five* wonderful petals."[42] It is possible that Wilde uses the idea of the glance in *Salome* in reference to Mallarmé and his unfinished poem *Le Noces d'Hérodiade*.

The two men had known each other since February 1891, when Wilde was writing a preface for his novel *The Picture of Dorian Gray*. Wilde first visited Mallarmé's *mardis* on February 24, at which he was very well received and to which he was happy to return the following week. In October 1891, Wilde was in Paris again and visited the *mardi* on the third of November. For this visit he prepared a copy of his newly published novel, *The Picture of Dorian Gray*, with a homage to Mallarmé's art. Wilde had a great appreciation of Mallarmé's work, and Mallarmé was very much impressed by Wilde's, especially *The Picture of Dorian Gray*. As Richard Ellmann points out:

> It [Wilde's novel] shared the preoccupation of Mallarmé's verse with the way that the borders of life and art, the real and the unreal, shift under the pressure of the imagination. . . . Both Mallarmé and Wilde saw literature as the supreme art, and one that could transform a painting into words, a life into an artifice.[43]

Wilde began to think about writing *Salome* before he met Mallarmé but it is possible that the meeting with Mallarmé accelerated the genesis of the play. Perhaps the writing of *Salome* and the choice to do so in French, both of which occurred at the time when Wilde became personally acquainted with Mallarmé, were the result of a hidden or subconscious desire to outdo Mallarmé. It was no secret that Mallarmé was writing *Hérodiade* and that he hoped to express through the poem his philosophy of art. It was also known that Mallarmé had difficulties finishing the poem. Thus there is the possibility that Mallarmé and Wilde exchanged ideas on the topic, and perhaps Mallarmé even shared with Wilde his idea of *viol occulaire*, although Wilde could also have learned about it from their common friends, the participants of the *mardis*, with whom he occasionally lunched and dined.

At the end of the play, using the language of the *Song of Songs* and speaking of the beauty of Jokanaan, Salome accentuates the importance of the ability to look and to be able to see what can be beautiful and what would become a reality once discovered through the process of seeing.[44] "The poet is one who looks," said André Gide. Salome to a degree is a poet, and she has a poetic vision of the world. John the Baptist's image is a product of her imagination and is therefore her work of art. When her work of art fails to turn out the way she intended she kills the work of art, becoming in that moment the classic figure of the frustrated artist. The ultimate consequence of this failure—the death of Salome—turns her into a symbol of the artist who, unable to fill his artistic aim, is condemned to cease all artistic activity. In this way the artist—and to a degree, Salome—becomes a martyr for his cause.

Salome's way of addressing the issue of truly seeing, and of thereby creating through the process of seeing, is strikingly expressed at the end of the play:

> Thy body was a column of ivory set upon feet of silver. It was a garden full of doves and lilies of silver. It was a tower of silver decked with shields of ivory. There was nothing in the world so black as thy hair. In the whole world there was nothing so red as thy mouth. Thy voice was a censer that scattered strange perfumes, and when I looked on thee I heard a strange music. . . . Well, thou hast seen thy God, Jokanaan, but me, me, thou didst never see. If thou hadst seen me thou hadst loved me. I saw thee, and I loved thee. Oh, how I loved thee! I love thee yet, Jokanaan, I love only thee. . . . I am athirst for thy beauty; . . . Ah! Ah! Wherefore didst thou not look at me? If thou hadst looked at me thou hadst loved me. Well I know that thou wouldst have loved me, and the mystery of love is greater than the mystery of death.[45]

In Mallarmé's poem the meaning of John's glance is perceived by Hérodiade/Salome as a visual rape. On a more symbolic level, John's glance and his exchanges with Hérodiade play the role of an initiation into the world of supreme Beauty, of the Absolute.[46] In Wilde's play, the ability to look and to see is also associated with Beauty and an initiation to it. If the character of Salome is an embodiment of an aesthetic beauty whereas the character of John embodies the ethical beauty, the union of the two is the realization of supreme Beauty. However, in the play the aesthetic beauty, Salome, is rejected by the ethical, John, whose ethics deny the potential wholeness. John's refusal to look and his inability to see lead to the non-realization of supreme Beauty and to the inversion of initiation, which is the death of Beauty's disjointed components. Thus for Wilde the complete Beauty, which for him symbolizes art, must embody both aesthetics and ethics. Without a union, Beauty is incomplete and will not survive.

Wilde never read Mallarmé's final version of the triptych of *Hérodiade* (Ouverture, Scène and Cantique de St. Jean). It was published long after both of their deaths. But Mallarmé did read Wilde's *Salome* and, as we saw earlier, greatly admired it. Could it be that it is Wilde's use of looking and seeing in *Salome* that helped Mallarmé establish his own relationship between the ability to look and the notion of Beauty as a part of his philosophy of art? Could Mallarmé's *Hérodiade* be a sort of homage to Wilde?

Notes

[1] All three citations are taken from Richard Ellmann, *Oscar Wilde* (New York: Alfred A. Knopf, 1988), 375.
[2] Ellmann, *Oscar Wilde,* 343.
[3] Ibid., 343-344.
[4] The quote is taken from Joseph Pearce, *The Unmasking of Oscar Wilde* (London: Harper Collins Publishers, 2000), 192. The French reads: "Elle est presque nue; dans l'ardeur de la danse, les voiles se sont défaits, les brocarts ont croulé ; elle n'est plus vêtue que de matières orfévries et de minéraux lucides ; un gorgerin lui serre de même qu'un corselet la taille, et, ainsi qu'une agrafe superbe, un merveilleux joyau darde des éclairs dans la rainure de ses deux seins; plus bas, aux hanches, une ceinture l'entoure, cache le haut de ses cuisses que bat une gigantesque pendeloque où coule une rivière d'escarboucles et d'émeraudes." Joris-Karl Huysmans, *A Rebours* (Bibliothèque de L'Académie Goncourt Les Éditions G. Crès et Cie 21, Rue Hautefeuille – Paris, 1922), 103-104, available online at http://fr.wikisource.org/wiki/À_rebours/Chapitre_V.
[5] Pearce, *The Unmasking of Oscar Wilde*, 192-193.
[6] See Part II, Chapter 5.
[7] See Part III, Chapter 7.
[8] See Part II, Chapter 6.
[9] Ellmann, *Oscar Wilde*, 340-341.
[10] Ibid., 343. Pearce, *The Unmasking of Oscar Wilde*, 193; and William Tydeman and Steven Price, *Wilde—Salome* (Cambridge: Cambridge University Press, 1996),

15.
[11] Ellmann, *Oscar Wilde*, 344-345.
[12] See the "Introduction" by Holbrook Jackson to *Salome* (New York: Heritage Press, 1945), 8.
[13] Oscar Wilde, "The Critic as Artist," in *Complete Works of Oscar Wilde* (Glasgow: HarperCollins, 2003), 1010.
[14] Joris-Karl Huysmans, *Against Nature*, trans. Margaret Mauldon (Oxford: Oxford University Press, 1998), 46.
[15] Oscar Wilde, *Salome* (Boston: Branden Pub. Co., 1996), 8.
[16] Ibid., 13.
[17] Note that it has nothing to do with the biblical story.
[18] Huysmans, *Against Nature*, 46.
[19] See Part I, Chapter 4.
[20] Huysmans, *Against Nature*, 46.
[21] Wilde, *Salome*, 2, 5.
[22] Ibid., 6.
[23] William E. Phipps, "The Plight of the Song of Songs," *Journal of the American Academy of Religion* 42 (Mar. 1974): 82.
[24] Italics are mine.
[25] Wilde, *Salome*, 10. Italics are mine.
[26] Ibid., 10.
[27] Ibid., 11.
[28] Ibid., 12.
[29] Ibid., 12.
[30] Introduction to *Salome*, ibid., 11.
[31] Wilde, "The Critic as Artist," 1010.
[32] Wilde, *Salome*, 11.
[33] Ibid., 12.
[34] Ibid., 13.
[35] Plato, *Plato in Twelve Volumes*, vol. 9, trans. Harold N. Fowler (Cambridge, MA, Harvard University Press; London, William Heinemann Ltd., 1925). See especially the section *Phaedrus*, available online through the Perseus DigitalLibrary (http://www.perseus.tufts.edu/hopper/text?doc=Plat.+Phaedrus&fromdoc=Perseus%3Atext%3A1999.01.0174).
[36] Rodney Shewan, *Oscar Wilde. Art and Egotism* (London: The Macmillan Press LTD, 1977), 140.
[37] Ibid., 140.
[38] Ibid., 141.
[39] Wilde, *Salome*, 35.
[40] See Part II, Chapter 6.
[41] Quoted in Shewan, *Art and Egotism*, 142-143.
[42] Ellmann, *Oscar Wilde*, 339.
[43] Ibid., 338-339.
[44] This is like art itself, in that once it is created it becomes real. This idea is fully in harmony with the idea of the power of the metaphor, which once created and

used becomes a reality for Salome.
[45] Wilde, *Salome*, 35-36.
[46] See Part II.

CHAPTER NINE

WILDE, BEARDSLEY, STRAUSS

As I mentioned earlier, Wilde's Salome became a kind of summation of every existing Salome, and eventually found its adaptation in different forms of art: visual art, opera, ballet, even in film. Here we will only examine the most striking manifestations of Salome in visual art and in opera: the drawings created by the English artist Aubrey Beardsley and Richard Strauss's opera *Salome*.[1]

Aubrey Beardsley

Aubrey Beardsley (1872-1898), a brilliant young graphic artist who had a complex and somewhat controversial relationship with Wilde, created a number of drawings for *Salome*. Those drawings did not directly illustrate the play but were based on Beardsley's perception of the spirit of the play. Although Wilde expected those images to be in "a Byzantine style like Gustave Moreau's" *Salomes*, he was struck by Beardsley's originality and interpretation of the play's images and characters.

Beardsley created his first drawing of Salome, *Salome with the Head of John the Baptist* (Fig. III-9-1), right after he finished reading Wilde's *Salome* in French, in 1893. That drawing drew attention to Beardsley. It represented Salome with the head of John the Baptist, with the appended caption: "*j'ai baisé ta bouche Iokanaan, j'ai baisé ta bouche.*" The drawing was executed in the Japanese style. At that time, Beardsley was under the influence of James McNeil Whistler's Peacock Room at the London town house of Frederick Leyland, a wealthy Liverpool ship owner.

In the drawing, both the bleeding head of John (similar to the head of John in Moreau's *The Apparition*) and Salome are fully androgynous. A lotus, the symbol of lust, is represented at the bottom of the drawing as a foundation for John and Salome's relationship. The lust symbolized by the lotus might be a reference to Beardsley's perception of John as someone who reacts violently to Salome's advances because he fears his own feelings; alternately, it may refer to Salome's lust for John and her frustrated passion.

Fig. III-9-1. Aubrey Beardsley, *Salome with the Head of John the Baptist*

Fig. III-9-1b. Aubrey Beardsley, *Climax*

This drawing was intended to illustrate Joseph Pennell's article on Beardsley, titled "A New Illustrator: Aubrey Beardsley." It was supposed to appear in the first issue of *The Studio* in April of 1893. Interestingly, the drawing found a large prepublication audience.

Wilde's friend Robbie Ross saw the work and recommended it to Wilde's prospective publisher, John Lane. In March 1893, Wilde himself saw it. He was so impressed that he presented Beardsley with a copy of the Paris edition of *Salome*, in which he inscribed: "For Aubrey: for the only artist who, besides myself, knows what the dance of the seven veils is, and can see that invisible dance. Oscar."[2] Beardsley's contract with Lane was signed on 8 June 1893, and it stipulated: "Beardsley would provide ten full-page drawings and a cover design for a fee of fifty guineas, the illustrations to be the 'exclusive property' of the publisher."[3]

When the drawings were finished they evoked controversial reactions. The publishers, especially George Moore, were scandalized by the drawings' supposed indecency, even as they admired their originality. Consequently, they asked Beardsley to make some modifications to his drawings. For example, the original drawing for the front page (Fig. III-9-2) represented an androgynous figure with female breasts and male genitals as well as a figure of a boy, probably a Page, with male genitals. The androgynous figure had Wilde's face and was his caricature, alluding to his homosexuality and lifestyle. The publishers, however, ignored the drawing's allusions to Wilde. They were more concerned with the representation of male genitals and insisted that Beardsley remove them.

The drawing *Enter Hérodiade* (Fig. III-9-3) had to be modified as well. In *Enter Hérodiade* Beardsley's candles bear a resemblance to male genitals in states of erection and ejaculation, accentuating Hérodiade's reputation and her love for men. A character in the original drawings is naked and displays elaborate male genitals. One of Hérodiade's servants has Wilde's face, implying that Wilde is at the service of vice. Once again, the publishers were not concerned with Wilde's caricature; they asked Beardsley to find a solution for the elaborate male genitals. In a reworked drawing he covered them with a fig leaf, much as the Vatican did with so many of their nudes from antiquity and with Michelangelo's frescos in the Sistine Chapel. On one copy of the proofs, Beardsley wrote:

Because one figure was undressed
This little drawing was suppressed.
It was unkind, but never mind,
Perhaps it all was for the best.[4]

Oscar Wilde's face appears in two more *Salome* drawings: *The Woman in the Moon* (Fig. III-9-4) and *The Eyes of Herod*. In *The Woman in the Moon* the moon has Wilde's face, once again emphasizing his androgyny since the moon is usually associated with femininity. For some reason, the

Fig. III-9-2. Aubrey Beardsley, Frontispiece, original

Fig. III-9-3. Aubrey Beardsley, *Enter Hérodiade*

Fig. III-9-4. Aubrey Beardsley, *The Woman in the Moon*

publishers ignored the naked man with exposed genitals in this drawing. In *The Eyes of Herod* it is Herod who has Wilde's face. This seems to be Beardsley's implication that Herod's character in *Salome* is an embodiment of Wilde himself, a symbol of debauchery. The spirit of the drawing seems somehow similar to Moreau's *Salome Dancing Before Herod* (Fig. II-5-7). *The Eyes of Herod* shows Herod's palace, a chandelier that looks similar to a huge lotus, two cupids holding the chandelier, a peacock (the bribe of Herod as well as the symbol of Whistler's Peacock Room in Japanese style) and finally Salome, naked but as majestic as Moreau's version of her, dancing the dance of Seven Veils.

Some of the original drawings that the publishers found indecent were withdrawn by Beardsley and replaced with completely different drawings that he described as "beautiful and quite irrelevant."[5] The original *The Toilette of Salome* (Fig. III-9-5), which represented a naked Salome surrounded by her naked servants—including one drawn with exposed genitals—was replaced by a very elegant drawing with a masked Pierrot (which existed in the original drawing as well) adjusting the hat of a fashionably dressed lady—Salome (Fig. III-9-5b). Common to both drawings, besides the masked Pierrot, were books that were considered scandalous, such as *Manon Lescaut*, Zola's *Nana*, *The Golden Ass* and a volume of de Sade. In both drawings they were provocatively located on the shelf below the beauty products.

A drawing of two androgynous figures, *John and Salome* (Fig. III-9-6), was replaced as well. The original drawing embodies the spirit of the relationship between Salome and John as Wilde had intended to convey through his language: perfect in their imperfection, "in love," while conversing with and insulting each other, Salome insolently arguing with the prophet. It was Salome's large navel, two large breasts and vampire face that caused the publishers' embarrassment. The drawing was eventually published in 1907.

In the original edition the drawing *John and Salome* was replaced with *The Black Cape* (Fig. III-9-7), which shows an elegant woman in a narrow-waisted, wide-skirted, multiple-caped black coat. As Stanley Wintraub pointed out, "It could have offended no one except a reader who expected the illustrations to have some connection to the text."[6]

The first drawing that Beardsley executed, *Salome with the Head of John the Baptist*, also changed and became *The Climax* (Fig. III-9-1b). In that drawing the inscription "j'ai baisé ta bouche Iokanaan, j'ai baisé ta bouche" was taken out, the Peacock style was a little bit less elaborate and the drawing was smaller. In essence, however, the drawing conveyed the same idea as its predecessor.

Fig. III-9-5. Aubrey Beardsley, *The Toilette of Salome.* Original version

Fig. III-9-5b. Aubrey Beardsley, *The Toilette of Salome*

Fig. III-9-6. Aubrey Beardsley, *John and Salome*

The Platonic Lament, The Peacock Skirt, The Stomach Dance, The Dancer's Reward and *Tailpiece* were also part of the collection. Perhaps the most striking are *The Peacock Skirt* (Fig. III-9-8), *The Dancer's Reward* (Fig. III-9-9) and *Tailpiece* (Fig. III-9-10). *The Peacock Skirt* was inspired by Wilde's Herod, who tried to bribe Salome with peacocks: "my beautiful white peacocks, that walk in the garden between the myrtles and the tall cypress-trees. Their beaks are gilded with gold and the grains that they eat are smeared with gold, and their feet are stained with purple."[7] Beardsley was also still under the inspiration of Whistler's peacocks in his decorations for Leyland. The drawing represents once again two conversing androgynous figures: one is either John or Herod—Beardsley liked the ambiguity—and the other is Salome. The figure of John/Herod is dressed in a peacock skirt and wears a crown made of peacock feathers. If the figure is John, according to ancient beliefs, these feathers are a symbol of immortality, of a flesh that does not decay, and therefore refer to the body of Christ and become a symbol of sainthood. It seems as though John is trying to bribe Salome by telling her that if she accepts the bribe, his life will be spared and then he and Salome might become very close friends and even more if she desires. Or, as it is in the play, it could be also Herod, androgynous, as Beardsley's satire of Oscar Wilde, who bribes Salome with his peacocks in an effort to convince her to spare the life of John.

The Dancer's Reward is the penultimate scene, after Salome kisses the lips of John the Baptist's head and perhaps understands the implications of his death: the impossibility of their union and realization of perfection. The androgynous Salome and the androgynous head seem to reflect here more than ever Wilde's interplay of the Lover and the Beloved.

Tailpiece—the final scene, in which a dead and naked Salome is held by a masked Pierrot, the symbol of theater, and by a naked devil, ready to put her in the coffin—plays on a number of possible interpretations. Could Beardsley mockingly imply that Wilde's play is similar in its provocative spirit to medieval plays performed by peripatetic artists and circuses on cathedral squares and perceived by the Church as the symbol of evil, anti-Christian traditions? Is Beardsley suggesting that Wilde's *Salome* could be seen as one of these controversial, provocative performances? Could it also imply that society would link daring theater performances with evil, since the perception of the theater as evil was a common view of the Church? Salome, a symbol of evil—and in this image held by the devil—is clearly a connection between the two. Furthermore, the figure of Salome stresses the link between evil and the theater: She is a figure of evil, a daughter of Eve and a sinful temptress and seducer, and the theater is the stage upon which her story is narrated. Moreover, the theater's role, like

Fig. III-9-7. Aubrey Beardsley, *The Black Cape*

Fig. III-9-8. Aubrey Beardsley, *The Peacock Skirt*

Fig. III-9-9. Aubrey Beardsley, *The Dancer's Reward*

Salome:
Tailpiece.

Fig. III-9-10. Aubrey Beardsley, *Tailpiece*

Salome's, is to seduce its audience. In this drawing the feminized Salome is no longer an androgynous figure. She is transformed into a woman only in death, when she becomes fully and entirely the possession of the devil, who, while putting her in a coffin, is ready to become one with her.

Although Wilde and Beardsley had a complicated relationship, Wilde paid a tribute to Beardsley's talent, imagination and drawings for *Salome* in a note to one of his acquaintances, the actress Mrs. Patrick Campbell, whom Beardsley wanted to draw. He wrote:

> Mr. Aubrey Beardsley, a very brilliant and wonderful young artist, and like all artists a great admirer of the wonder and charm of your art, says that he must once have the honor of being presented to you, if you will allow it.

So, with your gracious sanction, I will come round after Act III with him, and you would gratify and honor him much if you would let him bow his compliments to you. He has just illustrated my play of *Salome*, and has a copy of the *edition de luxe* which he wishes to lay at your feet. His drawings are quite wonderful.[8]

Beardsley's drawings illustrate the spirit of Wilde's *Salome* as perhaps Wilde intended and Beardsley perceived it. His Salome, the seducer, neither woman nor man, seems to have lost her innocence long ago. His androgynous John, as corrupt as Salome, seems to be her friend, someone who might have learned to become her lover if he were not beheaded. Yet the images of Salome and John and the ambiguity of the characters show Beardsley's insight into Wilde's play. These figures, together with Herod, Hérodiade, and even the image of the moon, imply a mockery of Wilde and of his ideas, personality and lifestyle. The biting satire of these images is certainly Beardsley's revenge for Wilde's patronizing treatment of him, treatment that Beardsley perceived as offensive and strongly reacted against in his art and life.

Richard Strauss's Opera *Salome*

Richard Strauss saw Wilde's drama in Berlin in 1902, in Max Renhardt's Kleines Theater, with Gertrud Eysoldt in the title role.[9] The play made a very strong impression on Strauss. He recalls it in his *Recollections and Reflections*: "After the performance I met Heinrich Grünfeld, who said to me: 'My dear Strauss, surely you could make an opera of this!' I replied: 'I am already busy composing it.'"[10]

The first performance of the "drama in one act" was given at the Dresden State Opera on 9 December 1905. It attracted great and widespread attention. In January 1907, seven years after Wilde's death, when the Metropolitan Opera presented for the first time Richard Strauss' opera *Salome,* based on Wilde's play, it provoked such a scandal that *Salome* did not return to the Met until 1934. One of the American spectators of 1907, a physician, vented in a letter to the *New York Times*:

> I am a man of middle life, who has devoted upward of twenty years to the practice of a profession that necessitates, in the treatment of nervous and mental diseases, a daily intimacy with degenerates . . . I say after deliberation, and a familiarity with the emotional productions of Oscar Wilde and Richard Strauss, that *Salome* is a detailed and explicit exposition of the most horrible, disgusting, revolting and unmentionable features of degeneracy (using the word now in its customary social, sexual significance) that I have ever heard, read of, or imagined . . . That which it depicts is

naught else than the motive of the indescribable acts of Jack the Ripper.[11]

The work encountered resistance on various grounds, and the scent of scandal adhered to it for years; but slowly it established itself. Today it is recognized that the "shocker" of 1905 represents one of the most important turning points in operatic history, marking the end of the post-Wagnerian epoch and opening the way for the development of the twentieth century, above all the work of Arnold Schoenberg and Alban Berg.[12]

The German translation was the work of Hedwig Lachmann, and this was the text used by Strauss, whose only alterations of Wilde's play took the form of some sizable cuts. At the time the one-act opera was an innovation. After Strauss, many young composers such as Ravel, Stravinsky, Schoenberg, Hindemith and Puccini found the one-act opera the most suitable format in which to defy the conventional, traditional operatic norms.

The dramatic structure of the opera has a foundation in the musical architecture and Wagnerian notion of the *Gesamtkunstwerk*, "in which the musical, verbal and scenic elements cohere to serve one dramatic end."[13] As Laurence Gilman asserts:

> In spite, however, of its unprecedented difficulties and its inveterate novelty of effect, the work is based, in its main outlines, upon the principles of musico-dramatic structure enunciated and exemplified by Wagner. It is a true lyric-drama: that is to say, the music is always and uncompromisingly at the service of the dramatic situation, enforcing and italicizing the meaning of the text and action.[14]

Musically, the opera can be divided into three major parts: the meeting of Salome and Jokanaan, Herod's soul-searching and the catastrophe. The orchestra between these parts assumes something of the function of a Greek chorus. Strauss uses some twenty leitmotifs. He wrote the following about his music in the opera:

> I had long been dissatisfied with the absence of truly eastern color and fierce sunlight in any operas about the Orient and the Jews. Necessity taught me how to write really exotic harmony, which shimmered like shot silk, especially in strange cadences. The desire for the most vivid characterization possible drove me to bitonality, because rhythm alone, such as Mozart uses so ingeniously, did not seem to me to be strong enough to characterize the contrast between Herod and the Nazarenes, for examples. It should be regarded as an isolated experiment on a special subject, but not recommended for imitation.[15]

Karl Bohm was the first conductor to lead Strauss's performances. Although Wilde's text and the libretto were quite similar, the music led the development of Salome's character in a certain direction. Laurence Gilman, in his book *Strauss' "Salome,"* states:

> In harmonic boldness and in elaborateness and intricacy of orchestration it is his [Strauss's] most extreme performance. His use of dissonance is as persistent as it is nonchalant. The entire score is a harmonic *tour de force*—a practically uninterrupted texture of new and constantly varied sequences and chord formations. Much of it is designed quite frankly and obviously as sheer noise, intentional cacophony.[16]

The motives that constantly repeat themselves are those related to Salome's personality, her behavior and the impressions that she makes on her surroundings.[17] For example, at the beginning of the opera, in the second measure, the melody that is performed by the clarinet reflects Narraboth's passionate view of Salome and her charm and beauty. This is a motive of Salome. Then there is a motive of Salome's Charm played by violins, violas and a celesta at the moment of Salome's entrance on the stage when she tells us about Herod's obsessive glance upon her. This theme comes back when Salome speaks of the moon and describes her as "a virgin." Another motive that pertains to Salome's personality is Salome's Grace, which appears for the first time when the Page foreshadows a forthcoming disaster.

The motives of Salome, Salome's Charm and Salome's Grace are used individually and interwoven at various points of the opera. For example, when Salome, speaking of Jokanaan, says, "What a strange voice! I would speak with him," we hear the intertwined motives of Salome, Salome's Charm and Salome's Grace. Later, when she insists on wishing to speak with Jokanaan and when Narraboth gives in to her, those themes return. The theme of Salome's Charm comes back alone when Salome answers Jokanaan's question of who she is. We can hear the theme of Salome when Herod expresses his concern to Hérodiade about Salome being too pale, when Herod invites Salome to drink wine with him, when we hear the voice of Jokanaan prophesying the coming of Christ and when Herod begs Salome to dance for him.

Gilman explains that sometimes Salome's themes are present in a distorted version. For example, this is the case when she looks into the cistern, impatiently watching for the results of her request. Sometimes Salome's themes are accompanied by other themes, as when the theme of Salome's Charm is accompanied by the themes of Jokanaan, Narraboth's Longing and Jokanaan's Prophecy. Additionally, every time there is a reference to Salome's dance we hear a tambourine, which adds color to her leitmotifs.

According to Laurence Gilman, the twenty leitmotifs could be summarized in the following order of appearance: *Salome*; *Narraboth's Longing*; *The Jews; Jokanaan; Salome's Charm; Herod's Desire; Salome's Grace; Prophecy; Ecstasy; Yearning; Anger; Enticement; Kiss Theme; Fear; Herod; The Wind; Herod's Graciousness; Dispute; The Dance;* and *Herod's Pleading*. Each motive is a reflection of the theme pertaining either to the character or to the event. The music reflects the personality, the aspirations, the moods and the spirit of the events that occur in the opera. Although the opera's text is almost analogous to the play's, the music brings another dimension and interpretation to the play. Strauss's music transforms the story from decadence to tragedy, and the character of Salome becomes a tragic hero who undergoes the process of epiphany and purification.

* * *

From the above discussion we can see that the visual and musical renditions of Wilde's *Salome* accentuate and illuminate different aspects of the play and of Salome as a character. The play's complexity offers many possible interpretations. In turn, artists across different media explored particular aspects of those interpretations. Thus, Aubrey Beardsley's illustrations stress the satiric side of Wilde's play and emphasize the complexity of the characters' androgyny. Beardsley's transformation of Salome from an androgynous being into a woman in his *Tailpiece* (Fig. III-9-11) subtly follows the nineteenth-century view of women: To be a woman is to be possessed by and in a relationship with the devil.

In comparison, Strauss's opera, through the complexity of the music, explores the play's characters and makes Salome into an almost Shakespearean figure. The Salome of Strauss is akin to a tragic hero, a victim of pride and passion who is caught in an unfolding of events beyond her control. These renditions of Wilde's work in different media highlight the play's great depth and multidimensionality.

Notes

[1] For information about Salome in ballet and film, see William Tydeman and Steven Price, *Wilde—Salome* (Cambridge: Cambridge University Press, 1996).
[2] Stanley Weintraub, *Beardsley, a Biography* (New York: George Braziller, 1967), 56.
[3] Ibid., 57.

[4] Robert Ross, *Aubrey Beardsley* (London: John Lane, The Bodley Head, 1921), 88.
[5] Weintraub, *Beardsley*, 62.
[6] Ibid., 68.
[7] Oscar Wilde, *Salome* (Boston: Branden Pub. Co., 1996), 31.
[8] Weintraub, *Beardsley*, 71.
[9] For more information, see Appendix One.
[10] Richard Strauss, *Recollections and Reflections* (The University of Virginia: Greenwood Press, 1974), 150.
[11] The citation is taken from Alex Ross, *The Rest Is Noise. Listening to the Twentieth Century* (New York: Farrar, Straus and Giroux, 2007), 27-28.
[12] There were 697 editions published between 1905 and 2011 in twelve languages and held by 2,685 libraries worldwide.
[13] Andrew Porter, "Music drama," in *The New Grove Dictionary of Music and Musicians*, ed. Stanley Sadie, 20 vols. (London: Macmillan, 1980), vol.12, 830.
[14] Laurence Gilman, *Strauss' "Salome." A Guide to the Opera with Musical Illustrations* (London: John Lane, the Bodley Head; New York: John Lane Company, 1907), 56.
[15] Strauss, *Recollections and Reflections*, 150.
[16] Gilman, *Strauss' "Salome,"* 55.
[17] Strauss gives names to some leitmotifs but does not do so consistently. Gilman and Roese assigned their own—sometimes contradictory—names to leitmotifs, whereas Derrick Puffett is skeptical about the value of labeling. See Derrick Puffett, *Richard Strauss "Salome"* (Cambridge: Cambridge University Press, 1989), 69 and the whole chapter "*Salome* as Music Drama," 58-87.

Conclusion

When one considers that the dance of Herodias' unnamed daughter in the Gospel of Mark is simply an instrument through which Herodias brings about the beheading of John the Baptist, the scope of the enormous mythical elaboration of the dancing figure over the centuries is astonishing. Once the name Salome becomes attached to the dancing girl, the mythologizing seems to take off, with "Salome" providing an ever-malleable image onto which may be projected ideas of women and womanhood. Although this book has focused on a few case studies, from the Church Fathers to the early twentieth century, the underlying constant in all of the studies is the way theologians, writers, artists and composers have found ways of projecting their fears and desires regarding women onto the "Salome" of their imaginations.

Although Salome has always been linked to some versions of evil, her character came to bear many associated themes. Often she was allied to something in women's behavior that society was struggling against or that particular groups, like artists, found desirable—even if they found it dangerous as well. Thus for the Church Fathers and the artists and theologians in the Middle Ages Salome symbolized what women should shun, whether in the form of the Bacchae left over from pagan times or simply in the image of the seductive dancer or acrobat.

In the Renaissance, as we saw, Salome's image was considerably different from that of her medieval predecessor. Although she and her dance were always the instigators of John the Baptist's death, she was also depicted as a muse, a symbol of an artistic search for Beauty and an embodiment of femininity and inspiration.

One of the novelties of the Renaissance was that artists began to use as models women who played important roles in their personal lives. For some Renaissance artists this meant their lovers or daughters, who were then depicted as Salome to bring personal and philosophical meaning into the story. For example, Filippo Lippi's model for Salome was Lucrezia Buti, the love of his life and the mother of his children. In representing three different instances of the Salome story—dancing, receiving the head of the Baptist and handing the head to her mother, Herodias—Lippi also represented Lucrezia at three stages of her life.

When Titian painted one of his Salomes, he used as a model his daughter Lavinia; for another he painted his own features in the head of John the Baptist on a platter. As we saw, his paintings seem to bear an allegorical meaning and to express his views on the relationship of an artist to his creations.

One of the most interesting discoveries in the study has been the way in which the story of Salome and John the Baptist inspired some artists, poets and writers to imagine themselves and their relation to the tale. Despite their apparent differences, there is a common thread in their work: The theme of Salome is used to convey their philosophy of art and to express painful relationships in their lives. It was certainly the case for painters such as Titian, Emile Bernard and Gustave Moreau, living in two different countries, Italy and France, and in different times. It was also the case of the Symbolist poet Stéphane Mallarmé. Although in appearance these representations followed the already established Renaissance tradition of self-portraits in disguise and in *decapité*, each of them brought in new meanings and new connotations. Mallarmé, for example, at a time when Hérodiade and Salome were perceived only as *femmes fatales*, attributed to his Hérodiade a new role. For him she embodied the double role of a poet and of a poem in the process of being created. Gustave Moreau, in the image of the floating head of John the Baptist in his watercolor *The Apparition*, symbolically expressed the idea of an eternal life on earth given to artists who, through the genius of their art, capture and herald beauty and the nobility of the divine and their own role in it.

We saw that Moreau's representation of the disembodied head of John the Baptist was part of the nineteenth-century fascination with the myth of the beheading. This theme goes hand in hand with the myth of Orpheus, also painted by Moreau, in which the meaning of the head of Orpheus found by the young girl of Thrace is similar to that of the floating head of John the Baptist.

However, my study also demonstrated that the myth of the beheading holds another meaning. Salome, or more broadly, woman, by severing man's head – sometimes equaled to a castration – the seed of his thought and his creativity, deprives man of his masculine power and reduces him to her own condition, the condition of nature, of an animal.[1] Although in this book I only examine the works of Gustave Moreau, the works of Gauguin and especially Odilon Redon also produced a number of representations of the disembodied head, attaching to it a variety of different meanings.

In the nineteenth century, Salome again became an evil force. If in the Middle Ages Salome was only an appendix to John the Baptist's story and in the Renaissance, although she remained part of his story, she "mellowed" and was often painted not as an evil force, but as a muse and nymph, in the nineteenth century, in response to women's growing claims for equality, she became an independent figure, often represented without reference to the Baptist. She was turned into a symbol of women gaining independence and displacing men from their comfortable positions of power. For society, she became the symbol of the power of destruction for the sake of a new world that she would embody, the world often represented through works of art and literature as a world of evil, blood, ugliness and the frightening unknown. She, the whore of Babylon, was depicted as an apocalyptical danger awaiting the world if it gives in to her temptations.[2]

Although thousands of religious, literary and artistic works have invoked the figure of Salome over the centuries, I have examined only a few exemplary cases, but they are enough to show how a simple biblical fragment mushroomed into a vast myth that powerfully reinforced fears and desires about women. Far from her humble origins as the nameless daughter of Herodias, Salome has become in some ways a figure as enduring and important as the man whose execution she was used to bring about. Since that first task of hers she has been put in the service of countless other masters, all appropriating the image of a woman who, in many ways, never was.

Notes

[1] See Jean de Palacio's article "Motif privilégié au jardin des supplices : Le mythe de la décollation et le décadentisme," *Revue des Sciences Humaines* 153 (Aspects du décadentisme européen), (January-March 1974).

[2] Literary criticism, especially in the twentieth century, contributed to a variety of interpretations of the story of Salome's dance and John the Baptist's beheading. Exploring the various critical interpretations is beyond the scope of this book, but one of the more interesting studies is "Scandal and the Dance: Salome in the Gospel of Mark" by René Girard. It interprets the story from the point of view of mimetism or mimetic desire—when one desires something because someone else does. Girard believes that Herodias' desire to have John's head reinforces Salome's desire. Salome's desire then induces and reinforces the desire of the guests, and so on. Girard's interpretation of Salome's story allows him to connect it to the broader phenomenon: the phenomenon of popular revolts and manifestations.

APPENDIX ONE

LOVIS CORINTH

The German artist Lovis Corinth (1858-1925) painted a striking *Salome* in 1899-1900. He may have been inspired by Wilde's play *Salome* but he certainly influenced the propagation of the mythical image of Salome.[1]

Fig. App 1-1. Lovis Corinth, *Salome*

Painted between 1899 and 1900, Corinth's *Salome* almost looks to have been inspired by one of the final scenes of Wilde's play. It is the moment when Salome, while kissing John's lips, comes to the realization of his irrevocable death and her subsequent loss.

> Ah! thou wouldst not suffer me to kiss thy mouth, Iokanaan. Well! I will kiss it now. I will bite it with my teeth as one bites a ripe fruit. Yes, I will kiss thy mouth, Iokanaan. I said it; did I not say it? I said it. Ah! I will kiss it now . . . . But wherefore dost thou not look at me, Iokanaan? Thine eyes that were so terrible, so full of rage and scorn, are shut now. Wherefore are they shut? Open thine eyes! Lift up thine eyelids, Iokanaan! Wherefore dost thou not look at me? Art thou afraid of me, Iokanaan, that thou wilt not look at me?[2]

The painting *Salome* (Fig. App 1-1) is considered to be a new phase in Corinth's career: his move to being viewed as "a painter of flesh." Corinth had a keen interest in portraying flesh—sometimes in its most carnal state—which seems to have begun in 1893. In that year he painted *The Slaughterhouse* (Stuttgart, Staatsgalerie), followed in 1905 by *Cattle Slaughtered at the Slaughterhouse* (Ratisbonne, Kunstforum Ostdeutsche Galerie). There is a sense that toward the end of the century, Corinth was in search of a means to represent the naked body. The portrayal of *Salome* fits into this period.

Corinth's image of Salome, contrary to Beardsley's, is striking for its feminine sensuality and fleshiness. In the center of the painting a half-naked Salome bends over the platter. She is shown with large, voluptuous lips and desiring eyes. Her breasts are bare and nearly touch John's head. Instead of holding the head, as she does in Wilde's play, she is presented it by a naked slave. The executioner, also naked save for a loincloth, holds the bloodied sword and stares at Salome; his desire for her seems evident.

Salome bends toward John's head as a lover would bend to a beloved. She appears to look through or beyond the head, as if she were looking at it under the influence of narcotics. If the play did inspire Corinth, he certainly selected the moment that could be perceived as an illustration of Salome's state of mind at the end of the drama: She is close to madness while realizing the results of her unrestrained desire for John.

Corinth's work is striking for its use of light and colors. It gives the impression that the depicted event is occurring on a large terrace of a palace illuminated by the bright Mediterranean sun. On the one hand, the color of the bodies seems to blend with the color of the sunlit terrace; on the other hand, colors such as those of the dresses, hair decorations and makeup are strongly contrasted with the colors of the environment. This contrast creates a powerful dramatic effect: the sunny, well-lit background of the painting, a symbol of the transcendental, much like the gold background of a medieval painting, underscores the dark necrophilia of the mesmerized Salome, who is still trying to tempt the disembodied head of John. The vivacity and the contrast of colors bring a stunning naturalistic power to this picture and make it quite different from the thousands of pictures of Salome that were produced in the nineteenth century.

Corinth's *Salome* played an important role in his artistic career. After he completed the painting in 1900 he applied for the exhibition of the Munich Secession. He had not exhibited with that group since 1893 because of his complicated relationship with some of its members. His attempt to exhibit his *Salome* with them was unsuccessful. He was subsequently offered an opportunity to exhibit *Salome* at the second exhibition of the Berlin Secession, where it was a sensational success. The painting's reproduction was printed with *Rosenhagen's Review,* and it contributed to Corinth's reputation.

Corinth's involvement with Salome continued when, in 1902-1903, he collaborated with Max Reinhardt's theater on the production of Oscar Wilde's play.[3] In his theater productions Reinhardt strove to move away from the naturalism of the theater and to express the essence of the play through action and décor. Corinth's role was very important, since he was a décor and set designer for Reinhardt from 1902 to 1907. Corinth considered *Salome* to be the most controversial of the plays on which he collaborated with Reinhardt. He designed the costumes for the play, and the sculptor Max Kruse created the sets.

Salome, as translated by Hedwig Lachmann, was first performed before a private audience at the Kleines Theater on 5 November 1902. It premiered in Berlin on 29 September 1903 at the Neues Theater. As Horst Uhr points out: "Corinth's costumes added barbaric splendor to this ominous mood. In their garish magnificence, the multicolored robes, encrusted with colored stones, expressed the high pitched depravity that propelled the lurid plot."[4]

During that time Corinth also produced portraits of actors in their roles. In January 1903 he painted Gertrud Eysoldt (1870-1955) in the role of Salome (Fig. App 1-2). Eysoldt was a stunningly versatile actress who was able to depict Salome's contradictory personality and its combination of childlike innocence and lustful cruelty. Corinth worked to capture the ambivalence of Salome's personality and her emotions as performed by Eysoldt. After the first performance at the Kleines Theater the actress posed for Corinth in his studio wearing the jewelry and the costume he had designed for her. Uhr describes her portrait as Salome in the following citation:

Without any further references to Wilde's play, Corinth in this portrait represented a generalized image of depravity, partly, perhaps, in response to the then current vogue for pictures of the prototypical *femme fatale* but surely also out of his own interest in the universal human dimension.[5]

Fig. App 1-2. Lovis Corinth, *Gertrud Eysoldt as Salome*

Corinth made considerable contributions to the propagation of the story of Salome. His painting *Salome* is one of the manifestations of her perverse, sensual and even necrophiliac nature. In exposing and emphasizing the flesh of Salome, Corinth depicts a type of *femme fatale*, itself a concept linked to the story and figure of Salome.

Notes

[1] I say "may have" because it is possible that Lovis Corinth became acquainted with Wilde's play only in Hedwig Lachmann's translation, in 1902, a few years after he painted his *Salome*. Corinth was not in Paris in February 1896 for the first staging of Wilde's *Salome* at the Théâtre de l'Oeuvre. Though he spoke and read French there is no record to suggest that Corinth read the play in French when it first came out. We can only be sure that he became acquainted with it when it was published in a German translation.

[2] Oscar Wilde, *Salome* (Boston: Branden Publishing Company, 1996), 34.

[3] In 1902 Reinhardt became a director at the Kleines Theater in Berlin. This was the beginning of the most avant-garde period in the history of the Berlin theater. By 1903 the Kleines Theater was too small to hold the audiences for Reinhardt's productions. Consequently, he rented the much larger Neues Theater. In 1905 he became responsible for the Deutsches Theater and the year after for the Berlin Kammerspiele. Reinhardt's goal was to move away from the naturalism in the theater and to build a theater which would express the essence of the play through action and décor. Hence the stage designer was a very important person in Reinhardt's productions.

[4] Horst Uhr, *Lovis Corinth* (Berkeley, Los Angeles, Oxford: University of California Press, 1990), 166.

[5] Ibid., 167.

APPENDIX TWO

SALOME IN RUSSIAN CULTURE

Three prominent Russian poets of the twentieth century composed works in which Salome was a central figure. Alexander Blok created an image of Salome in some of his poems, partly as a result of his trip to Italy and partly under the influence of Mallarmé and Wilde. Blok was under the spell of the Italian practice of artists depicting their self-portraits in *decapité*. In his first poem in which Salome appears—about Venice and a Venetian triptych—the image of Salome walking and carrying the head on the platter, which is the head of the poet himself, is a central feature.[1]

The cold wind coming from the lagoon,
The silent coffins of gondolas,
This night, sick and young,
I am lying by the lion's column.

On the tower, singing wonderful songs,
Giants beat the midnight hour.
Mark drowned in the moonlight lagoon
Its colorful iconostasis.

In the shade of the palace gallery
Lightly illuminated by the moon,
Hiding, Salome is walking
With my bloody head.

Everything is asleep – palaces, canals, people,
Only the sleeping ghosts step,
Only the head on the black plate
Staring with sadness at the surrounding world.[2]

In a verse that was not included in the final version of the poem, Blok, using the image from Wilde's *Salome* when she finally kisses the mouth of the beheaded John the Baptist, depicts Salome kissing his own head.[3]

> I will not escape my dark destiny,
> I recognize my fall:
> The dancer in the transparent tunic
> Kissing my head.

Blok also evokes her image in his 1914 poem "Antverpen" ("Antwerp"), written as a result of his travels to Holland in 1911.

> Look at the darkness of centuries
> In a quiet city museum:
> There the king is Quentin Matsys;
> There in the folds of the Salome dress
> The golden flowers are woven.

Although Blok endows it with its own significance and relates it to the beginning of the First World War, this poem is heavily influenced by Dutch art,[4] especially by Quentin Matsys's painting of Salome, and is essentially an ekphrasis of that work.[5]

In 1916 Osip Mandelshtam wrote a poem entitled "Solominka," inspired by the Georgian princess Salomea Andronikova (1888-1982). Andronikova was a literary and political figure in pre-revolutionary St. Petersburg who, because of her stunning beauty, was perceived as a *femme fatale* and with whom Mandelshtam was very much in love. In his poem, Mandelshtam blends the notion of a loveless Salome with that of a beautiful Ligeia, the character in Edgar Allan Poe's short story of the same name. Mandelshtam does not add or take away from the already established image of Salome. Rather, he mainly uses wordplay based on the character's name—the Russian word *solominka* translates as "little straw"—while playing with the idea of cruelty, already an indelible part of the image of Salome but in this case associated with the author's pains resulting from unrequited love for Salomea Andronikova.

> I.
>
> Solominka, when you cannot sleep,
> You wait anxiously in your huge room
> For the heavy ceiling to lower its sad
> Weight over your sensitive eyes.
>
> Dry little straw, sonorous Solominka,
> Drinking death has put you at rest.
> The dear little straw is dead.
> No, not Salome, Solominka.

Sleepless objects grow heavy
And so quiet, as if there were less of them.
The white pillows glimmer faintly in the mirror.
The bed is reflected in its round pool.

The twelve months sing the hour of death
And pale-blue ice streams through the air.
No, it is not Solominka in solemn satin,
In the huge room above the Neva.

Solemn December lets out its breath
As if the heavy Neva were in the room.
No, not Solominka—It is Ligeia dying:
I have learned you blessed words.

II.

I have learned you, blessed words:
Lenore, Solominka, Ligeia, Seraphita.
Pale-blue blood seeps from the granite.
The heavy Neva is in the room.

Solemn December shines above the Neva.
The twelve months sing the hour of death.
No, it is not Solominka in solemn satin
Slowly inhaling the wearisome peace.

In my blood it is Decemberish Ligeia,
Whose blessed love sleeps in the sarcophagus.
But that little straw, perhaps Salome,
Was killed by pity, never to return.[6]

In 1946 Anna Akhmatova dedicated a poem to the much admired dancer Tat'iana Vecheslova. In this poem the character of a dancer and the power of her dance are reflections of the already existent reputation of Salome as a *femme fatale*. This is a figure who does everything as she pleases and who uses her sensual, irresistible beauty and the fatal power of her dance to seduce and destroy at will.[7]

Smoky full moon incarnate,
White marble in the twilight walkways,
Fatal girl, a dancer,
The best of all cameos.
She is a cause of people's perishing,
For her Genghis sent an ambassador.

She is one of a kind, who carries the head of the Baptist
On the bloodied plate.[8]

Fig. App 2-1. Valentine Serov, *Ida Rubenstein as Salome*

In Russia the image of Salome also appeared in the performing and visual arts. For example, in 1908 Ida Rubenstein, tutored by the choreographer Michail Fokine, danced in a single private show the role of Salome based on Oscar Wilde's play *Salome*. For her performance she stripped nude while executing the dance of Seven Veils. In 1910 Russian painter Valentin Serov painted *Ida Rubenstein as Salome* (Fig. App 2-1). In 1911 the Russian artist Marianna Werefkin, a member of the German expressionist movement Blue Rider, painted *Salome with the Head of John the Baptist* (Fig. App 2-2). And in 1913 the Russian artist and set-designer Sergei Sudeikin (Soudeikine) designed the sets and costumes for Diaghilev's production of *La tragédie de Salomé* by the French composer Florent Schmitt.

Fig. App 2-2. Marianna Werefkin, *Salome with the Head of John the Baptist*

Notes

[1] For a detailed analysis of this poem, see the chapter on Salome, *Саломея*, in Olga Matich's book *Erotic Utopia: The Decadent Imagination in Russia's Fin de Siècle*, (Moscow: NLO, Новое литературное обозрение, 2008), 149-163.

    Холодный ветер от лагуны,
    Гондол безмолвные гробы.
    Я в эту ночь – больной и юный –
    Простерт у львиного столба.

    На башне, с песнею чудесной
    Гиганты бьют полночный час.
    Марк утопил в лагуне лунной
    Узорный свой иконостас.

    В тени дворцобой галереи,
    Чуть озаренная луной,
    Таясь, проходит Саломея
    С моей кровавой головой.

    Все спит – дворцы, каналы, люди,
    Лишь призрака скользящий шаг,
    Лишь голова на черном блюде
    Глядит с тоской в окрестный мрак.
    (p. 150, Matich)

[2] The translations of all Blok's poems in Appendix 2 are mine. R.N.

[3]   Мне не избегнуть доли мрачной –
    Свое паденье признаю:
    Плясунья в тунике прозрачной
    Лобзает голову мою.
    (p. 156, Matich).

[4] For more information see Matich, 160-162.

[5]   А ты – во мглу веков вглядись
    В спокойном городском музее:
    Там царствует Квентин Массис;
    Там в складках платья Саломеи
    Цветы из золота вплелиль.

[6]   Когда, соломинка, не спишь в огромной спальне
    И ждешь, бессонная, чтоб, важен и высок,
    Спокойной тяжестью – что может быть печальней –
    На веки чуткие спустился потолок,

    Соломка звонкая, соломинка сухая,
    Всю смерть ты выпила и сделалась нежней,

Сломалась милая соломинка неживая,
Не Саломея, нет, соломинка скорей!

В часы бессонницы предметы тяжелее,
Как будто меньше их – такая тишина!
Мерцают в зеркале подушки, чуть белея,
И в круглом омуте кровать отражена.

Нет, не соломинка в торжественном атласе,
В огромной комнате над черною Невой,
Двенадцать месяцев поют о смертном часе,
Струится в воздухе лед бледно-голубой.

Декабрь торжественный струит свое дыханье,
Как будто в комнате тяжелая Нева.
Нет, не соломинка – Лигейя, умиранье, –
Я научился вам, блаженные слова.

II

Я научился вам, блаженные слова,
Ленор, Соломинка, Лигейя, Серафита,
В огромной комнате тяжелая Нева,
И голубая кровь струится из гранита.

Декабрь торжественный сияет над Невой.
Двенадцать месяцев поют о смертном часе.
Нет, не соломинка в торжественном атласе
Вкушает медленный, томительный покой.

В моей крови живет декабрьская Лигейя,
Чья в саркофаге спит блаженная любовь,
А та, соломинка, быть может Саломея,
Убита жалостью и не вернется вновь

1916 © Осип Мандельштам / Osip Mandelshtam
http://www.peoples.ru/art/literature/poetry/oldage/mandelshtam/poetry_solominka.shtml
English version translated by Kevin Kinsella and available at:
http://www.thedrunkenboat.com/mandelshtam.htm

[7]
    Дымное исчадье полнолунья,
Белый мрамор в сумраке аллей,
Роковая девочка, плясунья,
Лучшая из всех камей.
От таких и погибали люди,

> За такой чингиз послал посла,
> И такая на кровавом блюде
> Голову крестителя несла.

This poem was originally written on a piece of cardboard, on which was glued a photograph representing the nude Vecheslova. Later the poem became part of Akhmatova's poetry collection *Nechet*.

[8] The translation is mine. R.N.

SELECTED BIBLIOGRAPHY

The Age of Rossetti, Burne-Jones and Watts. Symbolism in Britain 1860-1910. London: Tate Gallery Publishing, 1998.
Akhmatova, Anna. *Sbornik stikhov "Nechet:"* http://www.ahmatova.ru/book/783/
Alberti, Leon Battista, ed. and trans. Rocco Sinisgalli. On Painting. New York: Cambridge University Press, 2011.
Albouy, Pierre. *Mythes et mythologies dans la littérature française.* Paris: A. Colin, 1969.
Apollinaire, Guillaume. *L'hérésiarque et compagnie.* Paris: Livre de poche, 2003.
—. *Alcools.* Paris: Gallimard, 1955.
Arasse, Daniel. *On n'y voit rien.* Paris: Editions Denoel, 2000.
Ashley, Michelle Lee. *Subversive sexuality within fin-de-siècle dramatic literature.* Master's Thesis, Southern Illinois University, 2010.
Atkinson, Kenneth. *Queen Salome: Jerusalem's warrior monarch of the first century B.C.E.* Jefferson, NC: McFarland & Co., 2012.
Austin, Lloyd James. *Essais sur Mallarmé.* Manchester and New York: Manchester University Press, 1995.
Bach, Alice; Exum, J. Cheryl; Dillon, Leo; and Dillon, Diane. *Miriam's well: stories about women in the Bible.* New York: Delacorte Press, 1991.
Bach, Alice. *Women, seduction, and betrayal in biblical narrative.* Cambridge: Cambridge University Press, 1997.
Bal, Mieke. *Narratology: Introduction to the theory of narrative.* Toronto: University of Toronto Press, 2nd ed., 1997.
—. *Lethal love: Feminist literary readings of biblical love stories.* Bloomington: Indiana University Press, 1987.
Ballarin, Alessandro; Savy, Barbara Maria; and Romanino, Girolamo. *La Salomè del Romanino ed altri studî sulla pittura bresciana del Cinquecento.* Cittadella: Bertoncello artigrafiche, 2006.
Ballerini, Isabella Lapi. *On the Scaffolding with Filippo Lippi: Prato Cathedral of Santo Stefano, Visits on the Scaffolding of the Restoration Worksite for Filippo Lippi"s Frescoes.* Prato: Provincia Di Prato Agenzia Per Il Turismo, 2001.
Barasch, Moshe. *Giotto and the Language of Gesture.* Cambridge:

Cambridge University Press, 1990.
Barthes, Roland. *Mythologies*. New York: Hill and Wang, 1995.
Baudelaire, Charles. *The Flowers of Evil*. Translated by James McGowan. Oxford: Oxford University Press, 1998.
Bénichou, Paul. *Selon Mallarmé*. Paris: Gallimard, 1995.
Bennett, Michael Y., ed. *Refiguring Oscar Wilde's Salome*. Amsterdam: Rodopi, 2011.
Bentley, Toni. *Sisters of Salome*. New Haven: Yale University Press, 2002.
Bernard, Emile. *Aventure de ma vie (My Life Adventure)*. Unpublished manuscript, Musée du Louvre.
The Bible. Revised Standard Version of the Bible. 1952. 2nd edition, 1971. Available online at: http://www.biblestudytools.com/.
Blok, Aleksandr. *Polnoe sobranie sochinenii v 3 tomakh (Complete Works in 3 volumes)*. Moskva: Progress-Pleiada, 2009.
Bochet, Mark. *Salome. Du voilé au dévoilé*. Paris: Les Editions du CERF, 2007.
Bonafoux, Pascal. *Portraits of the Artists. The Self-Portrait in Painting*. New York: Skira, Rizolli, 1985.
Brant, Jo-Ann A.; Hedrick, Charles W.; and Shea, Chris, eds. *Ancient fiction: the matrix of early Christian and Jewish narrative*. Leiden: Brill, 2005.
Brenner, Athalya. *A Feminist companion to the Song of Songs*. Sheffield: Sheffield Academic Press, 2001.
Brooke, George J., and Kaestli, Jean-Daniel, eds. *Narrativity in Biblical and related texts = La narrativité dans la bible et les textes apparentés*. Leuven: Leuven University Press, 2000.
Brunel, Pierre, and Vion-Dury, Juliette, eds. *Dictionnaire des mythes du fantastique*. Limoges: Presse Universitaire, 2003.
Brunel, Pierre, and Dotoli, Giovanni, eds. *La femme en Méditerranée*, Actes du Colloque de Bari, 8 June 2007. Biblioteca della Ricerca, Alain Baudry et les éditeurs, 2007.
Bühler, Pierre, and Habermacher, J.-F., eds. *La narration: quand le récit devient communication*. Postface de Paul Ricoeur. Geneva: Labor et Fides, 1988.
Campbell, Jean-Currie. *The Legend of Salome in the History of the Arts*. Thesis. Northampton: Smith College, Massachussettes, 1931.
Cansinos-Asséns, Rafael. *Salomé en la literatura: Flaubert, Wilde, Mallarmé, Eugenio de Castro, Apollinaire*. Madrid: Editorial-América, 1919.
Capodieci, Luisa. "Gli ornamenti simbolici: l'uso degli elementi decorativi nella *Salome tatuata* di Gustave Moreau." *Ricerche di Storia dell'Arte*

57 (1995): 5-22
—. "Salomé." In *Gustave Moreau: Les aquarelles*. Paris: Somogy Editions d'Art, 1998.
Chambers, E. K. *The Medieval Stage*. Oxford: Oxford University Press, 1978.
Cheney, Liana De Girolami; Faxon, Alicia Craig; and Russo, Kathleen Lucey. *Self-Portraits by Women Painters*. Aldershot: Ashgate, 2000.
Clark, Kenneth. *An Introduction to Rembrandt*. New York, Hagerstown, San Francisco, London: Harper & Row, Publishers, 1978.
Cohn, Haim. *The Trial and Death of Jesus*. New York: Ktav Publishing House, Inc., 1977.
Cole, Brendan. "Nature and the Ideal in Khnopff's *Avec Verhaeren: Un Ange* and *Art, or the Caresses*." *The Art Bulletin* 91 (September 2009): 325-342.
Cole, Bruce. *Giotto and Florentine Painting 1280-1375*. New York: Icon Editions, Harper & Row, 1976.
Cooke, Peter. "History Painting as Apocalypse and Poetry: Gustave Moreau's *Les Prétendants*, 1852-1897, with Unpublished Documents." *Gazette des beaux-arts* (January 1996): 27-48.
—. "La pensée esthétique de Gustave Moreau à travers ses écrits." *Dossiers de l'art* 51 (1998): 16-26.
Cooke, Peter, ed. *Gustave Moreau. Ecrits sur l'art*. Fontfroide: Fata Morgana, 2002.
Cooke, Peter. *Gustave Moreau et les arts jumeaux: peinture et littérature au dix-neuvième siècle*. Berne: Peter Lang, 2003.
—. "Gustave Moreau's 'Salome': the poetics and politics of history painting." *The Burlington Magazine* 149 (August 2007): 528-536.
Corley, Kathleen E. "Were the Women around Jesus Really Prostitutes? Women in the Context of Greco-Roman Meals." In *Society of Biblical Literature seminar papers*, edited by David J. Lull, 487-521. Atlanta: Scholars Press, 1989.
Curl, James Stevens. *Egyptomania. The Egyptian Revival: A recurring Theme in the History of Taste*. Manchester, New York: Manchester University Press, Manchester, 1993.
Daffner, Hugo. *Salome: ihre Gestalt in Geschichte und Kunst, Dictung, bildende Kunst, Musik*. Munich: Hugo Schmidt, 1912.
D'Arcais, Francesca Flore. *Giotto*. New York: Abbeville Publishers, 1995.
Décaudin, Michel. "Un Mythe 'fin de siècle': Salomé." *Comparative Literature Studies*, Vol. IV, N 1 and 2, 1967: 109-117.
—. "Salomé dans la littérature et l'art de l'époque symboliste." *Bulletin de l'Université de Toulouse* 152 (March 1965): 1-7.

Del Mastro, M. L. *All the women of the Bible*. Edison, NJ: Castle Books, 2004.
De Palacio, Jean. "Motif privilégié au jardin des supplices : le mythe de la décollation et le décadentisme." *Revue des Sciences Humaines* 153 (1974): 39-62.
—. "La Féminité dévorante : sur quelques images de la manducation dans la littérature décadende." *Revue des Sciences Humaines* 168 (December 1977): 601-618.
De Vos, Dirk. *Rogier van der Weyden*. Paris: Hazan, 1999.
—. *Rogier Van Der Weyden: The Complete Works*. New York: Harry N. Abrams, 2000.
Dierkes-Thrun, Petra. *Salome's modernity: Oscar Wilde and the aesthetics of transgression*. Ann Arbor: University of Michigan Press, 2011.
Dijkstra, Bram. *Idols of Perversity. Fantasies of Feminine Evil in fin-de-siècle culture*. New York, Oxford: Oxford University Press, 1986.
Doody, Margaret Anne. *The True Story of the Novel*. Rutgers University Press, 1996.
Dottin-Orsini, Mireille, *S Comme Salomé. Salomé dans le texte et m'image de 1870 à 1914,* une exposition documentaire du Centre de promotion de la recherche scientifique. Université de Toulouse-Le Mirail, 1986.
—. "Lectures fin-de-siècle de l'iconographie de Salomé." *Bible et Imaginaire* 11 (1991): 121-137.
—. "Portrait de femme fatale en vampire", *Littératures*, 26 (1992): 41-57.
—. "Salomé de Henri Regnault (1870): genèse et réception d'un tableau légendaire." *"Textes, Images, Musique", Cahiers de "Littératures"* (1992): 30-45
—. *Cette femme qu'ils dissent fatale*. Paris: Bernard Grasset, 1993.
—. "Salomé-Hérodiade." In *Dictionnaire des mythes littéraires*, edited by Pierre Brunel, 1176-1187. Paris: Editions du Rocher, 1994.
—. *Salomé*. Paris: Éditions Autrement, 1996.
Drewska, H. "Quelques interprétations de la Légende de Salomé dans les Littératures contemporaines." Thesis: Montpellier, 1912.
Downey, Katherine Brown. *Perverse Midrash: Oscar Wilde, André Gide, and censorship of biblical drama*. New York: Continuum, 2004.
Dumesnil, René. Introduction to *Oeuvres, II* by Gustave Flaubert, 575-583. Paris: Bibliothèque de la Pléade, Editions Gallimard, 1952.
Eco, Umberto. *Art and Beauty in the Middle Ages*. New Haven: Yale University Press, 2002.
Eimerl, Sarel. *The World of Giotto, c. 1267-1337*. New York: Little Brown & Company, 1967.
Ellmann, Richard. *Oscar Wilde*. New York: Alfred A. Knopf, 1988.

Fairlie, Alison. *Imagination and Language. Collected essays on Constant, Baudelaire, Nerval and Flaubert.* Cambridge: Cambridge University Press, 1981.
Filippo et Filippino Lippi. La Renaissance à Prato. Paris: Silvana Editoriale, Musée du Luxembourg, 2009.
Fisher, Burton D. *Salome, adapted from the Opera Journeys lecture series by Burton D. Fisher.* Coral Gables, FL: Opera Journeys, 2002.
Flaubert, Gustave. *Oeuvres, II.* Paris: Bibliothèque de la Plèade, Editions Gallimard, 1952.
—. *Trois Contes.* With an afterword and notes by Pierre Mark de Biasi. Paris: Seuil, 1993.
—. *Trois Contes.* Paris: Booking International, 1994.
—. *Voyage en Orient.* Foreward by Claudine Gothot-Mersch. Paris: Gallimard, 2006.
Flavius, Josephus. *The Works of Josephus Flavius.* Translated by William Whiston. Available online at: http://www.ccel.org/j/josephus/works/ant-18.htm
The Florence Baptistery Doors. Introduction by Kenneth Clark, photographs by David Finn, commentaries by Georges Robinson. New York: A Studio Book, The Viking Press, 1980.
Fossi, Gloria. *Filippo Lippi.* Florence: Scala, 1989.
Fowlie, Wallace. *Mallarmé.* Chicago: The University of Chicago Press, 1953.
Freedman, Luba. *Titian's Independent Self-Portraits.* Florence: Leo S. Olschki, 1990.
Gautier, Theophile. *Le Roi Candaule.* Paris: Librairie des amateurs, A. Perroud, Libraire-editeur, 1893.
—. *Jettatura.* Boston: D.C. Heath and Co., Publishers, 1904.
Gilman, Laurence. *Strauss' "Salome." A Guide to the Opera with Musical Illustrations.* London: John Lane, the Bodley Head; New York: John Lane Company, 1907.
Giusti, Anna Maria. *The Baptistery of San Giovanni in Florence.* Translated by Steven Grieco. Florence: Mandragora, 2000.
Gibsen, Michael. *Symbolism.* Koln, London, Los Angeles, Madrid, Paris, Tokyo: Taschen, 2003.
Girard, René. *Le Bouc émissaire.* Paris: Grasset, 1982.
—. "Scandal and the Dance: Salome in the Gospel of Mark." *Ballet Review* (Winter 1983): 67-76.
Green, Rosalie, ed. *The Hortus deliciarum of Herrad of Hohenbourg (Landsberg, 1176-96): A Reconstruction.* London: Warburg Institute/Brill, 1979.

Grojnowski, Daniel. "L'ordre moral et le désordre : Les Salomé de Gustave Moreau," Toulouse, 1981.
—. "Salomé, l'art et l'argent." *Cahier de l'Herne J-K Huysmans* 47 (1985): 165-173.
Gormley, Beatrice. *Salome*. New York: Alfred A. Knopf, 2007.
Guido Reni 1575-1642. Los Angeles: County Museum of Art, Nuova Alfa Editoriale, 1988.
Haase, Myra. *Reconciling Contradiction. The Myth of Salome*. Thesis. Indianapolis: Christian Theological Seminary, 1994.
Hägg, Tomas. *The novel in antiquity*. Berkeley: University of California Press, 1983.
—. *The art of biography in Antiquity*. New York: Cambridge University Press, 2012.
Harris, Bruce S., ed. *The Collected Drawings of Aubrey Beardsley*. New York: Bounty Books, 1967.
Hartt, Frederick. History of Italian Renaissance Art. Painting, sculpture, architecture. New York : H.N. Abrams, 1969.
Hausamann, Torsten. *Die tanzende Salome in der Kunst von der christlichen Fruhzeit bis um 1500*. Zurich: Juris Druck, 1980.
Heffernam, James. *The Museum of Words: The Poetics of Ekphrasis from Homer to Ashbery*. Chicago: University of Chicago Press, 1993.
Heine, Heinrich. *Atta Troll*. Translated by Herman Scheffauer. New York: B.W. Huebsche, 1914.
Henry, Nicolas. *Mallarmé et le symbolism*. Paris: Librairie Larousse, 1986.
Hermann, L. "Hérodiade." *Revue des Etudes juives* 12 (1973): 49-63.
Heywood, J. C. *Salome. A dramatic poem*. New York: Hurd and Houghton, 1867.
Hoare, Philip. *Oscar Wilde's last stand: Decadence, conspiracy, and the most outrageous trial of the century*. New York: Arcade Pub., 1998.
Hoehner, Harold W. *Herod Antipas*. Cambridge: Cambridge University Press, 1972.
Holmes, Megan. *Fra Filippo Lippi. The Carmelite Painter*. New Haven and London: Yale University Press, 1999.
Humbert, Jean-Marcel; Pantazzi, Michael; Ziegler, Christiane; and Ziegler, Christine, eds. *Egyptomania. Egypt in Western Art 1730-1930*. Ottawa: National Gallery of Canada, 1994.
Horst Uhr, *Lovis Corinth*. Berkley, Los Angeles: University of California Press, 1990.
Hourticq, Louis. *La jeunesse de Titian*. Paris: Librairie Hachette, 1919.
Huot, Sylviane. *Le mythe d'Hérodiade chez Mallarmé: genèse et evolution*. Paris: A. G. Nizet, 1977.

Husslein-Arco, Agnes, and Koja, Stephan. *Lovis Corinth: A Feast of Painting*. New York, London: Prestel Pub, 2010.
Huysmans, Joris-Karl. *Against Nature*. Translated by Margaret Mauldon. Oxford: Oxford University Press, 1998.
Jackson, Holbrook. Introduction to *Salome*, by Oscar Wilde. New York: Heritage Press, 1945.
Jensen, Morten Hørning. *Herod Antipas in Galilee: the literary and archaeological sources on the reign of Herod Antipas and its socio-economic impact on Galilee*. Tübingen: Mohr Siebeck, 2006.
Jolowicz, H. F. *Historical Introduction to the Study of Roman Law*. 2nd ed. Cambridge: Cambridge University Press, 1952.
Kaplan, Julius. *Gustave Moreau*. Los Angeles: Los Angeles County Museum of Art, 1974.
Karayanni, Stavros Stavrou. *Dancing Fear and Desire: Race, Sexuality and Imperial Politics in Middle Eastern Dance*. Ontario: Wilfrid Laurier University Press, 2004.
Kemperdick, Stephan, and Sander, Jochen, eds. *The Master of Flémalle and Rogier van der Weyden: an exhibition organized by the Städel Museum, Frankfurt am Main, and the Gemäldegalerie, Staatliche Museen, Berlin*. Ostfildern: Hatje Cantz, 2009.
Kemperdick, Stephan. *Rogier van der Weyden, 1399/1400-1464*. Cologne: Könemann, 1999.
Knapp, Bettina L. "Flaubert: Dance and the Archetypal Harlot, Wife, and Castrator." In *Arabesqué*, 8-9. New York: Ibrahim Farrah, 1985.
Kokkinos, Nikos. "Which Salome did Aristobulus Marry?" *Palestine Exploration Quarterly* 118 (1986): 33-50.
Kornitz, Blaise Hospodar de. *Salome: Virgin or Prostitute?* New York: Pagean Press, 1953.
Kuryluk, Ewa. *Salome and Judas in the cave of sex: the grotesque: origins, iconography, techniques*. Evanston, IL: Northwestern University Press, 1987.
Lacambre, Geneviève: *Gustave Moreau : Maître Sorcier*. Paris: Gallimard & Réunion des musées nationaux, 1997.
—. *Gustave Moreau, 1826-1898*. Paris: Réunion des Musées Nationaux, 1998.
—. *Gustave Moreau: Magic and Symbols*. New York: Harry N. Abrams, 1999.
Lacambre, Geneviève; Feinberg, Larry J.; de Contenson, Maurie-Laure; and Druic, Douglas. *Gustave Moreau: Between Epic and Dream*. Princeton: Princeton University Press, 1999.
Lacan, Jacques. "Seminar on 'The Purloined Letter'." In *Écrits*, translated

by Bruce Fink, 6-51. New York: Norton, 2006.
Ladinsky, Ant. "Salomeia" ("Саломея"), *Novoselye* (Новоселье), (27-28, 1946) New York: 22-31.
Laforgue, Jules. *Moralités legendaries*. Paris: Flammarion, 2000.
Large, Victor. "The Reader in the Strategy of Fiction." In *Expression, Communication and Experience in Literature and Language*, edited by Ronald G. Popperwell, 86-102. Proceedings of the XIIth Congress of the International Federation of Modern Languages and Literatures. London: The Modern Humanities Research Association, 1973.
Le Monde de l'Art. Association artistique russe du début du XXe siècle, Introduction by Vsevolod Petrov and Alexadre Kamenski. Leningrad: Editions d'art Aurora, 1991.
Lietzmann, H. *A History of the Early Church*. 4 volumes in 2. New York: Meridian Books, 1961.
Lièvre-Crosson, Elisabeth. *Du Réalisme au symbolisme*. Milan: Les Essentiels, 2000.
Lillie, W. "Salome or Herodias?" *Expository Times* 65 (1953-4): 251
Lincoln, Kirstein. *Dance. A Short History of Classic Theatrical Dancing*. Princeton: Princeton Book Co., 1987.
Liss, Hanna, and Oeming, Manfred, eds. *Literary construction of identity in the ancient world: proceedings of a conference, Literary Fiction and the Construction of Identity in Ancient Literatures : Options and Limits of Modern Literary Approaches in the Exegesis of Ancient Texts*. Heidelberg, July 10-13, 2006. Winona Lake, IN: Eisenbrauns, 2010.
Lobstein, Dominique. "Anthony Roux: Portrait d'un Collectionneur et Mécène." *Dossier de l'Art* 51 (October 1998): 58-72.
Lorrain, Jean. "Salomé et ses Poètes." *Le Journal*, 11 February 1896.
Lovis Corinth. Paris: Musée d'Orsay, Réunion des Musées Nationaux, 2008.
Lowe, Margaret and Burns, Colin. "Flaubert's 'Herodias' – a new evaluation." *Montjoie* I (May 1953: 9-15.
Luthi, Jean-Jacques, and Israël, Armand. *Emile Bernard: 1868-1941: fondateur de l'Ecole de Pont-Aven et précurseur de l'art moderne*. Paris: Editions de l'Amateur, 2003.
Mallarmé, Stéphane. *Poesies*. Paris: GF Flammarion, 1989.
—. *Collected Poems and Other Verse*. Translated by E.H. and A.M. Blackmore. Oxford: Oxford University Press, 2006.
Mandel'shtam, Osip. *Polnoe sobranie sochinenii v trekh tomakh (Complete Works in 3 volumes)*. Moskva: Progress-Pleiada, 2009.
Marchal, Bertrand. *Lecture de Mallarmé*. Paris: José Corti, 1985.
—. *Salomé : entre vers et prose : Baudelaire, Mallarmé, Flaubert,*

Huysmans. Paris: J. Corti, 2005.
Masseron, Alexandre. *Saint-Jean Batiste dans l'Art*. Paris: Artaud, 1957.
Matich, Olga. *Erotic Utopia: The Decadent Imagination in Russia's Fin de Siècle*. Moscow: NLO, Новое литературное обозрение, 2008.
Matthieu, Pierre-Louis. *Gustave Moreau, sa vie, son oeuvre*. Fribourg: Office du Livre, 1976.
—. *Monographie et Nouveau Catalogue de l'oeuvre achevé*. Paris: ACR Edition Internationale, 1998.
—. *Le Musée Gustave Moreau*. Paris: Réunion des musées nationaux, 2005.
Meltzer, Françoise. *Salome and the dance of writing: portraits of mimesis in literature*. Chicago: University of Chicago Press, 1987.
Merkel, Kerstin. *Salome: Ikonographie im Wandel*. Frankfurt am Main: P. Lang, 1990.
Michaud, J.M. *Le thème de Salomé dans la peinture de 1840 à 1930,* Mémoire de Maîtrise. Paris I: U.E.R. d'Art et Archéologie, 1979.
Michel, Emile. *Rembrandt: painter, engraver and draftsman*. New York: Parkstone International, 2008.
Moskowitz, Anita Fiderer. *The sculpture of Andrea and Nino Pisano*. Cambridge: Cambridge University Press, 1986.
Mourey, Gabriel. "Salomé aux cent visages." *L'Art et les Artistes* XI (April 1910): 3-15.
Neginsky, Rosina. *Zinaida Vengerova: In Search of Beauty. A Literary Ambassador Between East and West*. Frankfurt, London, New York: University of Heidelberg Series, Peter Lang, 2005.
—. *Juggler*. New Orleans: University Press of the South, 2009.
Neginsky, Rosina, ed. *Symbolism, Its Origins and Its Consequences*. New Castel: Cambridge Scholars Publishing, 2010.
Newsom, Calor A., and Ringe Sharon H., eds. *Women's Bible Commentary*. Louisville, KY: Westminster John Knox Press, 1998.
Niessen, Carl. *Max Reinhardt und seine Bühnenbilder*. Cologne: Wallraf-Richartz-Museum, 1958.
Odilon Redon 1840-1916. Chicago: The Art Institute of Chicago, 1994.
Osburn, Carroll D., ed. *Essays on women in earliest Christianity*. Joplin, MO: College Press Pub. Co., 1993-1995.
Panizza, Oskar. *Le Concile d'Amour: tragédie céleste, Zurich, 1895*. Grenoble: Presses universitaires de Grenoble,1983.
Panofsky, Erwin. *Problems in Titian, Mostly Iconographic*. New York: New York University Press, 1969.
—. *Early Netherlandish Painting: Volume One*. New York: Harper & Row, 1971.

Paolucci, Antonio. *The origins of Renaissance art: the Baptistery doors, Florence.* New York: George Braziller, 1996.
Pearce, Joseph. *The Unmasking of Oscar Wilde.* London: Harper Collins Publishers, 2000.
Phipps, William E. "The Plight of the Song of Songs." *Journal of the American Academy of Religion* 42 (March 1974): 82-100.
Pierobon, Frank. *Salomé ou la tragédie du regard. Oscar Wilde, l'auteur, le personnage.* Paris: Les Essais, Editions de la Différence, 2009.
Plato, *Plato in Twelve Volumes.* Translated by Harold N. Fowler. Cambridge, MA: Harvard University Press, 1925.
Poeschke, Joachim. *Donatello and His World. Sculpture of the Italian Renaissance.* Translated by Russell Stockman. New York: Harry N. Abrams, Inc., 1993.
—. *Italian Frescoes: The Age of Giotto, 1280-1400.* Abbeville Press, 2005.
Porter, Andrew. "Music drama." In *The New Grove Dictionary of Music and Musicians,* edited by Stanley Sadie, 20 vols. London: Macmillan, 1980.
Praz, Mario. *The Romantic Agony.* Cleveland: World Pub. Co., 1965.
—. *La Chair, la Mort et le Diable dans la littérature du XIXème siècle.* Paris: Denoel, 1977.
Pressly, Nancy L. *Salome, la belle dame sans merci: San Antonio Museum of Art, May 1-June 26, 1983.* With an essay on Oscar Wilde's Salome by Erik Bradford Stocker. San Antonio: San Antonio Museum Association, 1983.
Psichari, Jean. "Salomé et la décollation de St. Jean-Baptiste." *Revue de l'Histoire des Religions* 72 (1915): 131-158.
Puffett, Derrick. *Richard Strauss: Salome.* Cambridge: Cambridge University Press, 1989.
Rapetti, Rodolphe. *Symbolism.* Paris: Flammarion,
Reardon, B.P. "The Aspects of the Greek Novel." *Greece & Rome* 23 (Oct., 1976): 118-131.
—. "The Greek Novel." *Phoenix* 23 (Autumn, 1969): 291-309.
Renan, Ernest. *Vie de Jésus.* Paris: Michel Lévy freères, 1864.
Resseguie, James L. *Narrative Criticism of the New Testament: An Introduction.* Grand Rapids: Baker Academic, 2005.
Reverseau, Jean-Pierre. "Pour une étude du thème de la tête coupée dans la littérature et la peinture de la deuxième moitié du XIXème siècle." *Gazette des Beaux-Arts* (September 1972): 173-184.
Ross, Robert. *Aubrey Beardsley.* London: John Lane, The Bodley Head, 1921.
Ruda, Jeffrey. *Fra Filippo Lippi: life and work.* London: Phaidon, 1999.

Saladin, Linda. *Fetishism and fatal women: gender, power, and reflexive discourse.* New York: P. Lang, 1993.
Salome dans les collections françaises. Saint-Denis: Musée d'art et d'histoire, 1988.
Salomé. Un mito contemporaneo: 1875-1925. Madrid: Museo Nacional Centro de Arte Reina Sofia, 1995.
Sato, Tomoko, and Lambourne, Lionel, eds. *The Wilde years: Oscar Wilde & the art of his time.* London: Barbican Art Galleries & Philip Wilson, 2000.
Schmidgall, Gary. "Richard Strauss: Salome." In *Literature as Opera.* New York: Oxford University Press, 1977.
Shewan, Rodney. *Oscar Wilde. Art and Egotism.* London: The Macmillan Press LTD, 1977.
Shiner, Larry. *The Invention of Art. A Cultural History.* Chicago: University of Chicago Press, 2001.
Sinisgalli, Rocco, ed. and trans. *Leon Battista Alberti: On Painting.* New York: Cambridge University Press, 2011.
Slessor, Catherine. *The Art of Aubrey Beardsley.* Leicester: Silverdale Books, 2004.
Spear, Richard E. *The "Divine" Guido: Religion, Sex, Money and Art in the World of Guido Reni.* New Haven and London: Yale University Press, 1997.
Staley, Allen. *The New Painting of the 1860s: Between The Pre-Raphaelites and The Aesthetic movement.* New Haven, London: Yale University Press, 2011.
Steinmetz, Jean-Luc. *Stéphane Mallarmé: L'absolu au jour le jour.* Paris: Librairie Arthème Fayard, 1998.
Stokstad, Marilyn. *Medieval Art.* New York: Harper & Row, 1988.
Strauss, Richard. *Recollections and Reflections.* The University of Virginia: Greenwood Press, 1974.
Sturgis, Matthew. *Passionate Attitudes: the English Decadence of the 1890s.* London: Macmillan, 1995.
—. *Aubrey Beardsley: a biography.* Hammersmith, London: Harper Collins, 1998.
Suleiman, Susan R., and Grosman, Inge, eds. *The Reader in the Text. Essays on Audience and Interpretation.* Princeton: Princeton University Press, 1980.
Tal, Ilan. *Jewish Woman in Greco-Roman Palestine.* Peabody, MA: Hendrickson Publishers, Inc., 1995.

Taylor, Jane H.M., and Smith, Lesley, eds. *Women and the Book. Assessing the Visual Evidence.* London, Toronto: The British Library and University of Toronto Press, 1996.

Tintori, Leonetto, and Borsook, Eve. *Giotto. The Peruzzi Chapel.* New York: Harry N. Abrams, 1965.

Todorov, Tzvetan. *Eloge de l'individu.* Paris: Edition Adam Biro, 2004.

Tolbert, Mary Ann. *Sowing the Gospel: Mark's World in Literary-Historical Perspective.* Minneapolis: Fortress Press, 1989.

Toman, Rolf, ed. *The Art of the Italian Renaissance: Architecture, Sculpture, Painting, Drawing.* Konigswinter: Ullmann & Könemann, 2007.

Tooke, Adrianne. *Flaubert and the Pictorial Arts. From Image to Text.* Oxford: Oxford University Press, 2000.

Tydeman, William. *The Theater in the Middle Ages.* Cambridge: Cambridge University Press, 1978.

Tydeman, William, and Price, Steven. *Wilde—Salome.* Cambridge: Cambridge University Press, 1996.

Vasari, Giorgio. *Vasari's Lives of the Artists: Giotto, Masaccio, Fra Filippo Lippi, Botticelli, Leonardo, Raphael, Michelangelo, Titian.* Translated by Mrs. Jonathan Foster. New York: Dover Publications, 2005.

Vaucaire, Maurice. "Salomé à travers l'Art et la Littérature." *Nouvelle Revue* 15 (May 1907): 145-151.

Vengerova, Zinaida. "Feminism and Woman's Freedom." In *Russian Women Writers*, edited by Christine D. Tomei, translated by Rosina Neginsky, vol. 2. New York: Garland Publishing, 1999.

Vince, Ronald W. *Ancient and Medieval Theater. A Historiographical Handbook.* Westport: Greenwood Press, 1984.

Voragine de, Jacques. "La décollation de saint Jean-Baptiste." In *Légende Dorée*, chapter CXXIV. Paris: Nabu Press, 2010.

Yablonskaya, M. N. *Women Artists of Russia's New Age: 1900-1935.* Edited and translated by Anthony Parton. London: Thames and Hudson Ltd., 1990.

Wall, Geoffrey. *Flaubert: A Life.* New York: Farrar, Straus and Giroux, 2002.

Weintraub, Stanley. *Beardsley, a Biography.* New York: George Braziller, 1967.

White, J. S. *The Salome Motive.* New York: New York City Opera Co., 1947.

Wilde, Oscar. *Salome.* Boston: Branden Publishing Company, 1996.

—. *Complete Works of Oscar Wilde.* Glasgow: Harper Collins, 2003.

Williams, *Thomas A. Mallarmé and the Language of Mysticism* (Athens: University of Georgia Press), 1970.

Winn, Adam. *Mark and the Elijah-Elisha narrative: considering the practice of Greco-Roman imitation in the search for Markan source material*. Eugene, OR: Pickwick Publications, 2010.

Wolf, Norbert. *Giotto*. Taschen, 2006.

Wood, Jennifer Mary. *From Docile Dance to Femme Fatale: The Evolution of Salome*. A Thesis, Master of Arts (Art History).. University of Southern California, 1994.

Woods-Marsden, Joanna. *Renaissance Self-Portraiture*. New Haven & London: Yale University Press, 1998.

Zagona, Helen Genéve. *The legend of Salome and the principle of art for art's sake*. Geneva: Droz, 1960.

INDEX

Absolute 126, 128, 129, 132–138, 142, 182
Abunda (fairy queen) 106
Acrobat 26, 153, 158, 159, 171
Acropolis 118
Acts of Pilate 24
Affaire Salomé (L') 82
Alban Berg 203
Albert von Keller 80
Alcazar of Seville 69
Alexander Blok 215, 216, 220
 "Antwerp" ("Antverpen") 216
Alexandria 23
Alla Azimova 5
Alphonse Mucha 71
Alsace 153
Amazonian battle-scene 118
Ambroise Vollard 90
Ancient novel 15–18, 21
André Gide 182
Andrea del Sarto 29, 33
Andrea Orcagna 92
Andrea Pisano 39, 44, 45, 48–5
Andrea Solario 33
Andrée Fort 104, 121, 122
Androgyne 90
Androgyny, androgynous 5, 90, 123, 173, 174, 186, 189, 193, 197, 201, 202, 205
Angel Gabriel 25
Anna Akhmatova 217, 222
 Nechet 221
Annibale Carracci 70
Anti-Eve 25
Apocalypse 15, 116, 167
Appolinaire 90
Arabian scholars 156
Arabic manuscripts 158

Aramaic 20, 56
Aristide Maillol 71
Aristobulus 9, 10, 11, 20, 41, 42
Aristophanes 174
Aristote 118
 De Mundo 118
Armène Ohanian 104, 105, 120–122
 Laughs of a Serpent Charmer 105
Armenia, Armenia Minor 9, 42
Arnold Schoenberg 203
Arte di Calimala 43
Artemisia Gentileschi 93, 119
 Pittura (La) 93
Arthur Meyer 82
 Gaulois (Le) 82
Arthur Schopenhauer 76
Ary Renan 107
Asexual 65, 146
Astinée Aravian (see Armène Ohanian)
Aswan 160
 Atalanta and Hippomenes 70
Athena Parthenos 118
Aubrey Beardsley 5, 78, 179, 186–202, 205, 211
 Black Cape (The) 193, 198
 Climax 188, 193
 Front Page 189, 190
 Peacock Skirt (The) 197, 199
 Salome's Toilette 78
 Tailpiece 197, 201, 205
August Strindberg 76
 Aurora 70
Azizeh 159, 160
Babylon 116, 160, 209
Babylonian Talmud 21

Bacchae, Bacchants 24, 26, 152, 165, 207
Baghdad 160
Banquet 17, 50, 120
   Herod's banquet 1, 10–12, 19, 21, 25–27, 36, 44, 50, 51, 56, 57, 59, 68, 69, 90, 153, 162
Baptism 59, 61, 69, 136
Baptistery of San Marco 26, 29, 120
Barbara G. Lane 34, 40, 61
Barcelona 120
Bardi chapel 46
Baroque 2, 64, 65, 87
Baudelaire, Charles 106, 132, 145
   The Flowers of Evil 145
Beauty 1, 2, 4, 20, 25, 29, 35, 36, 40, 58, 64, 65, 67, 71, 72, 74, 82, 87, 98, 104, 116, 126, 128, 129–134, 137, 138, 143–145, 171, 177, 179–183, 193, 204, 207, 208, 216, 217
Beheading 1, 11, 16–18, 24, 26, 29, 31, 33, 46, 48, 53, 60, 69, 76, 89, 90, 95, 96, 105, 114, 120, 122, 128, 134–136, 138, 150, 162, 174, 207–209
Bellini 119
Beloved 171–179, 197
Benevento Cathedral 118
Benjamin 20
Berlin 69, 98, 119, 202, 212, 214
Berlin Kammerspiele 214
Berlin Secession 212
Bernardino Luini 33, 35–37, 168
Berthe Morisot 139
Bertrand Marchal 125, 140, 142
Bible 1, 8, 10, 18, 19, 20, 76, 105, 148, 165, 176, 178
Bilha 20
Birth 46, 59, 69, 88, 129, 136, 146, 147
Bishop of Carthage 40
Bishop of Poitiers 40
Blue Rider 218

Boissière 170
Bologna 64
Bolognese School 70
Book of Homilies 118
Botticelli 58
   Primavera 58
"Bridge" (Dance pose) 152, 153, 158, 159–161, 163
Browning, Robert 133
   "Porphyria's Lover" 133
Brunelleschi 68
Byzantine 156, 158, 186
Byzantium 24
Cabal's story 146
Cairo 101, 120, 160
Caliphs 156
Callisto Piazza 168
Cappella Maggiore 44, 56–59
Caravaggio 70, 93, 96
   Head of the Medusa (*The*) 93
   Cardinal Roberto Ubaldini 70
Carlo Cesare Malvasia 64
Carolingian manuscripts 42
Carolingian Renaissance 42
Carthusian monastery of Miraflores 69
Cassandra 74
Cathedral at Monreal 118
Cathedral at Trani 118
Cathedral of Clermont-Ferrand 26
Cathedral of Novgorod 118
Catholic Church 76
Cazotte 89
Celtic myth 163
Cesare da Sesto 32
Charlemagne 42
Charles Hayem 111, 124
Chateaubriand 110
Chimera 113, 145
Christ 17, 18, 25, 43, 59, 61, 62, 69, 93, 99, 134, 177, 197, 204
   Passion and execution of 17, 18, 61, 62
   Prefiguration of 62
Christianity 145, 177, 178
Church Fathers 1, 2, 4, 23, 24, 76,

80, 207
Church of Notre-Dame-de-
    l'Assomption du Mousky 101
Cicero 16, 118
Circuses 24, 26, 197
Clara Ward 168
Claricia 118
Classicism 29, 40, 48
Claude Monet 139
Cleopatra 74, 88
Code Napoléon 88
Codex Sinopensis 26, 27, 29
Convent of Hohenburg 118
Countess Greffulhe 124
Courtesans 11, 78, 89, 152, 160
Cranach 93
Cristofano Allori 93, 95, 96
Crucifix, crucifixion 17, 118
Crusades 25
Cupid 96, 98, 99, 101, 192
Dalila 72, 113, 123
Dance xv, xvi, xxii, 1, 5, 8, 10, 11, 12, 14, 16–18, 19, 21, 22, 24–26, 29, 40, 41, 43, 44, 46, 47, 48, 49, 50, 52, 53, 55, 57–59, 61, 62, 64, 66, 67, 68, 71, 74, 80, 88, 90, 95, 99, 104, 111, 113, 116, 117, 121, 122, 127, 128, 138, 150–153, 158–165, 168, 171, 172, 174, 189, 192, 197, 204, 205, 207, 209, 217, 218
Dance of Seven Veils 5, 172, 189, 192, 218
Dante Gabriel Rossetti 67, 72, 133, 176
Darwin 76
Decapitation 26, 27, 34, 56, 61, 134, 140, 163, 170, 177
Delilah 74
Des Esseintes 116, 117, 124, 171
Deutsches Theater 214
Devil 40, 76, 78, 197, 201, 205
Diaghilev 218
Diamonds 133
Diana (Greek Goddess) 106
Diana Apostolos-Cappadona 87, 88

Dieric Bouts 62
    Feast of Passover (Holy Sacrament Altarpiece) 62
Dijkstra 78, 80, 82, 89, 90
Dionysus (God of Wine) 24
Dirk De Vos 40, 42, 69
Disembodied head 139, 208, 212
Domenico di Zanobi 56
Donatello 29, 44, 45, 53–56, 67, 68
Dürer 93, 99, 168
Early Christian writings 24, 25
Ecriture du visuel 151
Edfou 161
Edgar Allan Poe 216
    Ligeia 216, 217
Edgar Saltus 169, 170
Edom 176
Edouard Manet 139
Edvard Munch 72
Egypt 101, 104, 121, 124, 158–162, 165, 166, 174
Egyptian courtesans 152, 160
Ekphrasis 150, 164, 216
Elkin Mathews 167
Emile Bernard 4, 96, 101–105, 120–122, 208
    Dancing Salome 96, 104, 111, 112, 114
    My Life Adventure 120–122
    Salome with the Platter 101, 102
Eros 127
Erwin Panofsky 59, 69, 96, 119
Esau 146
Esneh 160
Esther 21
Evangeliaire de Chartres 26, 28, 33, 42
Evangelists 3, 13, 16–18, 22
Eve 2, 3, 23, 25, 42, 72, 87, 104, 141, 197
Exposition universelle 124, 140
Far Eastern theogonies 116
Feast of Herod 29, 44–46, 53–55
Feminism, feminist movement, feminists 2, 4, 76, 88, 89, 122

Femme fatale 4, 36, 74, 76, 80, 85, 88, 110, 128, 172, 173, 176, 178, 181, 213, 216, 217
Fernand Khnopff 72, 88
Filippino Lippi 57, 68
Filippo Lippi xxi, xxii, 29, 38, 44, 45, 56–59, 67, 68, 69, 207
Fin-de-siècle culture 74, 89
First World War 3, 84, 85, 87, 216
Flaubert (Gustave) 5, 26, 80, 110, 125, 140, 150–166, 169, 171
  Education sentimentale 160
  "St. Julien l'hospitalier" 151, 153
  Trois Contes 164, 166
  "Un cœur simple" 151, 152
  Salammbo 110
  The Temptation of Saint Anthony (*La Tentation de saint Antoine*) 152, 160, 161
  Voyage en Egypte 161, 165
Florence xxi, 34, 38, 43–49, 53, 56, 58, 68, 92
Florence Baptistery 34, 38, 46–52, 56
  South Doors 38, 48–52
Florent Schmitt 218
  Tragédie de Salomé (*La*) 218
Floating head 111, 116, 123, 139, 208
Fra Angelico 56
Francesco Datini 68
Franz Von Stuck 72, 78–80
Frau Hulda (Fru Helle or Fru Helde) 98
Friedrich Fuchs 81
Fritz Erler 80
Galatée 72
Galilee 12, 17, 19, 80
Gandersheim 158
Gare Saint Lazare (Paris neighborhood) 139
Geminiano Inghirmi 56
Geneviève Lacambre 114, 123, 124, 139, 148
George Moore 189

Gerard de Nerval 106
German expressionist movement 218
Gertrud Eysoldt 202, 212, 213
Gesamtkunstwerk 203
Ghent 97
Ghiberti 56
  Gates of Paradise 56
Ghirlandaio 168
Giannino della Magna 56
Giorgione 119
Giotto 29, 38, 44–48, 50, 51, 53, 67, 68
Giovanni di Paolo 30, 31, 33
Glance 48, 65, 72, 90, 96, 101, 111, 117, 137, 138, 148, 181, 182, 204
Gomez Carrillo 168, 169
Gospel of Matthew 10, 41
Gospels 1, 8–10, 12, 13, 15–18, 23, 41, 99
Gothic art 48
Goupil Gallery 124
Grand Café 168
Greco-roman culture 12, 23
  meals 11, 20
Greek chorus 203
  classics 156
  language 10, 20
  vases 160
Grenada 101
Guido Reni 64–67, 70
  Atalanta and Hippomenes 70
  Aurora 70
  Cardinal Roberto Ubaldini 70
  Massacre of the Innocents 70
  Salome with the Head of John the Baptist 64–67
Gustav-Adolf Mossa 73, 75, 77, 78
Gustave Klimt 72
Gustave Moreau 4, 71, 72, 82, 96, 105–117, 122, 123, 124, 138–140, 148, 150–152, 162, 168, 171, 186, 192, 208
  Apparition (*The*) 96, 107, 109, 111, 113, 114, 116, 117,

138–140, 150–152, 162, 171, 186, 208
Chimères (Les) 113
Dalila 113
Oedipus and the Sphinx 113
Orphée 71
Salome Dancing Before Herod 107, 108, 110, 111, 116, 124, 150, 151, 192
Salome in the Garden 114, 115
Salome in the Prison 114
Sulamite (La) 71
Gynocide 89
Hague (The) 69
Hair 21, 57, 58, 64, 65, 72, 117, 132–134, 175–177, 182, 211
Halo 111, 113, 117, 124, 134, 136, 139, 140
Hamlet 180
Handel xvi
Hanénah (Annette) Saati 101–104, 120–122
Hans Memling 33
Head on the platter 34, 38, 51, 58, 63, 65, 101, 215
Hedwig Lachmann 203, 212, 214
Hegel, Hegelianism 130, 134, 142, 143, 144
Heinrich Heine 105–107, 122, 169
Atta Troll 105, 106, 122, 169
Helen of Antiquity 116, 171, 172
Helen of Troy 88
Hellenized Jews 12
Henri-Léopold Levy 80
Sketch for Salome (A) 80
Henrik Bornemann the Younger 93
Herald 125, 126, 129
Herod Antipas 1, 5, 8, 10–14, 17, 18, 19, 20, 21, 22, 24, 25, 26, 27, 29, 30, 33, 36, 39, 41, 43, 44, 45, 46, 48, 49, 50, 51, 52, 53, 54, 55, 56, 57, 59, 61, 62, 68, 69, 80, 90, 98, 106, 107, 108, 110, 111, 114, 116, 124, 139, 150, 151, 153, 162, 170, 171, 172, 177, 179, 189, 192, 197, 202, 203, 204, 205
Daughter of 22
Herodias, Hérodiade, 1, 3, 4, 5, 8–26, 29, 33, 36, 38, 39, 40, 41, 41, 48, 50, 51, 53, 55, 57, 61, 62, 68, 80, 83, 117, 125–146, 150–153, 161, 162, 163, 169, 171, 172, 182, 189, 191, 202, 204, 207, 208, 209
Herrad de Landsberg xv, 118, 153–159, 165
Hieroglyphs 111, 158
Hilaire de Poitiers 40
Hindemith 203
Hippolyte Flandrin 114
Holland 216
Holofernes 74, 93, 96, 119, 120
Horst Uhr 212, 214
Hortus Deliciarum 118, 153, 165
Lucifer Falling 153, 156
Priest of the People 153
Stairs that lead toward the skies 153, 157
Whore of Babylon Inverted (The) 153, 154
Whore of Babylon Falling (The) 153, 155
Hourticq 98, 119
Hugo von Habermann 80
Hysteria 116, 171
Icelandic myth 163
Ida Rubenstein 218
Ideal realm 135
woman 1, 25, 133
Idumean night 146
Impressionism 111, 113
India 124, 152
Isabella Lapi Ballerini 57
Isabella the Catholic 69
Isis 111, 124, 158–164
Italian Baroque 64
Italy xxi, 48, 101, 111, 120, 208, 215
J.C. Heywood 169
Jack the Ripper 203

Jacob Grimm 105
  German Mythology 105
Jacobus de Voragine 24
  Golden Legend (*The*) 24
James McNeil Whistler 139, 186, 192, 197
  Peacock Room 186, 192
Jan van Eyck 63
Jean Chrysostome 40, 41
Jean Lorrain 82, 114, 170
Jean-Luc Steinmetz 125, 140
Jean-Sylvain Bieth 84, 85
Jeanne Chmaal 89
Jewess 80, 82
Jewish law 11–13
Jewish Wedding (Delacroix painting) 110
Jewish women 11, 20
Jews 3, 12, 13, 17–19, 22, 82, 90, 203
Jezebel 74
Joachim Poeschke 55, 68
John Lane 167, 189
John Ruskin 179
John the Baptist xxi, xxii, 1–4, 8, 9, 11–14, 16–18, 19, 20, 23–27, 29–40, 41, 43, 44–48, 50–52, 55–69, 71, 78, 80, 82, 85, 90, 95–99, 101, 105–107, 110, 111, 113, 114, 116, 120, 122, 123, 124, 125, 126, 128, 132, 134–140, 145, 150–153, 162–164, 167, 169, 170, 172, 173-183, 186, 187, 189, 193, 196, 197, 202, 207–209, 210–212, 215, 218, 219
Johannestag 106, 107
Jokanaan 171–177, 182, 203, 204
Ioakanann 151, 163
Mouth (of John the Baptist) 78, 98, 117, 172, 173, 176, 177, 182, 211, 215
Passion/Martyrdom of 1, 16, 17, 29, 36, 40, 44–48, 52, 56, 61, 64, 66, 67, 71

John the Evangelist 46
Joris-Karl Huysmans 116, 117, 124, 139, 150, 151, 168, 171–173, 183, 184
  Against Nature (*A Rebours*) 116, 117, 124, 139, 150, 168, 171–173, 183, 184
Josephus Flavius 8, 9, 12, 14, 19
  Antiquities of the Jews 8, 9
Juan de Flandres 69
Judaism 12
Judas 36, 61
Judith 74, 80, 88, 93, 95, 96, 119, 120
Juggler xvii
Jules Desbois 80
Jules Kaplan 110, 123
Jules Lefebvre 82
Karl Bohm 204
Katia Granoff 120
King Aretas 10, 14
King Juan II of Castile 69
King William II of the Netherlands 69
Kingdom of Burgundy 69
Kingdom of Chalcis 9
Kleines Theater (the) 202, 212, 214
Kuchiouk-Hanem 159, 160
Lamia 74
Land of Hebrews 80
Last Supper 51, 62
Late Antiquity 23, 97
Laurence Gilman 203–206
Lavinia (daughter of Titian) 99, 100, 119, 120, 208
Laws of God 14
Lechery 116, 171
Leconte de Lisle 151
Leitmotif(s) 203, 205, 206
Lenore 217
Leon Battista Alberti 54, 58, 59, 68
  De Pictura 58
Leon Daudet 82
  Action française 82
Leonardo da Vinci 92
  Mona Lisa 82

Letter of Herod to Pilate 24
Levy-Dhurmer 72, 78
Lilith 74
Liverpool 186
Lloyd James Austin 137, 141, 142
Lorenzo Monaco 38, 39
Lotus 111, 114, 124, 186, 192
Louis Fort 90
Louise Michel 89
Louvre 36, 82, 96, 121
Love affair 90, 98, 101, 104, 126, 135, 137, 178
Lover 171–179, 197
Lovis Corinth 210–214
  Cattle Slaughtered at the Slaughterhouse 211
  Slaughterhouse (The) 211
Luca Assarino 64
Lucius Flamininus 16–18
Lucrezia Buti 57, 58, 207
Luisa Capodieci 111, 123
Luke 1, 19, 93
Lust 72, 78–80, 90, 92, 116, 133, 153, 162, 169, 171, 172, 186, 212
Luxor 160
Madonna 36, 57, 63, 72
Maenads 24, 90
Magasin pittoresque 110
Malaga 120
Mallarmé (Stéphane) 4, 96, 110, 125–148, 167, 169, 171, 172, 181–183, 208, 215
  Cantique de saint Jean (The Song of Saint John) 125, 131, 134–140
    Gift of the Poem (Don du poème) 146
    Noces d'Hérodiade (Les) 4, 96, 125–138, 181
    Mardis 181, 182
    Ouverture 125, 126, 128–131, 140, 183
    Scène 125, 127, 128–134, 137, 140, 183
Mandet de Riom 33

Marianna Werefkin 218, 219
Marie Deraim 89
Mark 6:14-29 1, 19
Mary Magdalene 2, 25, 169
Master of the Nativity of Castello 56
Matthew 14:1-12 1, 18
Maurice Maeterlinck 167, 170, 172
Max Kruse, sculptor 212
Max Rehnardt 202
Max Reinhardt 212
Maxime du Camp 160
Medusa 88, 176
Messaline 72, 123
Messiah's kingdom 13, 61
Metropolitan Museum of Art 82
Michail Fokine 218
Michelangelo 70, 92–94, 124, 189
  Last Judgment 93, 94
Middle Ages 1, 2, 3, 24, 26, 40, 41, 44, 48, 66, 97, 118, 127, 158, 207, 208
Minerva 118
Mireille Dottin-Orsini xxi, 36, 76, 82, 89, 90
Moon 172, 175, 176, 179, 189, 192, 202, 204, 215, 217
Mosaics 26, 38, 43, 44–48, 51, 53, 67, 117
Moulin Rouge 171
Mozart 203
Munich Secession 212
Musée d'Orsay 71
Muses 74
Myth(s) 1–5, 18, 21, 44, 74, 86, 87, 93, 107, 124, 127, 162, 163, 208, 209
Nabataean royal family 10, 14
Naples 120
Napoléon I 88
Napoléon III 114
Napoleonic Wars 88
Narraboth 172, 204, 205
Naturalism 111, 113
Necrophilia 211, 213
Neoclassical 87

Nero 42
Neues Theater (The) 212, 214
Neva 217
New Testament Apocrypha 24
New York 82
New York Times (*The*) 202
Nicephorus Callistus 41
   Ecclesiastic History 41
Nicolo di Montefonte 118
Nile 158, 160
Nivardus 97, 98, 105, 119
Northern Renaissance 4, 59
Nothingness 126
Nubian gospel 170
Nurse 125, 128–131, 142, 143, 147
Odilon Redon 123, 139, 208
   Fallen Glory 123
Old Testament 11, 21, 51, 56
Orient 120, 121, 152, 160, 165, 166, 203
Orientalism, Orientalist 81, 120
Original sin 25
Orpheus 90, 123, 208
Orsanmichele, Florence 55, 92,
Oscar Wilde 5, 78, 85, 167–185, 186, 189, 192, 193, 197, 201–206, 210-214
   "The Critic as Artist" 180, 184
   Picture of Dorian Gray (*The*) 181
Osip Mandelshtam 216, 221
   "Solominka," *solominka*, little straw 216–217, 220, 221
Oskar Panizza 76
   Love Council (*The*) 76
Otsy 101, 120
Oxford 179
Pablo Picasso 80, 81, 90
   Barbarous Dance (*The*) 90
   Cirque Médrano 90
   Santimbanques (*The*) 90
Pagan, Pagans, Paganism 15, 24 80, 158, 178, 179
Palazzo Farnese 70
Palestine 20, 41, 160, 166

Pall Mall Gazette 169
Parnasse contemporain (*Le*) 125
Pasiphaé 123
Paul de Limbourg 69
Paul Gauguin 71, 93, 123, 208
Pauline Mink 89
Pericles 118
Peruzzi Chapel 44–48, 53, 67
Peter Cooke xxii, 123, 124
Phidias 117, 118, 145
Philip (Herod Antipas' half brother) 8, 9, 10, 13, 18
Pierre Loti 167
Pierre-Joseph Prudhon 89
Pierre-Mark de Biase 161
Pierrot 193, 197
Plato 170, 174, 178, 184
   Phaedrus 178, 184
   Symposium 174, 178
Pliny 118, 119
Plutarch 16, 22, 118
Polyptychs 46
Pontius Pilate 152
Pope Leo III 42
Prato xxi, 29, 38, 44, 56, 57, 68
Pre-Adamite people 146
Pre-Raphaelite artists 67, 132, 176
Precious stones 117, 133
Pride 92, 172, 173, 205
Princesse de Chimay 168
Prostitutes 11, 12, 17, 20, 78, 160
Prudence 92
Prussia 82
Puccini 203
Puvis de Chavannes 71, 122
Queen Constance 180
Quentin Matsys 216
Raphael 70, 110
Ratisbonne, Kunstforum Ostdeutsche Galerie 211
Ravel 203
Realism 111, 113, 123
Regnault, Henri 82, 83, 107, 110, 128, 168
Rembrandt 93, 110
   Prodigal Son (*The*) 93

Renaissance xxi, 1, 2, 3, 4, 23, 29, 35, 40, 42, 44–70, 71, 74, 85, 87, 92, 96, 101, 107, 110, 111, 119, 207, 208
René Dumesnil 153, 165
René Girard 6, 209
Revue blanche (La) 76
Reuben 20
Richard Spear 65
Rigo 168
River Jordan 59, 69
Robbie Ross 189
Robert Campin 59, 63, 69
Robert de Montesquiou 137
Rococo 87
Rogier van der Weyden 4, 33, 34, 36, 40, 42, 44, 45, 59–64, 67, 68, 69
   Medici Madonna 63
   Saint Columbia Altarpiece 63
   St. John's Altarpiece 40, 44, 59–64, 69
Roman court 9
Roman Empire 15, 80
   law 13
Romanino 98, 119
Romans 13, 14, 17, 18, 22
Rome 22, 42, 70, 96, 101, 165
Rosenhagen's Review 212
Rouen 26, 42, 153, 159, 160–164
Russia, 5, 6, 85, 88, 120, 121, 215–220
Russian culture 5, 6, 215–222
   poets 215-222
Saint Margaret 57
Saint Paul's Letter to the Romans 148
Saint-Etienne de Toulouse 29
Saint-Lazare d'Avallon (Burgundy) 26
Sainte-Odile convent 153
Salome (paintings titled)
   Dancing Salome (Emile Bernard) 96, 104, 111, 112, 114
   Salome Dancing Before Herod (Gustave Moreau) 107, 108, 110, 111, 116, 124, 150, 151, 192
   Salome in the Garden (Gustave Moreau) 114, 115
   Salome in the Prison (Gustave Moreau) 114
   Salome with the Head of John the Baptist (Guido Reni) 64–67
   Salome with the Head of John the Baptist (Vasilii Myazin) 85, 86
   Salome with the Platter (Emile Bernard) 101, 102
   Salome's Toilette (Aubrey Beardsley) 78
   Sketch for Salome (A) (Henri-Léopold Levy) 80
Salomea Andronikova, 215
Samson 74, 176
Samuel Palmer 93
San Cugat Del Vallès (Catalonia) 26
San Zeno (Verona) 26, 118
Santa Croce 44–46, 48
Santo Stefano Cathedral 44, 56–59
Scapegoat 6, 18
Scherer 130, 142, 143
Second World War 85
Self-portrait (s) 4, 58, 92, 93, 95, 96, 98, 104, 111, 117, 118, 119, 125, 127, 139, 208, 215
   Assistenza 93
   in *décapité* 4, 93, 95, 96, 111, 119, 208, 215
   Selbstandiges Selbstbildnis 93
   Selbstbildnis zu Studienzwecken 93
   self-portraits in disguise 4, 58, 93, 95, 208
   Verkapptes Selbstibildnis 93
Seneca 17
Seraphita 217
Sergei Chepik 85, 86
Sergei Sudeikin (Soudeikine) 218

Sirène 123
Sistine Chapel 93, 189
Social life 12, 23, 88
Song of Songs (The) 173–177, 179, 182, 184
Spain 69, 101, 120, 156
Sphinx 113, 123
Spontaneous evocation (« évocation spontanée ») 163
St. Augustine 41, 99
  16th Sermon 41
St-Georges de Boscherville 26
St. Bartholomew 93, 124
St. Francis 46
St. Pharaildis 97, 98
St. Verelde 97, 98
Stephan Kemperdick 63, 69
Strauss, Richard 5, 85, 87, 186, 202–206
Stravinsky 203
Striptease dancer 5
Studio (The) 189
Sybille 142
Syphilis 76, 78
Syria 160
Taddeo di Bartolo 92
Tat'iana Vecheslova 217, 222
Tertullian 40
Tetrarch 8, 12, 17, 19, 80, 117, 152
Théâtre de l'Oeuvre 214
Théophile Gautier 106, 110, 148, 151, 169
Time of Ahasuerus 21
Titian 4, 92, 93, 96–101, 118–120, 168, 207, 208
Lavinia as Bride 120
Lavinia as Matron 120
Toledo 156
Tournai 69
Transcendental 59, 61, 64, 67, 132, 211
Truth 92, 113, 134
Tuberculosis 120
Tuscany 44
Twelve Patriarchs 20
Universe 118, 138, 145
Valencia 120
Valentine Serov 218
Valerius Maximus 16, 17
Vampires 2, 76, 78, 193
Vanity 92, 107
Vasyli Myazin 85, 86
Venice 26, 120, 215
Venus of Milo 145
Viol occulaire 126, 132, 137, 145, 182
Virgin Mary 1, 2, 23, 25, 63, 65, 76
Vitellius 152
Void (*Néant*) 126, 129, 141, 142
Vulgate 10, 20
Walter Pater 179
Wild Hunt (Wilde Jagd or *Wildes Heer)* 98
"Woman's race" 74, 84, 89, 90
Working women 88, 89, 122
Young Syrian 171, 172, 179
Zachary 63
Zinaida Vengerova 88, 89